MASTERING READING THROUGH REASONING

SECOND EDITION

DR. ARTHUR WHIMBEY

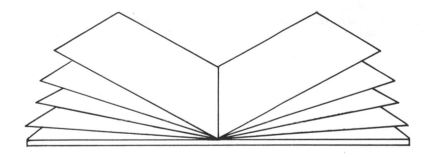

INNOVATIVE SCIENCES, INC.

Editorial Development:
John J. Glade

Editing and Styling:
Christine Shearn
Joseph N. Lane

Design:
John J. Glade

©1995 by Innovative Sciences, Inc.
975 Walnut St., Suite 342, Cary, NC 27511

99 98 97 96 95   1 2 3 4 5

ISBN 1-884582-00-1

Library of Congress Catalog Card Number: 94-73456

Copyright Notices and Acknowledgments

This is the second book for which I am deeply grateful to my editor, John Glade. The fact that the first book, ANALYTICAL READING & REASONING, is now being successfully studied by many thousands of students in hundreds of schools nationwide is due in no small part to John's guidance during its development. For the present book, John drew upon his own experience as a writer, curriculum developer and teacher in contributing to the form, content and rationale of the work.

Grateful acknowledgment is given to the following authors and publishers for the use of passages from these copyrighted reading selections:

From *A Child's Geography Of The World* by V.M. Hillyer and E.G. Huey. Copyright 1929 by The Century Co.; copyright 1951 by Appleton-Century-Crofts, Inc., renewed 1957 by Mercantile Safe Deposit and Trust Co. Reprinted by permission of E.P. Dutton, Inc.

From Boak/Slosson/Anderson/Bartlett: *The History of Our World*, Copyright ©1965 Houghton Mifflin Company. Reprinted with permission of Houghton Mifflin Company.

From Mary Lou Burket, "A Pet for Your Health." From *Children's Digest*, copyright ©1983 by Benjamin Franklin Literary & Medical Society, Inc., Indianapolis, Indiana. Used with permission of Mary Lou Burket.

From Edward H. Carlson, *Kids and the TI 99/4A*, Reston, Virginia: Reston Publishing Company. Copyright ©1983 by Datamost Inc. and used with their permission.

From Children's Better Health Institute. Review of *Toad Food & Measle Soup* by Christine McConnall reprinted by permission from "Book Beat" by Betty Winn Fuller, from *Children's Digest*, copyright ©1983 by Benjamin Franklin Literary & Medical Society, Inc., Indianapolis, Indiana. Reprinted with permission of Children's Better Health Institute.

From Sam Epstein and Beryl Epstein, *The First Book of Words*, copyright ©1954 by Franklin Watts, Inc. Reprinted with the permission of Franklin Watts, Inc.

From John T. Fodor, Lennin H. Glass, Ben C. Gmur, Virginia D. Moore and Elizabeth Neilson, *Keeping Healthy*, ©1977, River Forest, Illinois: Laidlaw Brothers. By permission of Laidlaw Brothers, A Division of Doubleday & Co., Inc.

From Robert Jordan, *Conan The Destroyer*, copyright ©1982 by Conan Properties, Inc. Reprinted with the permission of the publisher Tom Doherty Associates, Inc., New York City, New York.

From Gerald Leinwand, *The Pageant of American History*, ©1975, Newton, Massachusetts: Allyn and Bacon, Inc. Reprinted with the permission of the publisher Allyn and Bacon, Inc.

From *Living World History* by T. Walter Wallbank and Arnold Fletcher. Copyright ©1958 by Scott, Foresman and Company. Reprinted with permission of Scott, Foresman and Company.

From Edith McCall, Evelyn Rapporlic and Jack B. Spatafora, *Man—His World and Cultures*, Westchester, Illinois: Benefic Press. Copyright ©1974. All efforts to contact the copyright holder of this material have proved unsuccessful. An appropriate fee for this use will be reserved by the publisher.

From *Old-Fashioned Candymaking*, ©1974, by June Roth, with permission of Contemporary Books, Inc., Chicago.

From Clarence Samford, Edith McCall and Floyd F. Cunningham, *You and the World*, Westchester, Illinois: Benefic Press. Copyright ©1968. All efforts to contact the copyright holder of this material have proved unsuccessful. An appropriate fee for this use will be reserved by the publisher.

From Deanna Sclar, "The Fabulous Fordmobile and the Model A," *Boy's Life*, November 1980. Reprinted with permission of Deanna Sclar.

From excerpt from "The Ghost That Worked Overtime" by Claire Safran, published in the February 1983 issue of the *Reader's Digest*. Used with the permission of Claire Safran.

From *The World Book Encyclopedia*, Volume J-K, page 29. ©1984 World Book, Inc. Used with the permission of World Book, Inc.

From *The World Book Encyclopedia*, Volume L, page 312. ©1984 World Book, Inc. Used with the permission of World Book, Inc.

From A. van Breda, *Pleasure with Paper*, London: Faber and Faber Publishers, ©1972, pages 45-46 and 121-122. Reprinted by permission of Faber and Faber Ltd from *Pleasure with Paper* by A. van Breda.

Foreword

Public education in America has always been a major instrument in advancing the interest of the nation. Problems besetting the country have a way of becoming a focus for instruction. Throughout our history, reading instruction has been the most used tool for this purpose. Nila B. Smith has documented this fascinating practice in her *American Reading Instruction*. From salvation, to morality, to culture, to productive workers, our schools and their reading programs have been used to pursue the solutions to our perceived national problems.

In 1983 The Secretary of Education's Commission On Excellence issued its report "A Nation At Risk." The President of the United States immediately began to use the report to make a historically unprecedented number of appearances and statements that caught and held the public's attention on the quality of education in America.

Preceding the issuance of "A Nation At Risk," The National Assessment of Educational Progress (NAEP), the only nationally established and supported program to measure learner progress in designated areas of the curriculum, reported some alarming findings. While American students have been learning the "Basics" better than previously, their ability to apply them to advanced learning and to the real problems of life in America has diminished: this because they have not learned the "higher order" cognitive skills, such as critical analysis, synthesis, cause-effect reasoning, generalization, etc.

In one of his numerous suggestions for improving the quality of instruction, the Secretary of Education has identified the need for better textbooks in the schools. Texts must respond to the problems identified by the reports. In addition, they must more imaginatively and effectively engage the learner and the teacher. I believe that *Mastering Reading Through Reasoning* fulfills these requirements. It concerns itself with some of the most fundamental of the required higher order skills and it is so organized and lucid that learning the skills through its lessons will be stimulating and fulfilling.

Mastering Reading Through Reasoning is a book that will give learners and teachers a satisfying instrument through which to learn and teach higher order skills. Users will respond favorably to its organized, thoughtful and thorough way of guiding successful learning. It will help teachers develop their own exercises to further reinforce the learning of their pupils. Students will like it for it will focus their efforts and reward them with an immediate sense of accomplishment. Parents, business people, civic leaders and citizens who have no children in school will be assured by its purpose and clarity.

This is a book for our time! It will aid us significantly in our quest for Excellence!

PAUL B. SALMON, ED.D.
FORMER EXECUTIVE DIRECTOR
AMERICAN ASSOCIATION OF
SCHOOL ADMINISTRATORS

About the Author

> If I have succeeded in my inquiries more than others, I owe it less to any superior strength of mind, than to a habit of patient thinking.
>
> —Sir Isaac Newton

If any one phrase best sums up Dr. Arthur Whimbey's philosophy of instruction, it may be: "The key to academic and professional success lies in mastering the habit of patient thinking." For over 25 years, Dr. Whimbey has researched and developed teaching materials and study programs for training individuals in the skill of patient, systematic, accurate thinking.

In 1975 Dr. Whimbey (with Linda Shaw Whimbey) published *Intelligence Can Be Taught,* which introduced his philosophy for improving thinking and reasoning ability, popularly referred to as "The Whimbey Method." His unique method for boosting reading performance by developing reasoning abilities forms the basis for the present text as well as a higher level text entitled *Analytical Reading & Reasoning* (Innovative Sciences, 1983). Dr. Whimbey has also published articles in numerous magazines and journals including *Educational Leadership, Educational Psychology, Phi Delta Kappan, Saturday Review/World, Psychology Today,* and *Journal of Reading.* His method for improving intellectual performance has been successfully applied in high schools and colleges across the country, and has twice been reviewed in *The New York Times.*

Dr. Whimbey received his Ph.D. from Purdue University. Among the positions he has held are: NIMH Senior Postdoctoral Fellow, Institute of Human Learning, University of California at Berkeley; Coordinator of Communication Labs, Developmental Education Program, Bowling Green State University; Resident Scholar in the Center for Academic Skills, City College of New York; Visiting Professor, Reading Department, Xavier University; Resident Scholar, Department of Reading, Clark College; Academic Specialist, Bethune-Cookman College. He has also served on the editorial boards of the *Problem Solving Newsletter* and the *Human Intelligence International Newsletter.* Most recently, Dr. Whimbey has
Since writing the first edition of this textbook in 1985, Dr. Whimbey has continued to develop strategies for improving the intellectual skills of young adults, most recently at the Institute for TRAC (Text Reconstruction Across the Curriculum) Research.

Preface: To The Student

The goal of this book is to make you a better reader. Being a good reader is necessary for you to do well in school and to succeed in your life plans.

Since the first edition of this book was published in 1985, many thousands of students just like you have used this book and *have* become better readers, more successful students, and more successful in their chosen careers. This book will help you, too, but it will require serious study and hard mental work.

This book will help you in several ways. It will improve your vocabulary. It will help you better understand anything you read. It will strengthen your writing skills. But, in addition, this book will improve your thinking and reasoning skills. By becoming a better thinker, you will find it easier to learn, to take tests, and to do well in all of your classes.

Each unit in this book teaches an important reading skill. But the teaching is done in a different way than in other reading textbooks. Here, each unit aims at improving the way you *think* about reading material. In other words, at improving the way you use your mind to make sense of the words and ideas you read. Rather than have you concentrate on memorizing rules and definitions, the units will teach you how to *master reading through reasoning (thinking)* about written information.

The exercises in this book are reasoning exercises as much as reading exercises. They will challenge you to "figure out" the meanings of words, sentences, paragraphs and passages. As you work the exercises you should try hard to achieve 100% accuracy. You will be learning to think better as well as to read better.

We all know that thinking is fun. We enjoy solving crossword puzzles, riddles, brainteasers and other problems. Well, reading is simply thinking about *written* words and ideas. Reading is fun, too.

Contents

Cooperative Learning For Improving Reading Comprehension

OBJECTIVES

When you have completed this unit you will

- be able to use cooperative learning to discuss a reading exercise with a partner and reach agreement on the answer;

- be able to use cooperative learning to "think aloud" as you complete a reading exercise;

- be able to use cooperative learning to listen to and question a partner's solution to a reading exercise.

INTRODUCTION

The goal of this book is to improve your reading ability. To accomplish this goal, several special methods will be used to help you get the most from the exercises. One of these methods is called *cooperative learning*.

Cooperative learning means simply that you will often be cooperating, or working together, with a partner to learn reading skills. Working with a partner has been proven to be a very successful way to learn new skills. It is also more enjoyable than studying by yourself.

You will use cooperative learning in this book in two ways. You will learn about these two ways in this unit and have the chance to practice them.

PART I: Comparing and Discussing Answers

One way to use cooperative learning is to talk about the answers to exercises with a partner. First, you work the exercises by yourself. When you're finished, you get together with a partner to compare and discuss the answers. The key to this type of cooperative learning is *how* you discuss the answers with your partner.

A good discussion has several steps. For every exercise, each of you will take a turn telling your answer and explaining why you think that answer is correct. It is very important that you explain as carefully as you can why you believe your answer is correct. Tell your partner *what information* in the exercise helped you to get your answer. Also, explain *your reasoning* that led to your answer. In other words, explain in detail how you reached your answer.

Sometimes you and your partner will disagree about an answer. When that happens, you will talk it out together and try to decide which answer is the *best* answer. One thing you should not do is ask anyone else, "Who is right?" Your goal is to try to agree on the correct answer yourselves before asking anyone else.

The example below will help you to understand what makes a good answer discussion.

EXAMPLE: On the next page is a sample reading exercise from this book. The exercise has a short reading passage followed by a question about the passage. After the exercise is an example of how two students might discuss the exercise. Read and mark the answer to the exercise for yourself, then read the discussion.

Vocabulary preview: **conservation** (noun)—the act of protecting or saving something so it is not destroyed or lost.

1   Finland's principal resource is lumber.
2 The huge forests, under carefully con-
3 trolled conservation practices, are the
4 source of wood for manufacturing ply-
5 wood, paper, and insulating board.
6   Deposits of copper ore, iron ore, and
7 titanium have been found and are being
8 mined. The resources are used in the
9 manufacture of such things as electrical
10 goods, locomotives, and ships.
11   The capital of the Republic of Finland
12 is the city of Helsinki. Helsinki is also
13 Finland's most important port. Helsinki
14 has become increasingly important as a
15 tourist center. People come from all over
16 Europe to enjoy Finland's long winter
17 sports season.

According to the passage, Finland's forests

☐ (A) have supplied wood for manufacturing plywood, paper and insulating board, but are now almost used
up
☐ (B) have made Helsinki the center of
the lumber industry
☐ (C) have been used wisely to prevent
them from being used up

Student Discussion:

Student I   *I chose C.*

Student II   *I chose A. Lines 4 and 5 say Finland's forests are the source of wood for manufacturing plywood, paper, and insulating board.*

Student I   *That's true. But I think A is not the best answer because at the end of A it says the forests are now almost used up. However, lines 2 and 3 say that carefully controlled conservation practices are applied to the forests. And the vocabulary preview says conservation means protecting or saving something so it is not destroyed or lost. Therefore, I don't think the forests are almost used up. I chose C because it says the forests*

have been used wisely to prevent them from being used
up, and this agrees with lines 2 and 3 in the passage.

Notice how Student I's comments explain the answer and also help Student II learn to read more carefully.

This type of cooperative learning will help you get the most benefit from the exercises in this book. The following exercises will give you practice in comparing and discussing answers with a partner.

EXERCISE INSTRUCTIONS

Each exercise is a sample reading exercise. The exercise has a short reading passage followed by a question about the passage. Read the passage and mark the answer to the question. Then discuss the answer with a partner until you both agree on the *best* answer.

EXERCISE 1

1 Finland's principal resource is lumber.
2 The huge forests, under carefully con-
3 trolled conservation practices, are the
4 source of wood for manufacturing ply-
5 wood, paper, and insulating board.
6 Deposits of copper ore, iron ore, and
7 titanium have been found and are being
8 mined. The resources are used in the
9 manufacture of such things as electrical
10 goods, locomotives, and ships.
11 The capital of the Republic of Finland
12 is the city of Helsinki. Helsinki is also
13 Finland's most important port. Helsinki
14 has become increasingly important as a
15 tourist center. People come from all over
16 Europe to enjoy Finland's long winter
17 sports season.

1. Helsinki is an important city because

☐ (A) it is a major source of minerals
☐ (B) it is the Republic of Finland
☐ (C) it is a growing tourist center and a main port

EXERCISE 2

1 Canine heartworm disease, once found
2 only in the southwestern United States, is
3 spreading north and west. Today it is a
4 problem for dog owners in 42 states and
5 Canada.
6 Heartworm disease is carried by mos-
7 quitoes. When a mosquito bites an infect-
8 ed dog, and then bites a healthy one, it
9 deposits infective larvae under the second
10 dog's skin. The larvae make their way
11 into the bloodstream, then to the heart. In
12 time they become adult heartworms, six
13 to 14 inches long.

1. In the past, canine heartworm disease was found

☐ (A) just in 42 states and Canada
☐ (B) just in states like Georgia, South Carolina and Florida
☐ (C) just in states like California, Nevada and Arizona
☐ (D) just in states like New York, Maine and Connecticut

PART II: Thinking Aloud Problem Solving

The form of cooperative learning you practiced in Part I is useful for exercises in which you must do a lot of careful reading before answering questions. However, many units in this book have shorter exercises or problems in which you must give responses *as* you read, not just after you are done reading. For this shorter type of exercise, a form of cooperative learning called Thinking Aloud Problem Solving (TAPS) is very helpful.

Thinking Aloud Problem Solving is just what it sounds like: you think *out loud* while you complete an exercise. In using TAPS, partners take turns working the exercises. The student solving an exercise problem is called the "Problem Solver." The other student is called the "Listener."

The Role of the Problem Solver

The Problem Solver tries to do all of his (or her) thinking aloud. From the very beginning of the problem he tries to talk out all of his thoughts and decisions as he works out the answer. He explains step by step what he is doing, giving as much detail as possible. When necessary, he should draw diagrams or use any other methods that can help to show the Listener what he is thinking or why he thinks something is correct.

The Role of the Listener

The Listener should do more than just sit back and listen. Instead, he (or she) should carefully follow all of the Problem Solver's steps and check constantly to make sure those steps are correct. The Listener should ask questions if he can't understand something the Problem Solver is explaining. By asking questions, the Listener can help the Problem Solver to think more clearly and speak more clearly. Being able to clearly "speak what's on your mind" is a valuable skill in school and on the job, and so is being able to ask good questions.

EXAMPLE: Below is an example of how a Problem Solver might think aloud as she works an exercise that comes later in this book.

First try to complete the exercise for yourself. Then read the Problem Solver's "thinking aloud" solution.

EXERCISE

Instructions: Read these four sentences and number them in the best logical order. Write "1" by the sentence you think should come first, "2" by the sentence which should come second, and so on.

_____ **A. But the city has been rebuilt.**

_____ **B. However, during World War II large parts of Munich were destroyed.**

_____ **C. Today, Munich is again a center for German art, architecture and education.**

_____ **D. For many years before World War II the city of Munich was one of Germany's great cultural centers.**

Problem Solver's Thinking Aloud Solution:

First I will read the entire exercise, then I'll start working it.

Sentence A says, 'But the city has been rebuilt.' Since this sentence begins with the word 'but,' I don't think it should come first. 'But' is a word used to give a contrast. You need something before it to set up the contrast.

Sentence B says, 'However, during World War II large parts of Munich were destroyed.' 'However' is also a word that expresses a contrast, so this probably doesn't come first either.

Sentence C reads, 'Today, Munich is again a center of German art, architecture and education.' The word 'again' in this sentence suggests that something should come before this sentence. So I don't think this should be the first sentence.

Sentence D is, 'For many years before World War II the city of Munich was one of Germany's great cultural centers.' This could be a good first sentence. It seems to introduce a discussion of the city of Munich. I'll write the number 1 in front of this sentence.

_____   **A.**   **But the city has been rebuilt.**

_____   **B.**   **However, during World War II large parts of Munich were destroyed.**

_____   **C.**   **Today, Munich is again a center for German art, architecture and education.**

__1__   **D.**   **For many years before World War II the city of Munich was one of Germany's great cultural centers.**

Now I have to find the sentence which should come next. I'll start reading from the top again, 'But the city has been rebuilt.' I don't think this should be the second sentence. The word 'rebuilt' implies that the city was destroyed. A sentence which says something about destruction probably comes ahead of this one.

Sentence B is, 'However, during World War II large parts of Munich were destroyed.' This sentence mentions destruction, so it is probably the one that comes before sentence A.

Sentence B also gives a contrast to sentence D. The great city talked about in sentence D was partly destroyed. So it makes sense that sentence B should come second. I'll write a 2 by it.

_____   **A.**   **But the city has been rebuilt.**

__2__   **B.**   **However, during World War II large parts of Munich were destroyed.**

_____   **C.**   **Today, Munich is again a center for German art, architecture and education.**

__1__   **D.**   **For many years before World War II the city of Munich was one of Germany's great cultural centers.**

So far this makes sense. Sentence D talks about Munich before World War II, and sentence B then talks about Munich during World

War II. Now, what comes third?

Let me read sentence C again: 'Today, Munich is again a center of German art, architecture and education.' Because it says 'today,' this sentence sounds like it should be the last one in the set. Also, because it says 'Munich is again a center of art' and so on, it should come after the one about Munich being rebuilt. So sentence A should be the third sentence. I write 3 there.

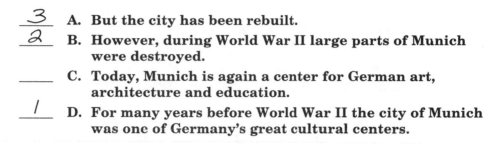

___3___ **A.** But the city has been rebuilt.

___2___ **B.** However, during World War II large parts of Munich were destroyed.

_____ **C.** Today, Munich is again a center for German art, architecture and education.

___1___ **D.** For many years before World War II the city of Munich was one of Germany's great cultural centers.

That means sentence C is number 4.

___3___ **A.** But the city has been rebuilt.

___2___ **B.** However, during World War II large parts of Munich were destroyed.

___4___ **C.** Today, Munich is again a center for German art, architecture and education.

___1___ **D.** For many years before World War II the city of Munich was one of Germany's great cultural centers.

Let me read all four sentences in the order I numbered them to make sure it all makes sense: 'For many years before World War II the city of Munich was one of Germany's great cultural centers. However, during World War II large parts of Munich were destroyed. But the city has been rebuilt. Today, Munich is again a center for German art, architecture and education.' That seems to make sense.

Did you notice how much detail this Problem Solver was able to explain as she thought aloud? As you work the exercises of this book, try to make your TAPS explanations as detailed as hers. You will be surprised how much you can learn by listening to your own thinking.

EXERCISE INSTRUCTIONS

These exercises will give you a chance to practice using TAPS with a partner. Take turns being the Problem Solver and the Listener. When you are the Problem Solver, make an effort to state as much detail as possible as you work the problem. When you are the Listener, remember to listen carefully for accuracy and to ask questions when necessary.

EXERCISE 1

Read these four sentences and number them in the best logical order. Write "1" by the sentence you think should come first, "2" by the sentence which should come second, and so on.

_____ A. Alaska is important as a source of furs, fish, oil and gold.

_____ B. Because of this location, several airports have been built where planes traveling to Japan and China can stop for fuel.

_____ C. But in this age of airplanes, it is important for another reason also.

_____ D. It is located at a good stopping place on the shortest air route from Seattle, Washington, to China or Japan.

EXERCISE 2

Read these four sentences and number them in the best logical order. Write "1" by the sentence you think should come first, "2" by the sentence which should come second, and so on.

_____ A. The secret to their survival seems to be in their bark, which is two feet thick, spongy, and filled with tannin.

_____ B. They have survived forest fires and avoided serious damage from insects.

_____ C. Some Sequoia trees in the Sierra Nevada Mountains have lived to be more than two thousand years old.

_____ D. Tannin is known to protect wood from insects and the spongy bark does not catch fire even when other flaming trees fall against a Sequoia.

> **The next two exercises are a little different. The Problem Solver might want to use scrap paper and draw a sketch or diagram as he/she thinks aloud and works through the exercise.**

EXERCISE 3

Read this paragraph, then answer the question beneath it.

The Ohio River is longer than the Tennessee River. The Arkansas River is shorter than the Mississippi River. The Arkansas River is longer than the Ohio River.

Which river is the shortest? _____

EXERCISE 4

Read this paragraph, then answer the question beneath it.

Tina has fewer CD's than Owen. Isaac has more CD's than Rolanda but he has less than Tina. Bob has more CD's than Tina but he has fewer than Owen.

Who has the most CD's? _____

Benefits of
Thinking Aloud Problem Solving
(TAPS)

Research has shown that TAPS is a very successful method for improving reading and reasoning skills. Why is TAPS such a good method?

TAPS helps you strengthen your reading and reasoning skills because it brings your skills 'out into the open' where they can be observed by others. When skills can be observed, they can then be improved.

For example, when you are dancing someone can watch you dance and notice which steps you do well — and also which steps you don't do so well. The watcher can then give you suggestions for improving parts of your dancing.

Likewise, when you use TAPS while working a reading exercise your reasoning and reading skills are brought out into the open — you and your partner can observe the steps you perform. Suggestions can then be made for improving parts of your reading and reasoning. You can learn to eliminate bad habits as well as boost successful skills.

Secondly, when you are reading aloud and explaining all your thoughts to a partner, you tend to read more carefully and thoroughly. This good habit by itself will improve your reading comprehension.

TAPS doesn't just help the one talking aloud either. You can learn a lot by observing your partner's thinking. By observing how your partner successfully reads and answers questions, you can see how someone else successfully deals with complex information and you can learn to use similar steps.

ADDITIONAL ASSIGNMENTS

1. In TAPS it is important for the Listener to ask questions that help the Problem Solver to think clearly. On the lines below, write at least three sample questions that a Listener could use to better understand what a Problem Solver is thinking or doing. One sample question has been provided as an example.

What details did you use to come to that conclusion?

_____

_____

_____

_____

_____

_____

_____

_____

2. Working with a partner has several benefits over working by yourself. Write two benefits on the lines below.

_____

_____

_____

_____

_____

_____

Reading For Context Clues And Vocabulary Growth

OBJECTIVES

When you have completed this unit you will

- be able to use four types of context clues to figure out a word's meaning;

- know the meanings of forty vocabulary Power Words;

- be able to use context clues to identify missing words in sentences;

- be able to solve analogies based upon vocabulary words.

INTRODUCTION

To understand what you read, you must first know the meanings of the words. Nothing can disturb your reading more, and confuse you more, than running into one unfamiliar word after another. So, a good first step in helping yourself better understand and enjoy what you read is to improve your knowledge of word meanings. In other words, to improve your vocabulary skill.

One way to increase your understanding of the vocabulary in reading material is to use a dictionary when you read. Anytime you come across a word you don't understand, look it up in a dictionary. But there is another method you can use that will often save you a trip to the dictionary. This is to use *context clues* that surround an unfamiliar word to figure out that word's meaning.

What are *context clues*? Context clues are hints you can find about one word's meaning by looking carefully at the other words in a sentence. For example, read the following sentence and try to decide what the word "consumed" means.

**Gerard was so hungry that for lunch he *consumed*
three sandwiches and a quart of milk.**

By looking carefully at the other words in this sentence you can easily figure out what "consumed" means. The sentence gives the context clues (hints) that Gerard was hungry and that he *did something with* three sandwiches and a quart of milk. From these context clues, you can figure out that "consumed" must mean "ate and drank." By doing this thinking you would not have to stop your reading and look up "consumed" in a dictionary.

The ability to use context clues to figure out a word's meaning is a valuable reading skill. In this unit, you will learn and practice how to use four different kinds (cases) of context clues. These four cases are:

CASE I: Meaning Stated With Punctuation
CASE II: Meaning Stated Without Punctuation
CASE III: Meaning Given By Contrast
CASE IV: Meaning Inferred From Ideas In The Sentence.

Each of these four cases has its own set of exercises in this unit. When you are ready, begin with CASE I on the next page.

CASE I: Meaning Stated With Punctuation

The simplest kind of context clue is when punctuation marks have been used to set off the meaning of a key word from the rest of the words in a sentence. Below is an example. Read this sentence carefully. Try to figure out the meaning of the word "elusive."

The "Swamp Fox" got his nickname because he was *elusive*—hard to pin down and catch.

The meaning of "elusive" is stated in the sentence. It is set off from the rest of the sentence by the dash. "Elusive" means "hard to pin down and catch."

Other forms of punctuation are also often used in sentences to state a key word's meaning. Study the following two sentences. Try to determine the meaning of the underlined word in each sentence.

Eating properly helps you <u>maintain</u> (keep up) your health.

The teacher asked Lou to stay after school because he pulled a <u>jape</u>, a practical joke, on the principal.

In the first sentence, parentheses are used to give the meaning of "maintain"—keep up. The second sentence has two commas that give the meaning of "jape"—practical joke.

The exercises on the next three pages will give you practice in figuring out a word's meaning using "meaning stated with punctuation" context clues.

EXERCISE INSTRUCTIONS

On the next three pages is a set of exercises called WORD POWER: CASE I. These exercises will build your skill in finding word "meaning stated with punctuation." They will also teach you 10 Power Words.

The Power Words are important words for you to add to your vocabulary. You will see these words often in your reading, so you should try hard to learn and remember their meanings. You should also try to use these words in your own speech. They will add power to your language skills.

Read the directions for the exercises carefully. Work slowly. Try to get every exercise correct.

Word Power Case I

Directions: Study each of the Power Words below. Note how each word is pronounced. In each of the sentences, the meaning of the Power Word is set off from the rest of the sentence by punctuation marks. Read each sentence to figure out what the Power Word means. Then complete the exercises on the next two pages.

Power Words	anecdote	legislation	assume	negligible	distinguish
	culture	rank	capacity	conflict	extraordinary

1. **anecdote** | **ăn′** ĭk dōt′ |
   - Telling a funny *anecdote* (a short story) is a good way to begin a speech.

2. **culture** | **kŭl′** chər |
   - Chinese *culture*—the beliefs, activities and possessions of those people—is quite different from American culture.

3. **legislation** | lĕj′ ĭs **lā′** shən |
   - *Legislation*—the making of laws—is done in the United States by senators and congressmen.

4. **rank** | răngk |
   - In the army a soldier's *rank*, his or her position in the order of command or authority, is shown by the number of stripes on the uniform.

5. **assume** | ə sōōm′ |
   - If you *assume* (accept as true) that everyone in the world is honest, you may lose everything you own.

6. **capacity** | kə **păs′** ĭ tē |
   - A bottle's *capacity*, the amount of liquid it can hold, can be measured in ounces or milliliters.

7. **negligible** | **nĕg′** lĭ jə bəl |
   - The company claimed that the amount of chemicals it dumped into the river was *negligible*—too small to have any effect.

8. **conflict** | **kŏn′** flĭkt′ |
   - Many soldiers lost their lives in the *conflict*, or war, between the North and the South.

9. **distinguish** | dĭ **stĭng′** gwĭsh |
   - Can you *distinguish* (tell the difference) between the Greek and the Roman buildings?

10. **extraordinary** | ĭk **strôr′** dn ĕr ē |
    - That child is an *extraordinary* (unusually good) artist.

ă pat / ā pay / â care / ä father / ĕ pet / ē be / ĭ pit / ī pie / î fierce / ŏ pot / ō go / ô paw, for / oi oil / ŏŏ book /
ōō boot / ou out / ŭ cut / û fur / *th* the / th thin / hw which / zh vision / ə ago, item, pencil, atom, circus

Meaning Comprehension Case I

Directions: In the blank next to each Power Word, write the letter of its correct definition.

Power Words

_____ anecdote

_____ culture

_____ legislation

_____ rank

_____ assume

_____ capacity

_____ negligible

_____ conflict

_____ distinguish

_____ extraordinary

Definitions

a. very unusual and special

b. too small to be important, not big enough to pay attention to

c. position in the order of command or authority

d. tell the difference, see how things are not alike

e. fight, war

f. the amount that can be held or contained in something

g. short story

h. the beliefs, activities and possessions of a group of people

i. the making of laws

j. accept as true, take for granted

Context Completion

Directions: Each sentence below has a blank where a word is missing. Choose the Power Word that goes in each blank and write it in the blank. Use each Power Word only once.

1. In the air force an officer with a high _____ may give orders to a lower officer.

2. Juan and Pedro are twins and look almost identical (completely alike), so it is hard to _____ them.

3. Jenny kept us laughing with one funny _____ after another about her stay at summer camp.

4. Before taking a trip to India it would be helpful to study the Indian _____ to see how the people think and live.

5. The gas tank in most cars has a _____ of about 15 gallons.

6. I didn't wear my boots because the amount of snow on the ground was _____ .

7. Easter Island is an _____ sight because of the huge heads carved in stone that stand on its hillsides.

8. In the future a small _____ between two nations might easily turn into a world-wide war.

9. Yesterday the State Senate voted in favor of _____ to change the legal drinking age to 21.

10. "I _____ that you did the homework," said the teacher, "so please tell the class the answer to the first exercise."

Muscle Builder Analogies

Directions: Each exercise below is an incomplete analogy. For each exercise, choose the Power Word that best completes that analogy. Write that Power Word in the blank. Write only Power Words in the blanks.

1. AGREEMENT is to ARGUMENT *as* PEACE is to _____

2. VERY LARGE is to GREAT *as* VERY SMALL is to _____

3. NOVEL is to LONG *as* _____ is to SHORT

CASE II: Meaning Stated Without Punctuation

In CASE I, you learned how the definition of a word is often stated in a sentence with the use of punctuation marks. In CASE II, the meaning of a key word is again stated in the sentence. But in this case it is NOT set off by punctuation marks.

Here is a sentence which contains the meaning of "aroma." Try to figure out the definition of "aroma" by reading the sentence carefully.

Farm country has its own special *aroma* and when I notice that smell I know I'm close to home and far from the city.

The sentence tells you that the meaning of "aroma" is "smell." First the sentence mentions the farm country's *aroma*, then it talks about the aroma as *that smell*. This context clue shows that "aroma" means "smell."

Here is another example. Can you figure out the meaning of "infection"?

Dying from an *infection* was common until modern medicines were developed that could stop the spread of disease in the body.

The context clue in this sentence tells you that an "infection" is an "unhealthy condition caused by the spread of disease in the body."

This kind of context clue is very common in textbooks. Read your textbooks carefully. You will find that many key words and terms have their definitions stated in simpler words within the same sentence or paragraph.

EXERCISE INSTRUCTIONS

On the next three pages is the WORD POWER: CASE II exercise set. These exercises will build your skill in figuring out word "meaning stated without punctuation." You will also learn 10 new Power Words to add to your vocabulary.

Word Power Case II

Directions: Study each of the Power Words below. Note how each word is pronounced. In each of the sentences, the meaning of the Power Word is stated within the sentence. Read each of the sentences to figure out what the Power Word means. Then complete the exercises on the next two pages.

Power Words

estimate	abroad	axis	affable	staff
commerce	imaginary	astronomers	intercede	objection

1. **estimate** | ĕs′ tə māt |
   - You should *estimate* how much time you need to study for a test because a careful guess can help you plan your studying.

2. **commerce** | kŏm′ ərs |
   - The president wanted to increase the country's *commerce* with other nations because the increased trade would give people jobs.

3. **abroad** | ə brôd′ |
   - Traveling *abroad* is educational because you can learn a lot from seeing how people in other countries live.

4. **imaginary** | ĭ măj′ ə nĕr′ ē |
   - The equator is an *imaginary* line which we pretend runs around the earth's middle.

5. **axis** | ăk′ sĭs |
   - The earth's *axis* is an imaginary line running through its center—from the North to the South Pole—around which the earth spins.

6. **astronomers** | ə strŏn′ ə mərs |
   - The ability of *astronomers* to study the stars and planets has improved with the invention of powerful telescopes.

7. **affable** | ăf′ ə bəl |
   - Although the boxer acted mean when he was in the ring, he was actually *affable* and always happy to talk to fans.

8. **intercede** | ĭn′ tər sēd′ |
   - The word *intercede* is made up of "inter," which is a prefix meaning "between," and "cede," which means "go."

9. **staff** | stăf |
   - The mayor's *staff* was made up of people that could best help her run the city.

10. **objection** | əb jĕk′ shən |
    - My argument that the project would be too expensive for us to do was also the *objection* of others.

ă pat / ā pay / â care / ä father / ĕ pet / ē be / ĭ pit / ī pie / î fierce / ŏ pot / ō go / ô paw, for / oi oil / oŏ book /
oō boot / ou out / ŭ cut / û fur / *th* the / th thin / hw which / zh vision / ə ago, item, pencil, atom, circus

Meaning Comprehension Case II

Directions: In the blank next to each Power Word, write the letter of its correct definition.

Power Words

_____ estimate

_____ commerce

_____ abroad

_____ imaginary

_____ axis

_____ astronomers

_____ affable

_____ intercede

_____ staff

_____ objection

Definitions

a. trade, business, the buying and selling of products between two areas

b. a group of people who work for and help a leader

c. guess carefully, approximate

d. friendly, easy to speak to, pleasant

e. people who study the stars and planets

f. outside one's country, in foreign lands

g. a reason or argument given against something

h. go between two people or groups to try to settle an argument between them

i. that on which a thing spins or turns

j. not real, pretended, existing only in the imagination

Context Completion

Directions: Each sentence below has a blank where a word is missing. Choose the Power Word that goes in each blank and write it in the blank. Use each Power Word only once.

1. Before mankind went to the moon, _____ knew quite a bit about the moon's surface through studying it with strong telescopes.

2. The president called a meeting of his _____ to discuss the country's budget.

3. A strike by truck drivers would interfere with the _____ between the United States and Mexico.

4. After graduating from high school Marcia traveled _____ for several months, then returned to America and went to college.

5. It is nicer to travel with someone who is _____ rather than with someone who is always in a bad mood.

6. A good carpenter can _____ how much wood is needed for a bookcase before measuring anything.

7. Mom would _____ whenever my two sisters argued and help them solve their disagreement.

8. Will you do what we ask or do you have an _____?

9. Many young children pretend to have special friends that are
_____ and can't be seen by other people.

10. The North and South Poles are the ends of the earth's _____ .

Muscle Builder Analogies

Directions: Each exercise below is an incomplete analogy. For each exercise, <u>choose the Power Word</u> that best completes that analogy. Write that Power Word in the blank. <u>Write only Power Words in the blanks</u>.

1. GEOLOGISTS are to ROCKS *as* _____ are to STARS

2. TRADE is to COMMERCE *as* FRIENDLY is to
_____

3. NIAGARA FALLS is to REAL *as* EQUATOR is to
_____

CASE III: Meaning Given By Contrast

CASES I and II showed how a word's meaning is often stated clearly in the other words of a sentence. In CASE III, a word's meaning is again given in the sentence. But in this case it is given by a *contrast* in the sentence. A *contrast* is a word or idea that *is the opposite of* the key word.

Read the sentence below. Study how the definition of "linger" can be understood from the contrast phrase "leave immediately."

You should not *linger* in the theater but should leave immediately when the movie is over.

You can conclude from the sentence that "linger" means *the opposite of* the phrase "leave immediately." Therefore, "linger" must mean "be slow to leave."

Here is another example. Read this sentence carefully and you will see that the meaning of "unintelligible" is given by TWO contrasts.

You should try to write clearly because if your writing is *unintelligible* people will not understand what you mean to say.

The word "unintelligible" is first contrasted with "clearly." Then it is also contrasted with the idea that "people will understand." (Notice that the word *not* gives the contrast of "people will understand.") Because of these two contrasts, you know that "unintelligible" means the opposite of "clearly" and "people will understand." Therefore, "unintelligible" must mean "unclear, not able to be understood."

The exercises on the next three pages will give you practice in determining a word's meaning by using the context clue of word "meaning given by contrast."

EXERCISE INSTRUCTIONS

Exercise set WORD POWER: CASE III is on the next three pages. Try hard to figure out the meaning of each Power Word by studying the contrast given in each sentence.

Word Power Case III

Directions: Study each of the Power Words below. Note how each word is pronounced. In each of the sentences, the meaning of the Power Word is given by a contrast within the sentence. Read each sentence to figure out what the Power Word means. Then complete the exercises on the next two pages.

Power Words	contradict	typical	interior	utter	previous
	unique	charitable	exterior	durable	discard

1. **contradict** | kŏn′ trə **dĭkt′** |
   - Everyone must have agreed with the speaker because I didn't hear anyone *contradict* her statements.

2. **unique** | yo͞o **nēk′** |
   - Each person is *unique* since no two people are exactly alike.

3. **typical** | **tĭp′** ĭ kəl |
   - Advertisers aim most of their ads at *typical* people rather than unusual or different people.

4. **charitable** | **chăr′** ĭ tə bəl |
   - The family painted the church as a *charitable* act and did not expect to be paid for their work.

5. **interior** | ĭn **tîr′** ē ər |
   - From the outside the house looked run-down, but the *interior* was richly decorated and beautiful.

6. **exterior** | ĭk **stîr′** ē ər |
   - After the explosion the *exterior* of the building was fine, but the interior was in ruins.

7. **utter** | **ŭt′** ər |
   - He is normally talkative, so people wondered why he didn't *utter* one word all evening.

8. **durable** | **do͝or′** ə bəl |
   - The wise shopper saves money by buying *durable* clothes because clothes that wear out quickly must be replaced more often, which can be costly.

9. **previous** | **prē′** vē əs |
   - John had trouble in his *previous* math class, but this year he has a better teacher and math seems easier.

10. **discard** | dĭs **kärd′** |
    - Each spring I clean out my garage and *discard* what is broken and useless and keep only the useful things.

ă pat / ā pay / â care / ä father / ĕ pet / ē be / ĭ pit / ī pie / î fierce / ŏ pot / ō go / ô paw, for / oi oil / o͝o book /
o͞o boot / ou out / ŭ cut / ü fur / *th* the / th thin / hw which / zh vision / ə ago, item, pencil, atom, circus

Meaning Comprehension Case III

Directions: In the blank next to each Power Word, write the letter of its correct definition.

Power Words

_____ contradict

_____ unique

_____ typical

_____ charitable

_____ interior

_____ exterior

_____ utter

_____ durable

_____ previous

_____ discard

Definitions

a. speak

b. inside, inner surface or part

c. like most others, average, usual

d. sturdy, long-lasting, able to withstand wear and tear

e. argue against, disagree with

f. throw away, get rid of as worthless

g. unlike anything else, one of a kind, unusual

h. outside, outer surface or part

i. kind and generous; done not for profit but to help others

j. earlier, coming before something else

Context Completion

Directions: Each sentence below has a blank where a word is missing. Choose the Power Word that goes in each blank and write it in the blank. Use each Power Word only once.

1. In many states people save empty cans for recycling rather than _____ them with the trash.

2. The _____ of the car is just as fancy and stylish as the outside.

3. Students never _____ a word of complaint— until the teacher is out of hearing!

4. Sails on boats are made of canvas because canvas is a _____ material that is not easily ruined by wind or water.

5. By definition an invention is _____ : There has never before been anything just like it.

6. Doing volunteer work in a hospital is a _____ thing to do and more people should serve their community in this way.

7. Because it had been super cold the _____ winter, people prepared for winter this year by buying extra-warm parkas and fur-lined boots.

8. The employee didn't agree with his boss, but decided not to _____ her during the meeting.

9. The inside of the briefcase was lined with suede and its
_____ was made from leather.

10. A _____ American family watches several
hours of T.V. every day, but there are a few families that don't
watch any T.V. at all.

Muscle Builder Analogies

Directions: Each exercise below is an incomplete analogy. For each
exercise, choose the Power Word that best completes that analogy.
Write that Power Word in the blank. Write only Power Words in the
blanks.

1. AGREE WITH is to CONTRADICT *as* INTERIOR is to
_____

2. DISCARD is to KEEP *as* FLIMSY is to _____

3. TYPICAL is to USUAL *as* _____ is to UNUSUAL

CASE IV: Meaning Inferred From Ideas In The Sentence

In context clue CASES I, II and III, you learned how the definition of a word is often *directly stated* in the other words in a sentence. When you come across an unfamiliar word in your reading, you should always look for these direct context clues.

However, in some sentences the meaning of an unfamiliar word will not be directly stated in the sentence. Yet, you can still often figure out the word's meaning by thinking carefully about the *ideas* in the sentence. By thinking about what the sentence is saying, you may be able to *infer* (conclude) what the unfamiliar word must mean. For example, try to infer the meaning of "elation" from the ideas in the following sentence.

> **The diver knew she had won first place when her last dive was scored a perfect 10.0, and her *elation* showed when she hugged her teammate.**

The sentence says that the diver won first place and she hugged her teammate. From these ideas you can *infer* that "elation" must mean "great happiness or joy."

Now try to infer the meaning of "negotiate" from the ideas in this sentence below.

> **The football star let his agent *negotiate* with the team owner about a change in his contract.**

From what you know about a football star, his agent, a team owner and a contract, you can infer that "negotiate" means "discuss with the hope of reaching an agreement" or "bargain."

When you come across an unfamiliar word and its definition is not directly stated in the sentence, try to infer its meaning from ideas in the sentence.

EXERCISE INSTRUCTIONS

On the next three pages is the WORD POWER: CASE IV exercise set. These exercises will boost your ability to find word "meaning inferred from ideas in the sentence." You will also master another 10 Power Words.

Word Power Case IV

Directions: Study each of the Power Words below. Note how each word is pronounced. In each of the sentences, the meaning of the Power Word can be inferred from the entire context of the sentence. Read each sentence to figure out the meaning of that Power Word. Then complete the exercises on the next two pages.

Power Words	essential	compelled	laborious	latter	barren
	issue	flaw	semicircle	detract	cunning

1. **essential** | ĭ **sĕn'** shəl |
   - Good tools are *essential* for a car mechanic because they turn otherwise hard jobs into easy work.

2. **issue** | **ĭsh'** ōo |
   - "Who has the right to vote?" was a main *issue* discussed by the Continental Congress.

3. **compelled** | kəm **pĕld'** |
   - The history exam is tomorrow morning, so Jocey feels *compelled* to study tonight.

4. **flaw** | flô |
   - Because the diamond had a *flaw* it was less valuable.

5. **laborious** | lə **bôr'** ē əs |
   - It took years of *laborious* digging to finish the Panama Canal.

6. **semicircle** | **sĕm'** ĭ **sûr'** kəl |
   - Some artists draw a circle freehand by first drawing a *semicircle* and then adding another semicircle to complete the full circle.

7. **latter** | **lăt'** ər |
   - The words "big" and "large" are synonymous (have the same meaning), but the *latter* word has two more letters.

8. **detract** | dĭ **trăkt'** |
   - Your sunglasses *detract* from your appearance because they hide your beautiful eyes.

9. **barren** | **băr'** ən |
   - The volcano's lava poured destructively down the mountainside and left the land *barren*.

10. **cunning** | **kŭn'** ĭng |
    - The raccoon is a *cunning* animal that can easily ruin a camping trip by stealing even the best hidden or locked up food.

ă pat / ā pay / â care / ä father / ĕ pet / ē be / ĭ pit / ī pie / î fierce / ŏ pot / ō go / ô paw, for / oi oil / ōo book /
ōo boot / ou out / ŭ cut / û fur / *th* the / th thin / hw which / zh vision / ə ago, item, pencil, atom, circus

Meaning Comprehension Case IV

Directions: In the blank next to each Power Word, write the letter of its correct definition.

Power Words

_____ essential

_____ issue

_____ compelled

_____ flaw

_____ laborious

_____ semicircle

_____ latter

_____ detract

_____ barren

_____ cunning

Definitions

a. lacking or unable to produce plants

b. topic for discussion, question or problem being debated

c. one-half of a circle

d. something which is wrong, a defect, an imperfection

e. forced or made (to do something), strongly influenced

f. difficult, demanding great effort and hard work

g. take away something, lessen in value

h. necessary, of great importance

i. clever, sly, crafty

j. the second of two things; something closer to the end than other things

Context Completion

Directions: Each sentence below has a blank where a word is missing. Choose the Power Word that goes in each blank and write it in the blank. Use each Power Word only once.

1. Half the moon was covered by a cloud, but the part that could be seen formed a bright _____ .

2. The shirt was not made perfectly but had a small _____ , so it was reduced in price.

3. A spy must be a _____ person who can pretend for a long time to be something he or she isn't.

4. This section of the coast will be _____ until the surf washes away the oil from the oil spill and plants can grow again.

5. Skill in basic math is _____ for almost all science courses, including chemistry and physics.

6. Rust and dents _____ from the value of a car.

7. I like peanut butter better than jelly because the _____ is too sweet for my tastes.

8. There are many people on each side of the _____ of saying prayers aloud in public schools.

9. Building big muscles requires years of _____
    weight lifting.

10. President Nixon said he felt _____ to resign
    the presidency although he didn't really want to do so.

Muscle Builder Analogies

Directions: Each exercise below is an incomplete analogy. For each exercise, <u>choose the Power Word</u> that best completes that analogy. Write that Power Word in the blank. <u>Write only Power Words in the blanks</u>.

1. TURTLE is to SLOW *as* FOX is to _____

2. UNNECESSARY is to ESSENTIAL *as* EASY is to
    _____

3. WISH is to WANTED *as* NEED is to _____

ADDITIONAL ASSIGNMENTS

1. Look up the definitions of the words below in a dictionary. Write the *first* definition given for each word on the line next to the word.

    banquet: _____

    coincide: _____

    customary: _____

    dishonor: _____

    miracle: _____

    quarry: _____

    segment: _____

    suspicious: _____

NOTE: In completing the following exercises, do not use any word more than once.

2. Pick one of the words from Exercise 1. Write a sentence on the lines below in which the meaning of that word is *stated with punctuation* (CASE I).

    _____

    _____

    _____

3. Pick one of the words from Exercise 1. Write a sentence on the lines below in which the meaning of that word is *stated without punctuation* (CASE II).

    _____

    _____

    _____

4. Pick one of the words from Exercise 1. Write a sentence on the lines below in which the meaning of that word is *given by contrast* (CASE III).

    _____

    _____

    _____

ADDITIONAL ASSIGNMENTS

5. Pick one of the words from Exercise 1. Write a sentence on the lines below in which the meaning of that word can be *inferred from ideas in the sentence* (CASE IV).

_____

_____

_____

Cloze:
Identifying Missing Words

OBJECTIVES

When you have completed this unit you will

- be able to use context clues to choose the best word (from four choices) to go in each of several blanks in an incomplete paragraph;

- be able to use context clues to put a list of words in blanks in an incomplete paragraph.

INTRODUCTION

This unit will add to the reading skills you developed in Unit 2. In Unit 2, you improved your skills in studying sentence contexts for word meaning. In this unit, you will apply these skills to reading longer passages and identifying omitted (missing) words. This process is called *cloze*. Reading passages to identify missing words will boost your ability to understand reading material fully, without missing any ideas.

EXERCISE INSTRUCTIONS

Each exercise is a passage with blanks for missing words. Each blank is numbered. Below the passage are four choices for each blank. Choose and then write the word that belongs in each blank.

Read the passage slowly and carefully. When you come to a blank, study the sentence context and think about the meaning of the entire passage. Sometimes a sentence that comes before the blank will give you a clue for the missing word. Other times you may have to read *past* the blank to get enough information to choose the correct word.

Try the example below.

EXAMPLE: Read the passage. Choose and then write the word that belongs in each blank.

As other parts of your body ¹_____, your bones grow too. ²_____ are the framework of your body. They give shape to your ³_____ . Without your bones, you could not ⁴_____ or sit. You would be much ⁵_____ a rag doll.

There are over 200 bones in your ⁶_____ . As a group, these ⁷_____ make up your *skeleton* [SKEHL-uht-uhn].

1. weaken   die   grow   subtract
2. Fingers   Bones   Toes   Eyes
3. body   house   cat   dog
4. fall   stop   add   stand
5. bigger   like   louder   different
6. closet   suitcase   body   house
7. veins   muscles   teeth   bones

Double check your work. Then compare your answers with the ones on the next page.

Answers: **The correct words are written in the blanks of the passage.**

As other parts of your body ¹___grow___, your bones grow too. ²___Bones___ are the framework of your body. They give shape to your ³___body___. Without your bones, you could not ⁴___stand___ or sit. You would be much ⁵___like___ a rag doll.

There are over 200 bones in your ⁶___body___. As a group, these ⁷___bones___ make up your *skeleton* [SKEHL-uht-uhn].

1. weaken   die   grow   subtract
2. Fingers   Bones   Toes   Eyes
3. body   house   cat   dog
4. fall   stop   add   stand
5. bigger   like   louder   different
6. closet   suitcase   body   house
7. veins   muscles   teeth   bones

When you understand these answers, begin the exercises that start on the next page. Work them carefully in the same way as the example. Try for 100% correct.

EXERCISE 1

You know that ¹_____ , flowers and vegetables are plants. But the smallest plants are ²_____ as bacteria (bak–TIR–ee–ya). They are so ³_____ that you cannot see them with just your eyes. You must use a microscope to ⁴_____ them. The largest ⁵_____ are only one-thousandth of an inch long, and most are much smaller than that. Bacteria are one-celled ⁶_____ . While most large plants can ⁷_____ their own food, many bacteria cannot. Therefore, they must depend on other ⁸_____ or animals for their ⁹_____ .

1. bees   bears   trees   tigers
2. known   largest   gone   dead
3. large   hot   small   cold
4. go   sell   hear   see
5. trees   bacteria   foods   microscopes

6. animals   dogs   humans   plants
7. drive   make   cut   walk
8. plants   cars   pencils   books
9. money   homes   food   clothes

EXERCISE 2

Some bacteria are ¹_____ to man. They cause illnesses (such as tuberculosis) which can possibly lead to ²_____ . But many bacteria are ³_____ . We use bacteria to ⁴_____ cheese, wine and yogurt, and linen from flax. Some bacteria ⁵_____ in the human body help in the digestion of food. Bacteria also break down dead ⁶_____ and animals into simple chemicals which can then be used again by ⁷_____ plants or animals. Finally, some bacteria ⁸_____ a chemical called nitrogen into a form which can be used by plants. Since plants need nitrogen to ⁹_____ , without these bacteria plants could not grow.

1. bacteria   useful   harmful   maybe
2. birth   death   bacteria   live
3. dead   harmful   large   useful
4. make   use   buy   answer
5. bought   in   found   above

6. animals   plants   dead   break
7. dead   plants   animals   living
8. change   travel   fly   swim
9. die   weaken   grow   fail

EXERCISE 3

My brother ¹_____ he is never wrong. Once
²_____ an argument I said, "You think you are always
³_____ , don't you?"

"No," ⁴_____ answered. "I was ⁵_____
once."

"When was that?" ⁶_____ asked.

"The ⁷_____ that I thought I was wrong and I
wasn't," he ⁸_____ smartly.

1. is   works   thinks   will
2. I   during   he   if
3. wrong   right   safe   threatened
4. I   she   he   they

5. right   always   wrong   never
6. I   he   that   wrong
7. reader   person   time   music
8. agreed   disagreed replied   asked

EXERCISE 4

Tooth decay is the breaking down of a ¹_____ . It
happens ²_____ of something called *plaque* [PLAK].
Plaque is partly made up of ³_____ that grow in groups
on teeth. It is also ⁴_____ up of sugar from foods. The
germs ⁵_____ on the sugar. As the germs feed,
⁶_____ make an acid. On a tooth on which there is
plaque, the acid may eat ⁷_____ the hard outside part
of the tooth. This may ⁸_____ a hole in the tooth. Such
a ⁹_____ is called a *cavity* [KAV-uht-ee].

If a cavity is not filled, the ¹⁰_____ may start breaking
down the inside of the tooth. The cavity may then become
¹¹_____ and larger. Finally, the whole
¹²_____ may be destroyed.

1. foot   hand   tooth   hair
2. therefore seldom   because   easy
3. gum   teeth   worms   germs
4. made   eaten   used   beaten
5. knock   lay   feed   fall
6. you   they   slowly   therefore

7. lunch   fish   through   tooth
8. sometimes never   come   cause
9. hole   man   day   bargain
10. tooth   dentist   acid   night
11. smaller   better   cavity   larger
12. germs   tooth   plaque   sugar

EXERCISE 5

Some ¹_____ have more than one meaning. They
sound alike, and they are ²_____ alike, but they can
fool you if you don't ³_____ fast.

This is a ⁴_____: July 4, 1776. But a date is also a
small brown ⁵_____ that is good to eat.

You ⁶_____ strike a match. But you can play a
⁷_____, too, on the tennis court or the hockey field.

A ⁸_____ is a round object that is thrown or bounced.
But a ⁹_____ is also a big dance.

The sound a ¹⁰_____ makes is a bark. But the outer
covering of a tree trunk is also ¹¹_____.

1.	foods	animals	words	songs	
2.	smelled	spelled	eaten	cooked	
3.	think	run	fly	walk	
4.	number	month	year	date	
5.	book	rock	fruit	door	
6.	make	are	eat	can	
7.	match	game	piano	role	
8.	globe	circle	ball	balloon	
9.	globe	circle	ball	balloon	
10.	cat	dog	bear	bee	
11.	wood	leave	bark	twigs	

EXERCISE 6

Vocabulary Preview: **Earl** (noun)—a royal title like "king" or "duke." The "Earl of Sandwich" was a man with a royal position in a section of England called Sandwich, just as the King of France held the highest royal position in France.

A number of words in our 1_____ are based on people's 2_____. For example, the Earl of Sandwich was a 3_____ man who didn't have time for 4_____. So he put a piece of meat 5_____ two pieces of 6_____ for a quick lunch. Thus the word 7_____ came into being. The milk you 8_____ is *pasteurized* to stop it from spoiling quickly. This is because Louis Pasteur discovered that germs cause 9_____ to spoil, and 10_____ are killed at very hot or cold temperatures. When milk is pasteurized it is 11_____ and then cooled. Just as the Earl of Sandwich and 12_____ had words based on their 13_____, you may someday have a word based on your name if 14_____ do something 15_____.

1. house language arithmetic city
2. feet hands names heads
3. busy hairy lazy crazy
4. books meals friends pets
5. there outside directly between
6. stone paper cardboard bread
7. Earl meat sandwich bread
8. eat drink walk fly
9. milk soda games weather
10. people germs milk vitamins
11. spilled drunk heated mixed
12. milk Sandwich Pasteur meat
13. foods homes laces names
14. they you we I
15. secretly nasty noteworthy wrong

EXERCISE 7

Sometimes there are two words that sound just alike but are not spelled the same way and don't <u>1_____</u> the same thing.

You can <u>2_____</u> a dish. But you can also step on the <u>3_____</u> if your bicycle is going too fast and you want to slow down.

If you go <u>4_____</u> a store, you go past it. But if you go into the store you can <u>5_____</u> something.

There is a <u>6_____</u> in his cage at the zoo. And if his fur is rubbed off in one place, he has a <u>7_____</u> spot.

You may wonder why a dog is wagging his <u>8_____</u>. And if you like, you can make up a <u>9_____</u> about him.

1.	sound	spell	mean	like	
2.	brake	drop	pedal	break	
3.	brake	drop	pedal	break	
4.	into	buy	take	by	
5.	into	buy	take	by	
6.	tiger	bear	bare	bald	
7.	tiger	bear	bare	bald	
8.	story	tail	song	tale	
9.	story	tail	song	tale	

EXERCISE 8

NOTE: Read the first **two** sentences before filling in blank #1.

Janus [JAY nuhs], in Roman mythology, was a god who had two faces that looked in ¹_____ directions. One face looked into the ²_____ and the other looked into the future. Janus served as the god of gates and doors and of entrances and ³_____. His name comes from the Latin word *janua*, ⁴_____ *gate*.

The Romans prayed to Janus at the beginning and ⁵_____ of any important action, especially a war. The ⁶_____ to Janus' temple in Rome always remained open in wartime. They were ⁷_____ only during the rare periods when Rome was at peace. The Romans called on Janus at the ⁸_____ of every prayer, even ahead of Jupiter, the king of the gods. January, the ⁹_____ month of the year, was named for Janus.

Other Indo-European peoples ¹⁰_____ a god who resembled Janus. For ¹¹_____, the early Hindus in India prayed to a ¹²_____ god named Vayu before starting any major undertaking.

1.   many   opposite   back   similar
2.   future   left   heart   past
3.   exits   middles   nights   flags
4.   stopping   meaning   starting   lasting
5.   bottom   future   end   top
6.   cars   buildings   walls   doors
7.   opened   closed   emptied   broken
8.   language   gods   Roman   beginning
9.   second   last   fourth   first
10. were   had   differed   passed
11. example   therefore   tomorrow   lasting
12. two-faced   one-faced   blue   nightly

EXERCISE 9

Vocabulary Preview: **playwright** (noun)—a writer of plays.
drama (noun)—a play presented by actors in a theater.
tragedy (noun)—a sad play.

Greek ¹_____ were among the world's greatest. They
invented what we ²_____ the *drama*. They
³_____ combined tragedy and comedy in one play. The
tragedies were all tragedy and the comedies were
⁴_____ comedy. The ⁵_____ great writers of
tragedy were Aeschylus (es′ kə ləs), Sophocles (sof′ ə klēz), and
Euripides (u rip′ ə dēz). The great ⁶_____ writer was
Aristophanes (ar is tof′ ə nēz), who poked fun at leaders and
politicians.

1. musicians   playwrights   soldiers   mathematicians
2. see   hear   tell   call
3. always   sometimes   never   frequently
4. every   sometimes   never   all
5. writers   three   two   tragedy
6. tragedy   mathematics   comedy   music

> The remaining exercises are a little different. Each sentence has
> a missing word. At the bottom of the passage, all of the missing
> words are listed. For each blank space of the passage, choose
> the missing word from the list and write it in the blank.

EXERCISE 10

Today I saw a young woman who seemed certain about her
future ¹_____. On her ²_____ was the sign:
Someday I will be a lawyer. I ³_____ how serious she
was about these plans. But the question was wiped from my mind
when she ⁴_____ off in an old, small Honda. On the
back ⁵_____ this sign: ⁶_____ I will be a
Cadillac.

was   Someday

drove   wondered

career   sweatshirt

EXERCISE 11

Vocabulary Preview: **compelled** (verb)—forced (to do something).

The *Omaha World-Herald* 1_____ a special Father's Day story each year. When the unpopular job of writing the story was assigned to a 2_____ named Ralph Hart, here is what he wrote:

"This is Father's 3_____. It is also the day when this reporter was to have his 4_____ in the paper about Father's Day. On Father's Day, a 5_____ can do as he wishes. This reporter 6_____ a father. He doesn't 7_____ to write a story. On Father's Day he can't be 8_____ to."

Hart's story appeared on page one of the paper and 9_____ many readers.

Day	compelled
want	story
is	father
amused	reporter
prints	

EXERCISE 12

Two famous women in science are a mother and her
1_____ . The mother, Marie Curie, 2_____
the Nobel Prize in physics in 1903. The Nobel Prize is the
3_____ award a scientist can win. Most
4_____ would be very 5_____ and happy to
win just one Nobel Prize in their lifetime. But Marie Curie won two
of 6_____ . The 7_____ one was awarded to
her in 1911, in the area of chemistry. Marie's daughter Irene
developed an 8_____ in her mother's work in radio-
activity. She 9_____ a leading scientist in the area
10_____ won the Nobel Prize for chemistry in 1935.
Marie Curie proved that a 11_____ can be an outstanding scientist and also a good 12_____ .

second	won
and	scientists
daughter	became
highest	woman
mother	proud
interest	them

ADDITIONAL ASSIGNMENTS

1. Pick a paragraph or short passage from one of your textbooks, an encyclopedia or a news article. On a separate piece of paper, copy the passage BUT *make these changes to it:* (1) omit one word from each sentence and put a blank where that word was; (2) number the blanks. Your written passage should look like the ones in this unit!

   Now, for each blank, write four word choices that might go in that blank. One choice should be the correct word. The other three choices should be *words that do not make sense in that blank.* Your list of choices for each blank should look like the ones in Exercises 1-9 in this unit.

   Ask a classmate or friend to read your passage and write the missing word in each blank. Discuss with that person *why* he or she chose each answer. Ask that person to explain the *context clues* he or she used to find the missing words.

2. *Write your own paragraph or short passage* on a topic that interests you. Then omit one word from each sentence and write choices like you did in Assignment 1.

   Ask a classmate or friend to read your passage and write the missing word in each blank. Discuss with that person the context clues he or she used to find the missing words.

3. Write another paragraph or short passage on a topic that interests you. Then omit one word from each sentence—BUT make sure you do not omit the same word twice!

   This time, *do not* write a list of choices for each blank. Instead, scramble the missing words so they are out of order and make a list of them underneath your passage. Your list of words should look like the one in Exercise 10 in this unit.

   Ask a classmate or friend to read your passage and write the missing word in each blank. Discuss with that person the context clues he or she used to find the missing words.

4. Study the meaning of the word "compelled" on page 41. Write a sentence on the lines below in which the meaning of "compelled" is *stated with punctuation* (see Unit 2, CASE I).

   _____

   _____

   _____

5. Study the meaning of the word "playwright" on page 40. Write a sentence on the lines below in which the meaning of "playwright" is *stated without punctuation* (see Unit 2, CASE II).

   _____

   _____

   _____

ADDITIONAL ASSIGNMENTS

6. Study the meaning of the word "tragedy" on page 40. Write a sentence on the lines below in which the meaning of "tragedy" is *given by contrast* (see Unit 2, CASE III).

_____

_____

_____

Reading And Writing Spatial Descriptions

OBJECTIVES

When you have completed this unit you will

- understand how words are used to describe the position, arrangement and direction of movement of objects;

- be able to make a diagram from a written passage describing a place, such as a park or a room;

- be able to make a diagram from a written passage describing the path of a moving object;

- be able to write instructions for following a given path or route;

- be able to draw objects from written descriptions of them.

INTRODUCTION

If you have ever tried to put together a toy model or to sew from a pattern, you know how hard it can be to follow exactly how the pieces fit together. Many textbooks contain information just like the directions for putting together a toy or sewing a piece of clothing. For example, they contain information about the geometry (shape and size) of things and the geography (location, distance, direction) of things. These kinds of descriptions are called *spatial* descriptions. They describe something's *position in space.* (In other words, the shape and size it has and where it is located.)

You must become good at following spatial descriptions in order to understand charts, graphs, maps, forms, patterns, diagrams and instruction sheets. Also, this will help you understand written passages about a thing and its parts (composition) and the arrangement of things. Even more, it will deepen your skill in arithmetic and geometry.

To boost your understanding of spatial descriptions, this unit will strengthen your:

— sense of direction
— sense of distance
— use of perimeter and area
— ability to visualize ("see") and draw things
— ability to arrange things in position.

This unit has three parts. The first part will develop your distance and direction skills. In the second part, you will get practice in drawing things from a written description. The third part will build your skill in arranging items in space.

PART I: Distance and Direction

Facts about distance and direction can often be hard to follow when you see them in writing. Words like east, west, north, south, left and right can be important for your understanding of what is being described. This part of the unit will improve your skill with this kind of information.

EXERCISE INSTRUCTIONS

The exercises that follow are written descriptions of distance and direction. You will be asked to show what is being described by drawing a diagram on a grid of squares (like graph paper). To demonstrate this procedure, here are two examples.

EXAMPLE 1

For this exercise, *let the length of one square equal one mile.* Also, *let the compass show the directions that lines follow.*

The diagram below shows a line that starts at point A and runs 3 miles east. It shows another line starting at point B and running 1 mile south. Study the diagram. Then try the exercise beneath it.

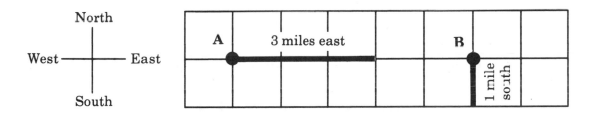

<u>Exercise:</u> *Let the length of one square equal 1 mile.*

Starting at point X, draw a line running 4 miles west.

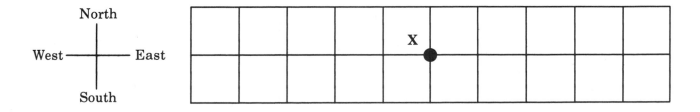

Check your answer with the diagram on the next page.

Answer: Here is how you should have drawn the line.

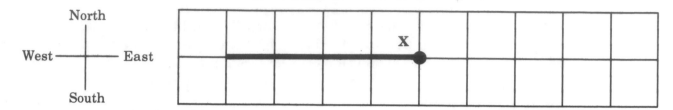

Note that the line runs across four squares because the length of a square in this exercise equals 1 mile. So, 4 squares equal 4 miles. Also, the line runs to the left from point X because the compass shows that *west* is to the left.

EXAMPLE 2

For the next exercise, *let the length of one square equal 5 miles.* First, study these sample lines. Then, try the exercise below.

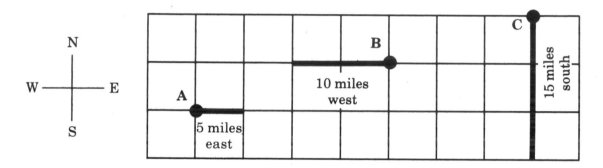

Exercise: *Let the length of one square equal 5 miles.*

Starting at point P, a car travelled 10 miles south, then 15 miles west, then 10 miles north, and then back to point P. Draw the route of the car.

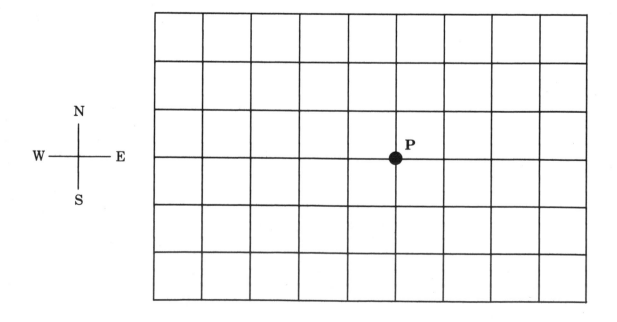

Answer: Here is the route of the car.

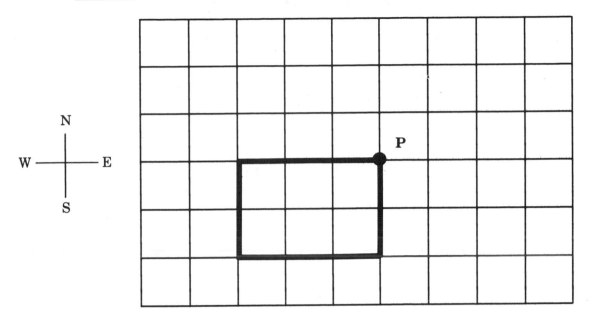

The first line drawn from point P runs two squares to the south because the length of a square in this exercise equals 5 miles. Then, the second line runs three squares to the west ("15 miles west"). The third line runs two squares to the north ("10 miles north"). The final line runs back to point P ("and then back to point P").

Begin now with the exercises on the next page.

EXERCISE 1:   Let the length of one square equal 2 miles. (Study these sample lines. Then, complete the exercise below.)

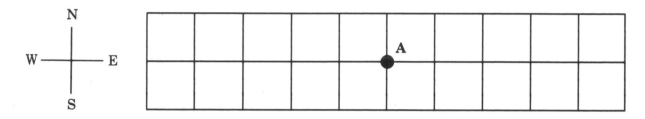

Starting at point A, draw a line running 6 miles east.

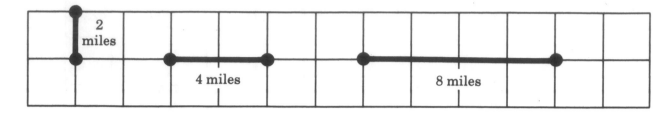

EXERCISE 2:   Let the length of one square equal 3 miles.

In going from our home to the mall we drive 6 miles west and then 12 miles south. Make a diagram of our route.

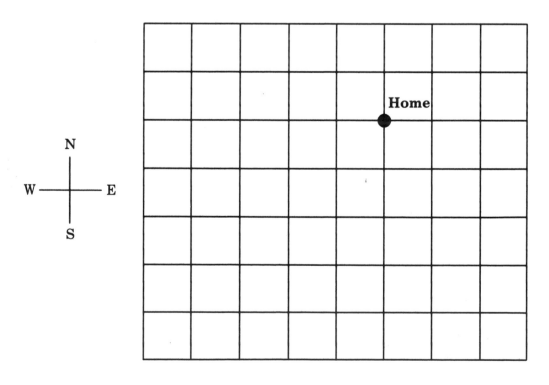

EXERCISE 3:   Let the length of one square equal 10 miles.

Starting at point P, a long-distance runner runs 10 miles north and stops for a rest. After a short time, she starts running again and goes another 10 miles north. Then she turns and runs 10 miles to the west. Draw the course she covers.

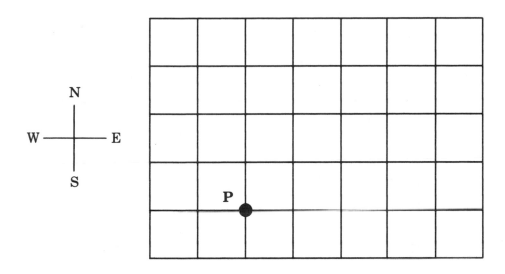

EXERCISE 4:   Let the length of one square equal 100 yards.

(A) Jody believes dogs need a lot of exercise. So, every day she takes her dog Tyler on the following walk. First, they leave the house and walk 300 yards east. Then Jody and Tyler turn and walk 200 yards north, and then turn again and walk 300 yards west. Finally, they turn and walk back to the house. Make a diagram of their walk.

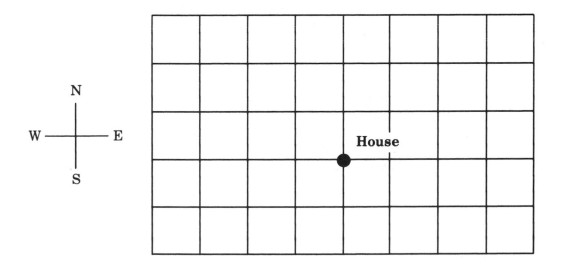

(B) How many total yards did they walk?   _____ yards

EXERCISE 5:   Let the length of one square equal 2 feet.

(A) Starting at point X, the borders of a garden run 10 feet east, 6 feet south, 2 feet west, 6 feet south, straight west to a point directly south of X, then straight back to X. Make a diagram of the garden. *Write the correct length in feet next to each side of the garden diagram.*

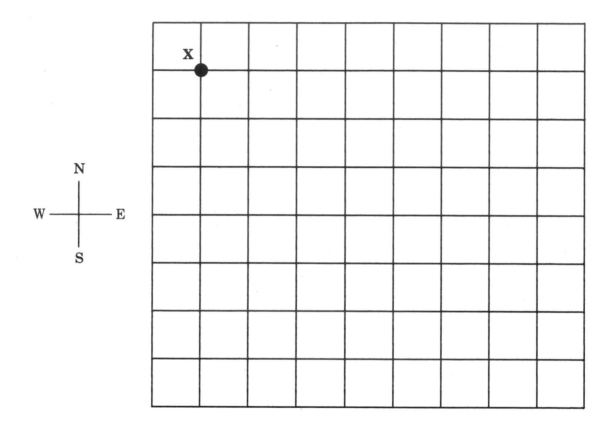

(B) The distance around the outside of the garden is called the *perimeter*. In order to put a chain fence around the garden, you would need to compute the perimeter to find how many feet of fence you need. To compute the perimeter, you add the length in feet of all the garden sides.

Compute the total distance in feet around the garden and write your answer in the blank.

Perimeter = _____ feet

EXERCISE 6:   Let the length of one square equal 2 miles.

(A)   Starting from its northeast corner, the borders of a park run 14 miles west, 4 miles south, 6 miles east, 2 miles south, 4 miles west, 6 miles south, 8 miles east, 4 miles north, east to a point directly south of the northeast corner, then directly back to the northeast corner. Make a diagram of the park *with the length written next to each section.*

(HINT: You may find it helpful to cross out each section of the park after you have drawn it on your diagram.)

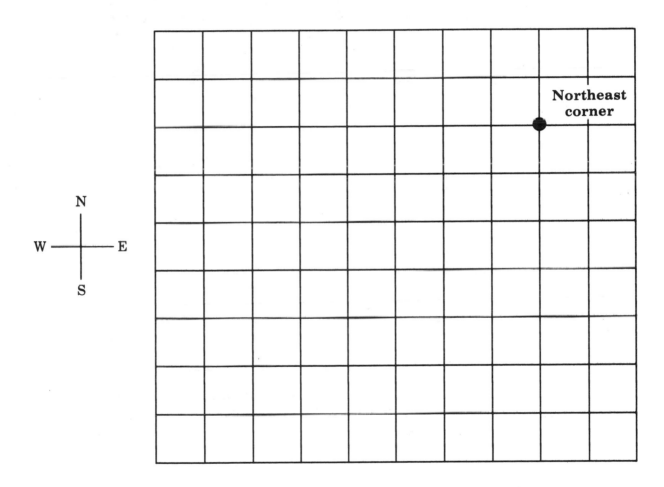

(B)   The total distance around the park is its *perimeter*. If a person drove completely around the park, without taking any shortcuts, the distance driven would be the park's perimeter.

Compute the perimeter and write it here.

Perimeter = _____ miles

EXERCISE 7: Vocabulary preview: **rectangular** (adjective)—having the shape of
a rectangle.

rectangle (noun)—a four-sided figure with
four 90° angles, such as these:

Let the length of one square equal 1 foot.

(A) The floor of a rectangular closet in Mrs. Ho's home is 5 feet long in
the east-west direction and 4 feet long in the north-south direction.
Make a diagram of the floor with the length written next to each
side. (Put the floor anywhere you want on the grid.)

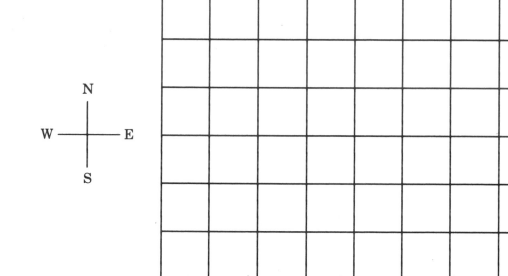

(B) Mrs. Ho wants to buy square tiles to put on the closet floor. Each
square tile is 1 foot long and 1 foot wide. How many tiles will she
need to cover the floor? Write your answer in *both* of the blanks
below.

Number of tiles = _____   *Area* of floor = _____ square feet

AREA: A tile that is 1 foot long and 1 foot wide is said to be 1 *square foot*.
The number of square feet in a floor is the *area* of the floor. You
will see the term *area* often in math books. It is used to describe the
size of floor space, wall space, land space, and so on.

This is called 1 square foot:

1 foot

1 foot

EXERCISE 8:   Let the length of one square equal 1 yard.

(A)   Starting at its southwest corner a room runs 5 yards north, 2 yards east, 3 yards south, 4 yards east, straight south to a point directly east of the southwest corner, and then straight west to the southwest corner. Pick a point in the southwest part of the grid to be the southwest corner of the room. Then make a diagram of the room with the length written next to each side.

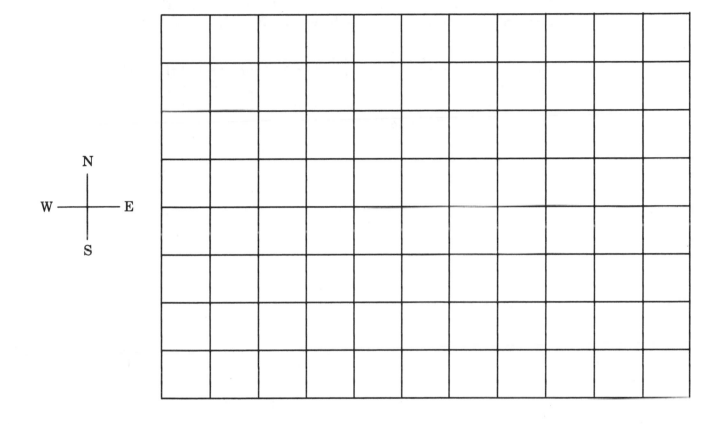

(B)   Each square of the grid is 1 yard long and 1 yard wide, so the *area* of each square is 1 *square yard*. This is called 1 square yard:

1 yard

1 yard

In order to know how much carpet it would take to cover the room's floor, you need to find the number of square yards (the area) of the room. Find the number of square yards and write it below.

Area of room's floor = _____ square yards

EXERCISE 9:   Let the length of one square equal 2 feet.

The lines of the grid below stand for tracks in a factory. A robot
moves along these tracks carrying materials throughout the factory. The robot cannot move off these tracks. Right now, the robot
is at the point shown. It is facing in the direction of the arrow (the
arrow is its nose).

Draw the path of the robot as it follows these instructions: Move
forward 2 feet, turn right, move forward 4 feet, turn right, move
forward 6 feet, turn left, move forward 8 feet, turn left, move forward 4 feet.

(HINTS: You may find it helpful to cross out parts of the instructions after you draw them. Also, turn this book if it helps you see
the direction the robot must turn when it obeys the instructions to
"turn right" or "turn left.")

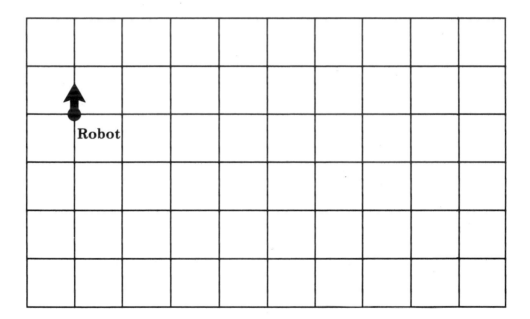

EXERCISE 10: Let the length of one square equal 2 feet.

A robot is on the tracks below, facing in the direction of the arrow. This robot does not know what "east" or "west" means. The only instructions it understands are "turn left", "turn right," and "move forward some number of feet."

Write instructions for the robot to follow the path shown by the heavy line. (Remember to start with an instruction for the robot to face the correct direction!)

INSTRUCTIONS FOR THE ROBOT:

_____

_____

_____

_____

_____

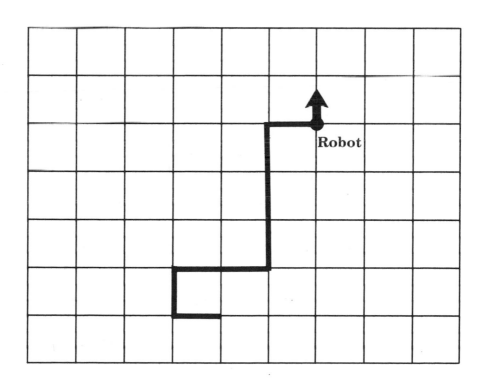

EXERCISE 11: Let the length of one square equal 2 yards.

A robot is on the tracks below, facing in the direction of the arrow. Because of an explosion, the tracks have been destroyed at the places marked by X's. To rescue some injured workers, the robot must get to point A as quickly as possible.

Write instructions for the robot to move along the tracks to point A by the *shortest route*.

INSTRUCTIONS FOR THE ROBOT:

_____

_____

_____

_____

_____

(Check your work: The total distance for the shortest route is 18 yards.)

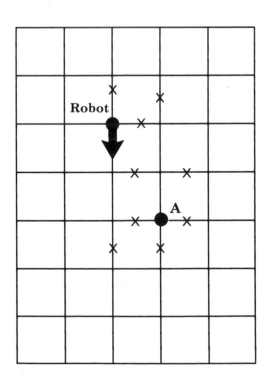

EXERCISE 12: Let the length of a **square's diagonal** equal 2 miles. Study these sample lines.

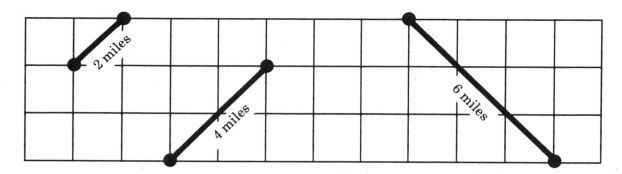

(A) Starting at point X, the borders of a farm run 6 miles southeast, 8 miles southwest, 4 miles northwest, 6 miles northeast, straight northwest to a position directly southwest of point X, and then straight back to point X. Draw the farm with the length written next to each side.

Northwest   Northeast

Southwest   Southeast

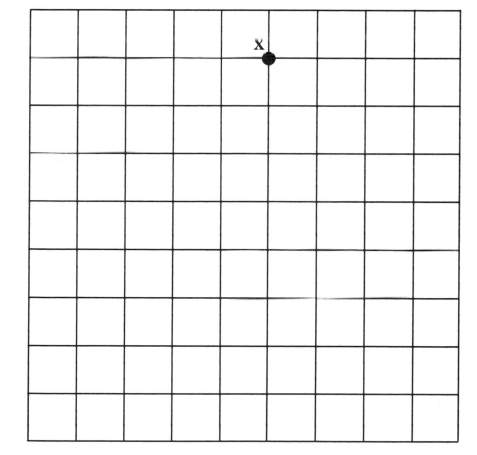

(B) What is the total distance around the farm (the farm's perimeter)?

Perimeter = _____ miles

EXERCISE 13: Let the length of a square's diagonal equal 2 miles, as shown in Exercise 12.

A robot is at the corner of the park shown in the diagram. This robot has been taught a different language than the robot you controlled in Exercises 10 and 11. This robot understands instructions such as "move northeast 6 miles" and "move southwest 4 miles." But—it *does not* understand the instructions "turn left" or "turn right."

Write instructions for the robot to move along the border of the park. The robot is lazy. Let it start moving in the direction it is facing (but tell it which direction that is!).

INSTRUCTIONS FOR THE ROBOT:

_____

_____

_____

_____

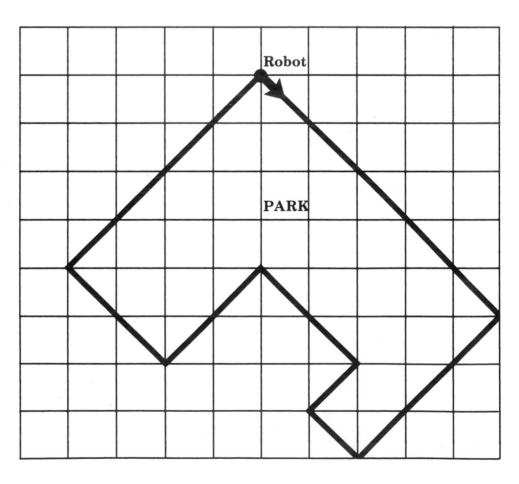

PART II: What's It Look Like?

You will often come across a written description of some object—and there will not be a diagram or picture to help you "see" what the object really looks like. A good reading practice is to make a sketch of what the object looks like to help your understanding. This section will give you practice in doing this.

EXERCISE INSTRUCTIONS

Each exercise is a written description of some object. In the blank space provided, draw a picture of the object.

EXERCISE 1

A *cogwheel* is a wheel with teeth like the teeth of a comb or saw along its outside edge. The teeth point away from the center of the wheel.

Draw a *cogwheel* in the space to the right.

EXERCISE 2

An *awl* is a hand tool with a small, round, solid handle that fits in the palm of the hand. Coming out of the bottom of the handle is a pointed piece of steel that looks like a nail and is about three inches long.

Draw an *awl* in the space to the right. (The picture does not have to be the correct size.)

EXERCISE 3

A *yawl* is a sailboat with two masts (posts that have sails attached to them). One mast is big and is located a little bit in front of the middle of the boat. The second mast is small and is located very near the back of the boat.

Draw a *yawl* in the space to the right.

EXERCISE 4

Vocabulary preview: **vertical** (adjective)—positioned up and down.
horizontal (adjective)—positioned from side to side.

A *patriarchal cross* is made up of one vertical and two horizontal pieces (which can be drawn as lines). One horizontal piece is one-half as long as the vertical piece, and crosses the vertical piece at each piece's center. The second horizontal piece is shorter than the other horizontal piece, and crosses the vertical piece above the other horizontal piece. The second horizontal piece crosses the vertical piece at the center of that second horizontal piece.

Draw a *patriarchal cross* in the space to the right.

PART III: What's the Arrangement?

Knowing how things are arranged (positioned in space) is often a key to understanding a passage that describes a scene or situation. Words and phrases such as inside, outside, above, below, around, to the left and to the right are important for understanding arrangements. This section will help you "see" arrangements that are described in words.

EXERCISE INSTRUCTIONS

Each of these exercises describes an arrangement of things. Read the description carefully, then draw the arrangement in the blank space provided.

To complete the exercises, you may need these definitions:

rectangle—A four-sided figure with four 90° angles, such as these:

square—A rectangle with all four sides the same length. For example:

triangle—a three-sided figure, such as these:

semicircle—One-half of a circle. For example:

EXERCISE 1

In the space to the right, draw a triangle inside a circle.

___

EXERCISE 2

In the space to the right, draw a rectangle inside a triangle and a circle around the triangle.

___

EXERCISE 3

Draw three separate triangles, with a semicircle in one and a square in each of the others.

___

EXERCISE 4

(A) Draw two large, separate rectangles, with three separate circles in each rectangle and two separate triangles in each circle.

(B) How many total triangles are there? _____

___

EXERCISE 5

Make a drawing from this description:

Inside a large square are four separate rectangles and a semicircle. Two of the rectangles each have a circle and a smaller rectangle inside of them. The third rectangle has only a triangle inside of it, and the fourth rectangle is completely empty.

EXERCISE 6 Make a drawing from this description. Write ALL lengths stated next to their correct places in your drawing. Label objects like the <u>s</u>moke <u>d</u>etector with their initials (s.d.).

The wall of a room is rectangular. It is 32 feet long and 8 feet high. A doorway in the middle of the wall is 3 feet wide and 7 feet tall. When you stand in this room and face the doorway, there is a window 5 feet to the left of the doorway. The window is a square, with each side equal to 2 feet. The bottom edge of the window is 3 feet up from the floor. Above the doorway is a smoke detector. One foot to the right of the doorway there is a light switch about 4 feet up from the floor. Also, about 6 feet to the right of the doorway, but down near the floor, there is an electrical outlet.

View of Wall from Inside Room

ADDITIONAL ASSIGNMENTS

NOTE: For Assignments 1 and 2 you will need four grids. Use four sheets of graph paper if you have them. If not, trace four copies of the grid in Exercise 8.

1. On a separate piece of paper, write a problem like PART I Exercise 6(A). In your problem be sure to include:

   — a compass showing directions
   — the distance covered by one square on the grid
   — a starting point for what will be drawn on the grid.

   Use one of your grids to help you write the problem by drawing on it what the correct answer will be.

   Give the problem to a classmate or friend to solve. Have that person write his or her answer on a second grid. Check his or her work using your answer drawing.

2. On a separate piece of paper, write a problem like PART I Exercise 9. In your problem be sure to include:

   — the distance covered by one square on the grid
   — a starting point for the robot
   — a starting direction in which the robot is facing.

   Use your third grid to help you write the problem by drawing on it what the correct answer will be.

   Give the problem to a classmate or friend to solve, using your fourth grid. Check that person's answer using your answer drawing.

3. Study the drawing below. On a separate piece of paper, write a description of this drawing. (For example, your description should be written like the one in PART II Exercise 4.)

4. Study the arrangement below. On a separate piece of paper, write a description of this arrangement (like the description in PART III Exercise 5).

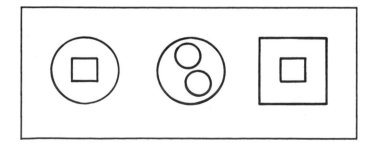

Comprehending
Descriptions of Order I

OBJECTIVES

When you have completed this unit you will

- understand how words called "comparatives" give information about the order (sequence) of things;

- be able to make a diagram showing the order of things described in a written passage;

- understand how the word "but" is used in compound sentences to give information about the order of things;

- be able to identify sentences that state the correct order of things described in a written passage.

INTRODUCTION

Reading materials in science, social studies and literature often describe the sequence (order) in which things happen or are arranged. Some common examples are:

— the order of people by age
— the order of history facts by date
— the order of mountains and rivers by size
— the order of cities, states and countries by land size or population
— the order of steps in a process
— the order of planets in the universe
— the order of places visited on a journey
— the order of events in a story's plot.

Sometimes an author describes the order of things very simply and it is easy to follow and understand. However, in many cases the order of things is written in a complex way that makes it more difficult to follow. But you must be able to figure out the order the author is explaining or you will not fully understand the material. Therefore, your skill in working through a description so that you understand the order of things is very important to reading and learning success. This unit will improve your ability to follow and understand written descriptions of the order of things.

PART I: Order! Order!

Many descriptions of order are written using words such as taller and shorter, older and younger, earlier and later, faster and slower, heavier and lighter, and so on. These words are called *comparatives*. They compare two or more things so that the order of those things is clear. For example, "John is a faster runner than Joe" means: the order of the speed of those two runners is first John and then Joe.

In this first part of the unit, you will build your skill in understanding written descriptions of order that use comparatives.

EXERCISE INSTRUCTIONS

Each exercise has a description of the order of certain things. Next to the description is a diagram with headings. Read the description carefully. Then write the things in their correct order on the diagram. Study the completed Example 1 below. Then try doing Example 2 on your own.

EXAMPLE 1:

Nina is two inches taller than Leo. However, Tessie is two inches shorter than Leo.

Write the names of the three people in order on the diagram.

taller
┼
┼
┼
shorter

Answer: The names have been written in their correct order on the diagram at right.

The description says that Nina is *taller* than Leo. So Nina is written above Leo on the diagram (closer to "taller").

The description says that Tessie is *shorter* than Leo. So Tessie is written below Leo (closer to "shorter").

taller
┼ Nina
┼ Leo
┼ Tessie
shorter

EXAMPLE 2: (Try this one yourself.)

Lead is heavier than gold. However, tin is lighter than gold.

Write the three metals in order on the diagram.

heavier
┼
┼
┼
lighter

Your diagram should look like the one on the next page.

Answer: Here is the correct ordering of the metals.

heavier

— lead
— gold
— tin

lighter

Do each of the following exercises this same way.

EXERCISE 1

Ida is five years older than René. Linus is five years younger than René.

Write the names of the three people in order on the diagram.

older

younger

EXERCISE 2

Mrs. Hall earns $3,000 more per year than Mr. Owens. Also, Miss Luke earns $3,000 less per year than Mr. Owens.

Write the three names in order on the diagram.

earns more

earns less

EXERCISE 3

The Mississippi River is about 2,000 miles longer than the Yukon River. Also, the Snake River is about 700 miles shorter than the Yukon River.

Write the three rivers in order on the diagram.

longer

shorter

EXERCISE 4

CAUTION: This exercise has a different pattern than the first three.

In a race, Tom ran slower than Yvette. However, Tom ran faster than Sara.

Write the three names in order on the diagram.

faster

slower

USE A "WORKING-DIAGRAM"

The last exercise began with this statement:

In a race, Tom ran slower than Yvette.

Because "slower" is at the bottom of the diagram, you know that you must put Tom *below* Yvette. But exactly how? All three of these might be correct:

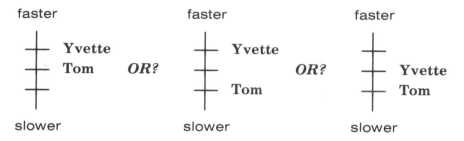

A good thing to do at this point is to make a "working-diagram" in the workspace. This working-diagram would show the information from the first sentence.

Then you should study the second sentence:

However, Tom ran faster than Sara.

This means Tom must be *above* Sara. So, Sara must be below Tom. Add this fact to your working-diagram.

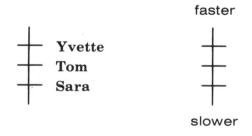

Now your working-diagram shows the correct order for the three names. Copy this ordering onto the answer diagram.

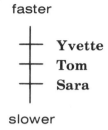

Use working-diagrams whenever they can help you organize information as you develop your answer.

EXERCISE 5

The peak of Mt. Bono in Alaska is about 2,000 feet higher than the peak of Mt. Whitney in California. However, the peak of Mt. Bono is almost 4,000 feet lower than the peak of Mt. McKinley in Alaska.

Write the three mountains in order on the diagram.

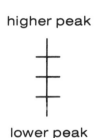

EXERCISE 6

Guglielmo Marconi invented the radio after Thomas Edison invented the electric light. Alexander Bell's invention of the telephone came before the electric light.

Write the *inventions* in order on the diagram.

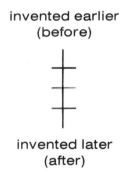

EXERCISE 7

Otto invented the gas engine after Morse invented the telegraph. However, Otto's invention was made before Edison's invention of the electric light.

Write the *inventions* in order on the diagram.

EXERCISE 8

Anne is two years older than Paulo. Maria is two years younger than Paulo. Bruce is two years older than Anne.

Write the four people in order on the diagram.

older

younger

EXERCISE 9

Beef has less calories than bacon. Also, turkey has more calories than cottage cheese. Finally, beef has more calories than turkey.

List the four foods in order on the diagram. [HINT: This exercise is tricky. Try it first on your own. Then read the explanation under *Working "Step-By-Step"* below.]

more calories

less calories

WORKING "STEP-BY-STEP"

Some paragraphs or passages will describe an ordering of many items. For example, in Exercise 10 there were four items. To understand these many-item descriptions, you must think about the information one step at a time. A helpful aid is to *first make a working-diagram for each sentence* (step) of the passage. *Then combine the working-diagrams* into a final answer diagram.

Let's see how this is done. Here is how you could work out the solution to Exercise 9 using step-by-step working-diagrams.

EXERCISE 9:

Beef has less calories than bacon. Also, turkey has more calories than cottage cheese. Finally, beef has more calories than turkey.

STEP 1— Show the first sentence with a working-diagram: *Beef has less calories than bacon.*

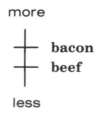

more

bacon

beef

less

STEP 2— Show the second sentence with another working-diagram: *Also, turkey has more calories than cottage cheese.*

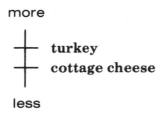

more

— turkey
— cottage cheese

less

STEP 3— Show the third sentence with still another working-diagram: *Finally, beef has more calories than turkey.*

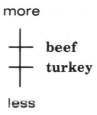

more

— beef
— turkey

less

STEP 4— Combine STEPs 1 and 3. In STEP 1, beef is at the bottom of the working-diagram. In STEP 3, turkey is below beef. Putting this together:

more

— bacon
— beef
— turkey

less

STEP 5— Combine STEPs 2 and 4. In STEP 4, turkey is at the bottom of the working-diagram. In STEP 2, cottage cheese is below turkey. Putting this together gives the final answer diagram:

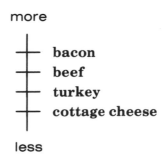

more

— bacon
— beef
— turkey
— cottage cheese

less

EXERCISE 10

Ralph is older than Andre. Also, Barry is younger than Patrice. However, Barry is older than Ralph.

List the four people in order on the diagram.

older

younger

EXERCISE 11

The Mississippi River is longer than the Arkansas River. The Tennessee River is shorter than the Ohio River. The Ohio River is shorter than the Arkansas River.

List the four rivers in order on the diagram.

longer

shorter

EXERCISE 12

NOTE: This exercise has **five** items to be ordered.

Carlos owns more records than Lewis. Denise owns more records than Marcia. But Marcia owns more records than Carlos. Furthermore, Al owns even more records than Denise.

Write the five names in order on the diagram.

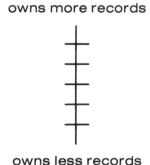

owns more records

owns less records

EXERCISE 13

CAUTION: Read carefully and make as many working-diagrams as helpful.

The first black writer to have a best selling novel was Richard Wright. His exciting *Native Son* sold 200,000 copies in three weeks. Wright was born after Langston Hughes, called the dean of black American letters. Hughes wrote *Tambourines To Glory*, a novel about two Harlem women who turned a street-corner revival meeting into a fortune. He also wrote *Mulatto*, a play translated into five languages. Hughes himself was born after Nella Larsen. Her novel *Quicksand* is about the travels and adventures of a black woman seeking a more meaningful life. Another black writer, Ann Petry, wrote *The Street*—about life in Harlem. The book won strong praise in the *New York Times*. Petry was born after Wright. On the other hand, there was James Weldon Johnson. His book *The Autobiography Of An Ex-Colored Man* was not truly autobiographical. But he did describe his experiences as a lawyer, journalist and politician in his autobiography *Along This Way*. Johnson was born before Larsen.

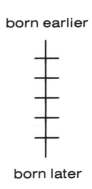

born earlier

born later

A. Five writers are mentioned in the passage. Write their *last names in order of birth* on the diagram.

B. What is the title of the first best selling novel by a black writer?

Write your answer here: _____

C. Which book is said to have won strong praise in the *New York Times*?

Title: _____

D. Read the last four sentences again carefully. Then, check (✓) the name of Johnson's autobiography.

_____ *The Autobiography Of An Ex-Colored Man*

_____ *Along This Way*

E. According to the passage, which work was a rags-to-riches story?

Title: _____

PART II: But . . .

The word "but" is often used in writing to join two sentences describing order into a single sentence. Read the following two sentences.

Gold is heavier than tin.
Gold is lighter than lead.

On a diagram, the order of the three metals would be:

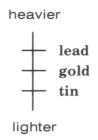

The word "but" can be used to join these two sentences into a single sentence. The single sentence will state the same order as do the two sentences above. Here is the single sentence:

Gold is heavier than tin but lighter than lead.

To check that this sentence states the same order as the two sentences, note that it could be broken down like this:

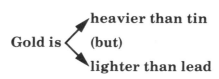

The two separate sentences are clearly contained in the single sentence. Therefore, the order of the metals is the same.

The exercises in this part of the unit will boost your ability to understand descriptions of order in which the word "but" is used. If you have any trouble with the exercises, try to break the sentences down as shown below.

Darwin was born before Einstein but after Newton.

— breaks into —

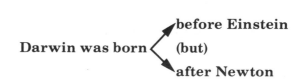

EXERCISE INSTRUCTIONS

For each exercise, read the description carefully. Then write the things in order on the diagram. Remember to use working-diagrams if needed.

EXERCISE 1

Abraham Lincoln was president about 80 years after George Washington was president. However, Abraham Lincoln was president about 80 years before Franklin D. Roosevelt was president.

A. Write the last names of the three presidents in order on the diagram.

B. Check (✔) the correct sentence.
    _____ a. Lincoln was president before Washington and Roosevelt.
    _____ b. Lincoln was president before Washington but after Roosevelt.
    _____ c. Lincoln was president before Roosevelt but after Washington.
    _____ d. Lincoln was president after Roosevelt but before Washington.

EXERCISE 2

Tina is four years older than Jon, but Tina is four years younger than Steve.

List the three people in order on the diagram.

EXERCISE 3

Tina is four years older than Jon but four years younger than Steve.

List the three people in order on the diagram.

EXERCISE 4

A. Check that your answers to Exercises 2 and 3 are the same.
    You know, then, that these two sentences mean the same:

    — **Tina is four years older than Jon, but Tina is four years younger than Steve.**

    — **Tina is four years older than Jon but four years younger than Steve.**

B. (Now try this problem.) Among famous 19th-century painters, Gauguin was born before van Gogh but after Whistler.

    Write the three painters in order on the diagram.

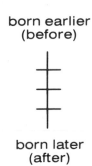

EXERCISE 5

Chicago has a smaller population than New York City but a larger population than Denver.

Write the cities in order on the diagram.

larger
population

smaller
population

EXERCISE 6

In the order of entering into the Union, California became a state ahead of Minnesota but following Iowa.

List the states in order on the diagram.

earlier

later

EXERCISE 7

Monica, who is seven years younger than Dena, is seven years older than Gwen.

Write the three people in order on the diagram.

older

younger

EXERCISE 8

The Great Pyramids of Egypt were built before the ancient Roman civilization reached its peak. Furthermore, the ancient Greek civilization reached its peak after the Great Pyramids were built but before the Roman peak.

earlier

later

A. Three historical highlights are listed below. List them in order on the diagram.

Roman peak   Egyptian pyramids   Greek peak

B. Check (✔) the correct sentence.

_____ a. Greece reached its peak before the Egyptian pyramids were built but after Rome reached its peak.

_____ b. Greece reached its peak after the Egyptian pyramids were built and after Rome reached its peak.

_____ c. Greece reached its peak after Rome reached its peak but before the Egyptian pyramids were built.

_____ d. Greece reached its peak before Rome reached its peak but after the Egyptian pyramids were built.

EXERCISE 9

During World War II, Japan attacked the United States at Pearl Harbor several years after Germany invaded Poland. Between these two events, Germany conquered France.

earlier

later

A.   Write the three events below in order on the diagram.

Pearl Harbor attack
Germany invaded Poland
Germany conquered France

B.   Check (✓) the correct sentence.

_____ a. Germany conquered France before Germany invaded Poland but after the Pearl Harbor attack.

_____ b. Germany conquered France before Germany invaded Poland and before the Pearl Harbor attack.

_____ c. Germany conquered France after Germany invaded Poland but before the Pearl Harbor attack.

_____ d. Germany conquered France after the Pearl Harbor attack but before Germany invaded Poland.

EXERCISE 10

The English pilgrims landed at Plymouth more than 100 years after da Gama landed in India. Magellan sailed around the world between these two events, whereas Columbus discovered America before da Gama reached India.

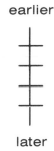

earlier

later

A.   Four landmarks in the discovery of new lands are listed below. Write them in order on the diagram.

Pilgrims land at Plymouth
da Gama reaches India
Magellan circles world
Columbus discovers America

B.   Check (✓) the correct statement.

_____ a. Da Gama landed in India before Magellan sailed around the world and before Columbus discovered America.

_____ b. Da Gama landed in India after Magellan sailed around the world and after Columbus discovered America.

_____ c. Da Gama landed in India after Magellan sailed around the world but before Columbus discovered America.

_____ d. Da Gama landed in India before Magellan sailed around the world but after Columbus discovered America.

EXERCISE 11

Shakespeare's tragedies are among the best plays ever written. *Hamlet* was written after *Romeo and Juliet,* while *Julius Caesar* was written between these two plays. *Othello* was written after *Hamlet, Macbeth* was written after *Othello,* and *Antony and Cleopatra* was written later still.

Write the six plays in order on the diagram.

written
earlier

written
later

EXERCISE 12

William Faulkner, who wrote about the American South, was born after Mark Twain (*Huckleberry Finn*). But Faulkner was born before Ernest Hemingway (*A Farewell to Arms*). Herman Melville (*Moby Dick*) was born before Twain but after Nathanial Hawthorne (*The Scarlet Letter*). John Steinbeck (*The Grapes of Wrath*) was born after all the other writers mentioned.

Write the last names of the six writers in order on the diagram.

born
earlier

born
after

EXERCISE 13

Among famous playwrights, Chekhov (Russian) was born after Shaw (English) but before O'Neill (American). Ibsen (Norwegian) was born before Shaw but after Goethe (German). The French playwright Beckett was born after O'Neill, and the American playwright Tennessee Williams was born after Beckett.

List the seven playwrights by name in order on the diagram.

born
earlier

born
later

ADDITIONAL ASSIGNMENTS

1. Study this sentence: Sharon is older than Janice but younger than Jerry.

   Now study the diagram to the right. Notice that the names have changed.

   On a separate piece of paper, write a sentence like the example above that describes the order that the diagram shows.

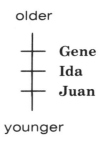

older

Gene
Ida
Juan

younger

2. Study this sentence: Charlie, who is a better swimmer than Sandra, is a worse swimmer than Arlene.

   Now study the diagram to the right. Notice that the names have changed.

   On a separate piece of paper, write a sentence like the example above that describes the order that the diagram shows.

better artist

Donna
Lionel
Gino

worse artist

For the next two exercises you will write your own problems. When finished, ask a classmate or friend to solve the problems. Watch to see if that person has trouble with the problems. Discuss with that person whether your problem is not written well, or whether he/she needs help with descriptions of order. Tutor him/her, if necessary, or rewrite your problem until it is a good one.

---

3. Write a problem about the order of names in length (number of letters). Use these four names: Andy, Belinda, Carmen, Daryl.

   (HINT: Review PART I Exercise 10 or PART II Exercise 10.)

   Have a classmate or friend solve your problem using the diagram on the right.

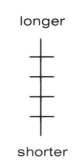

longer

shorter

ADDITIONAL ASSIGNMENTS

4. Reread PART II Exercise 11. Using information from that exercise, write a problem about the dates *four* of those Shakespearean plays were written.

   Have a classmate or friend solve your problem using the diagram on the right.

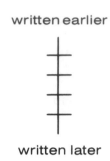

written earlier

written later

Reading For Full Comprehension I: Knowing The Best Title And Getting The Facts

OBJECTIVES

When you have completed this unit you will

- understand how titles are used to tell the "overall topic" of a reading passage;

- be able to choose the best title that tells the overall topic of a reading passage (from three choices);

- be able to identify titles that are too narrow and too broad for a given reading passage;

- be able to answer questions about facts stated in a reading passage;

- be able to use context clues to figure out the meaning of a word as it is used in a certain reading passage.

INTRODUCTION

One very important process in reading is called *analysis*. When you are doing analysis in reading, you are said to be *analyzing* the material or *reading analytically*.

Analysis is the process of separating the material of a passage into its parts (ideas and facts), and studying how those parts fit together to define and explain the subject (or topic).

For example, consider when you read a newspaper article that gives a bad review of a movie. The subject of the article is the writer's opinion about how bad the movie was. By *analyzing* the article, you can learn and understand the "parts" of that subject: what exact sections of the movie were bad; why were they bad; were there specific characters the writer didn't like; why didn't he/she like them; was there anything the writer did like; so on. Analyzing the passage gives you the details you need to truly understand the subject of the material.

In this unit you will strengthen your ability to make an overall analysis of the subject of a passage. In addition, you will sharpen your skill in identifying and analyzing the ideas and facts in the passage.

Each exercise consists of a short reading passage followed by a set of questions—in the familiar form of reading comprehension tests. The questions are of three types:

1. Questions that ask you to choose a best title for the passage.

2. Questions that ask about facts (details) and ideas discussed in the passage.

3. Questions that ask you about the meaning of a word as it is used in the context of the passage.

By studying this unit carefully, you will become better at analyzing reading passages for their overall topic and for their factual details. The skills you develop here will be of great value in all your reading, and in your test-taking, too.

EXERCISE INSTRUCTIONS

For each exercise, read the passage slowly and carefully. Try to understand every idea presented in the passage. This may mean that you sometimes stop to think or reread for a minute before moving ahead to the next ideas.

Some of the exercises have a "Vocabulary preview" before the passage. DO NOT SKIP the Vocabulary preview. It is hard to understand a passage if you don't know the meaning of some words. The Vocabulary preview can help. Also, if you come across any words you don't know as you read the passage, try to figure out what they mean by analyzing the sentence contexts—as you learned to do in Unit 2. If this doesn't work, stop your reading to look up the words in a dictionary.

In answering the questions about facts presented in the passage, again work carefully. Do not rush and answer questions without giving them enough thought. Be certain of each answer before you move on to the next question. Most people find that they must often reread sections of the passage to pin down the *best* answer to a question. YOUR GOAL IS 100% ACCURACY! Some of the questions will ask you for the *line numbers* of the lines where you found an answer. This will help you learn to pinpoint your search for information in a passage.

The first question after each passage will ask you to choose the best title for the passage. This will help you develop skill in seeing the OVERALL TOPIC of a passage. To illustrate the method for answering this "title" question, study the example below.

EXAMPLE: Study the Vocabulary preview. Then read the passage.

Vocabulary preview: **conservation** (noun)—the act of protecting or saving something so it is not destroyed or lost.

Finland's principal resource is lumber. The huge forests, under carefully controlled conservation practices, are the source of wood for manufacturing plywood, paper, and insulating board.

Deposits of copper ore, iron ore, and titanium have been found and are being mined. The resources are used in the manufacture of such things as electrical goods, locomotives, and ships.

The capital of the Republic of Finland is the city of Helsinki. Helsinki is also Finland's most important port. Helsinki has become increasingly important as a tourist center. People come from all over Europe to enjoy Finland's long winter sports season.

Now, read the explanation of the "title" question on the next page. Then answer the "title" question provided.

In the following "title" question, the three lettered phrases (A, B and C) describe the three possible titles listed.

One of the titles is *too broad*—it covers a broader, bigger topic than the passage is really about.

One of the titles is *too narrow*—it covers only a small part of what the passage is about.

One title is a *comprehensive title*—it covers what the entire passage is about, and only what the passage is about. It is neither too broad nor too narrow. The comprehensive title is the *best* title for the passage because it best states the OVERALL TOPIC of the passage.

Can you match the three descriptions to the three possible titles for the example passage?

Below are three possible titles for this passage. In each blank, write the letter of the phrase (A, B or C) which best describes that title.

_____ Helsinki: Capital of Finland
_____ Scandinavian Countries: Finland, Sweden, Norway and Denmark
_____ Finland: A Country of Many Resources

(A) too broad
(B) too narrow
(C) comprehensive title

Check your work with the answer on the next page.

Answer:

__B__ Helsinki: Capital of Finland

__A__ Scandinavian Countries: Finland,
Sweden, Norway and Denmark

__C__ Finland: A Country of Many
Resources

The title "Helsinki: Capital of Finland" is too narrow. Helsinki is only discussed in the third paragraph. The first two paragraphs explain other features of Finland.

The title "Scandinavian Countries: Finland, Sweden, Norway and Denmark" is too broad. The passage does not cover all four of these Scandinavian countries. It only covers one of them—Finland.

The title "Finland: A Country of Many Resources" does describe the OVERALL TOPIC of this passage. The passage deals with Finland's resources: lumber, minerals and weather good for sports. Therefore, "Finland: A Country of Many Resources" is a comprehensive title.

Begin working now on the exercises that follow. Remember, there will be questions about facts as well as the best title. Read carefully to get all the "fact" questions correct. Your goal is 100% accuracy.

PASSAGE A

Vocabulary preview: **conservation** (noun)—the act of protecting or
saving something so it is not destroyed or lost.

1   Finland's principal resource is lumber.
2 The huge forests, under carefully con-
3 trolled conservation practices, are the
4 source of wood for manufacturing ply-
5 wood, paper, and insulating board.
6   Deposits of copper ore, iron ore, and
7 titanium have been found and are being
8 mined. The resources are used in the
9 manufacture of such things as electrical
10 goods, locomotives, and ships.
11   The capital of the Republic of Finland
12 is the city of Helsinki. Helsinki is also
13 Finland's most important port. Helsinki
14 has become increasingly important as a
15 tourist center. People come from all over
16 Europe to enjoy Finland's long winter
17 sports season.

1. Below are three possible titles for this
passage. In each blank, write the letter for
the phrase (A, B or C) which best describes
that title.

_____ Helsinki: Capital of Finland
_____ Scandinavian Countries: Finland,
Sweden, Norway and Denmark
_____ Finland: A Country of Many
Resources

(A) too broad
(B) too narrow
(C) comprehensive title

2. According to the passage, Finland's forests

☐ (A) have supplied wood for manufacturing plywood, paper and insulating board, but are now almost used
up
☐ (B) have made Helsinki the center of
the lumber industry
☐ (C) have been used wisely to prevent
them from being used up

3. On which line(s) did you find the answer
to the last question?

LINE NUMBER(S): _____

4. Some of Finland's *mineral* resources are

☐ (A) huge forests
☐ (B) copper ore, iron ore and titanium
☐ (C) electrical goods, locomotives and
ships
☐ (D) long sports seasons and lumber

5. The passage states that

☐ (A) electrical goods, locomotives and
ships are used in the manufacture
of copper ore, iron ore and titanium
☐ (B) copper ore, iron ore and titanium
are used in the manufacture of
electrical goods, locomotives and
ships

6. Helsinki is an important city because

☐ (A) it is a major source of minerals
☐ (B) it is the Republic of Finland
☐ (C) it is the capital of the Republic of
France
☐ (D) it is a growing tourist center and a
main port

PASSAGE B

¹ Long before there was any Washington or any United States there
² were trader Indians living on the shores of the river that flows by
³ Washington. These Indians paddled their canoes up and down the
⁴ river and traded with other Indians, swapping things they had for
⁵ things they wanted—beads for furs, bows for arrows, corn for pota-
⁶ toes. In the Indian language the name for traders was potomac, so
⁷ we call the river after these trader Indians, the Potomac River. The
⁸ Potomac separates two states—Maryland and Virginia. They are
⁹ named after two queens. The Potomac Indians paddled their
¹⁰ canoes down the river until they came to a much broader body of
¹¹ water. This body of water was so big it seemed to them like the
¹² ocean, and they called it "the Mother of Waters," which in their
¹³ own language was "Chesapeake." Chesapeake Bay is not the ocean,
¹⁴ but it is the biggest bay in the United States.

1. Below are three possible titles for this selection. In each blank, write the letter of the phrase (A, B or C) which best describes that title.

   _____ Rivers and Bays in America
   _____ The Potomac River and Chesapeake Bay
   _____ Chesapeake Bay: The "Mother of Waters"

   (A) comprehensive title
   (B) too broad
   (C) too narrow

2. In line 1, the word "Washington" refers to

   ☐ (A) George Washington
   ☐ (B) Washington, D.C., our nation's capital
   ☐ (C) the state of Washington

3. The selection states that Virginia and Maryland were named

   ☐ (A) after two Indian words
   ☐ (B) after two states
   ☐ (C) after two queens

4. The word "potomac" is Indian for

   ☐ (A) river
   ☐ (B) the Mother of Waters
   ☐ (C) Washington
   ☐ (D) traders

5. According to the selection, which statement(s) are correct?

   I. The Potomac Indian traders could not be trusted.
   II. The Potomac River provided a means of transportation for the Indians.
   III. The Chesapeake Bay looked like an ocean to the Indians.

   ☐ (A) Statement I only.
   ☐ (B) Statement II only.
   ☐ (C) Statement III only.
   ☐ (D) Statements I and II.
   ☐ (E) Statements II and III.
   ☐ (F) Statements I and III.

6. Which body of water is narrower?

   ☐ (A) The Potomac River.
   ☐ (B) The Chesapeake Bay.

7. On which line(s) did you find the answer to the last question?

   LINE NUMBER(S): _____

PASSAGE C

Vocabulary preview: **vegetarian** (adjective)—made only of plants
and plant products, without any meat.

1 Leo's mother has turned into a vegetarian cook.
2 He hates the weird meals she serves. Leo is sure his
3 father does too because he notices the way his
4 father gulps down his food, then takes hurried bites
5 of bread to kill the taste.
6 On the night that Mrs. Nolan goes to a meeting,
7 Leo and his father head for the nearest hamburger
8 place. Guess what happens? We won't tell you, but
9 it does mean the end of the vegetarian cooking
10 experiment.
11 This chapter is the first of five funny tales about
12 Leo Nolan, his family, his friends, his pets, and his
13 school. All of these combine to make an interest-
14 ing story of the adventures of an appealing boy.
15 We think you will enjoy the story and the pictures
16 in Toad Food & Measle Soup. We won't tell you
17 how the book got its name. Read it and you'll find
18 out for yourself.

1. Below are three possible titles for this
   passage. In each blank, write the letter of
   the phrase (A, B or C) which best describes
   that title.

   _____ Review of *Toad Food & Measle Soup*
   _____ Humorous Books About Children
          and Young Adults
   _____ An Event in a Hamburger Place

   (A) too broad
   (B) too narrow
   (C) comprehensive title

2. In the *second* paragraph the writer tries to
   raise your curiosity by

   ☐ (A) telling you that one night Mrs.
          Nolan went to a meeting
   ☐ (B) telling you this chapter is the first
          of five funny tales about Leo Nolan
          and his family, friends, pets and
          school
   ☐ (C) asking you to imagine what might
          happen when Leo and his father go
          to a hamburger place without Mrs.
          Nolan

3. Does the second sentence support or contradict (argue against) this statement:
   Leo enjoys experimenting with new non-
   meat foods.

   ☐ (A) supports
   ☐ (B) contradicts

4. This passage seems to be

   ☐ (A) a three-paragraph book review,
          maybe from a magazine
   ☐ (B) three paragraphs taken from a
          book called *Toad Food & Measle
          Soup*
   ☐ (C) an argument to make you like
          vegetarian cooking
   ☐ (D) three paragraphs arguing that
          hamburgers are better than vege-
          tarian cooking

5. *Toad Food & Measle Soup* seems to

   ☐ (A) present a somewhat unfair view of
          vegetarian cooking in order to be
          funny (since some people do like
          this cooking)
   ☐ (B) present a fair view of vegetarian
          cooking (since everyone will agree
          with Leo and his father that this
          cooking is "weird" and tastes bad)

PASSAGE D

Vocabulary preview: **city-state** (noun)—a city with complete control of its own laws and government, even though it is part of a larger area.

1 Sparta was the most warlike of the
2 Greek city-states. Its government was
3 headed by kings who struggled to keep
4 the throne within their family. The idea
5 of god-kings which began in Egypt,
6 however, was not accepted in Greece.
7 The chief or king was advised by citizen
8 councils, which actually held most of
9 the power.
10 Every boy in Sparta was raised to
11 become a soldier. He was trained to
12 place the good of Sparta ahead of his
13 own welfare or that of any other person.
14 A boy's training began when he was
15 quite young. Girls, too, were expected to
16 be strong so that someday they might
17 become the mothers of Spartan soldiers.
18 To this day, the word "spartan" sug-
19 gests something very plain or a person
20 with great self-discipline.

1. Below are three possible titles for this passage. In each blank, write the letter of the phrase (A, B or C) which best describes that title.

_____ The Major Greek City-States
_____ Sparta's Training of Youth
_____ Sparta's Government and Training of Youth

(A) comprehensive title
(B) too narrow
(C) too broad

2. The passage states that Sparta's king

☐ (A) was very powerful in government
☐ (B) was not very powerful in government affairs

3. In Sparta a young man was taught to be a good soldier and to

☐ (A) save the lives of other soldiers, because human life is more important than the protection of the country
☐ (B) place the protection of his country above the protection of his own life
☐ (C) save his own life, because his life was more important than the protection of his country

4. On which line(s) did you find the answer to the last question?

LINE NUMBER(S): _____

5. Which sentence is true, according to the passage?

☐ (A) The boys in Sparta were raised to be strong while the girls were raised to be delicate and weak.
☐ (B) The girls in Sparta were raised to be strong while the boys were raised to be delicate and weak.
☐ (C) Both boys and girls in Sparta were raised to be strong.
☐ (D) Since a good soldier must be intelligent, in Sparta the boys were raised to be intelligent rather than just strong and the girls were raised to be intelligent but weak.

6. The term "Spartan" would apply to

☐ (A) an athlete having a simple diet and strict training schedule
☐ (B) a person who enjoyed Greek foods in huge portions
☐ (C) a colorful plaid cloth worn by the Scottish at parties

PASSAGE E

¹   Our Earth is just one of nine planets that rotate around the
² sun. Among the other eight, Mercury is the closest to the sun.
³ Moving outward one finds Venus, Mars, Jupiter, Saturn, Ura-
⁴ nus, Neptune and finally Pluto. Our Earth is between Venus and
⁵ Mars.
⁶   The sun, the nine planets, and various smaller bodies which
⁷ travel around the sun are together called the solar system. One
⁸ of the smaller bodies is the moon which circles around the Earth.
⁹ In addition, Mars has two moons, Saturn has ten, Jupiter has
¹⁰ four large moons and eight smaller ones, and there are more
¹¹ moons circling other planets.
¹²   Besides the planets and their moons, there are also comets,
¹³ meteors, and asteroids which travel around the sun and are part
¹⁴ of the solar system. Of course, there are many heavenly bodies
¹⁵ which are not part of the solar system, such as the thousands of
¹⁶ stars you see at night. Scientists have learned a great deal about
¹⁷ the stars by using giant telescopes and electronic equipment. But
¹⁸ a complete summary of all that is known about these more dis-
¹⁹ tant heavenly bodies is not possible in this short description of
²⁰ the solar system.

1. Below are three possible titles for this selection. In each blank, write the letter of the phrase (A, B or C) which best describes that title.

   _____ Complete Description of All Heavenly Bodies
   _____ The Solar System
   _____ The Moons of the Planets

   (A) too narrow
   (B) too broad
   (C) comprehensive title

2. In order to be included as part of the solar system, a heavenly body must

   ☐ (A) be a planet
   ☐ (B) be a moon circling a planet
   ☐ (C) travel around the sun
   ☐ (D) be a distant star

3. On which line(s) did you find the answer to the last question?

   LINE NUMBER(S): _____

4. How many planets are closer to the sun than is the Earth?

   ☐ (A) 9   ☐ (C) 3
   ☐ (B) 8   ☐ (D) 2

5. According to the selection, how many moons does Jupiter have?

   ☐ (A) 24
   ☐ (B) 12
   ☐ (C) 10
   ☐ (D) 8
   ☐ (E) None of the above.

6. The number of moons for each of *four* planets is given in the selection. What is the *total number* of moons for these *four* planets?

   ☐ (A) 25
   ☐ (B) 24
   ☐ (C) 12
   ☐ (D) 10

7. As used in the context of line 1, the word "rotate" means

   ☐ (A) travel in a circle
   ☐ (B) replace
   ☐ (C) expand
   ☐ (D) grow

PASSAGE F

Vocabulary preview: **corridor** (noun)—narrow passageway or hallway.

1 Nick Ramon looked up from the papers on
2 his desk and listened. There it was again. The
3 sound of footsteps moving slowly past his
4 office. A door opening along the corridor.
5 Then the creak of a chair, as if someone had
6 just sat down.
7 Nick was working late again, anxious to
8 finish a report. An hour ago everyone else had
9 left the offices of the Community Develop-
10 ment Corporation, a social-service agency in
11 Brownsville, Texas. Had somebody returned?
12 Pushing back his chair, Nick paced down
13 the corridor, looking into each one of the
14 suite's ten small windowless offices. They were
15 empty—just as they'd been all those other
16 times that he had heard noises. The front and
17 back doors were locked. When Nick looked
18 out the window of the reception area, he saw
19 only his car parked in front of the long, low-
20 slung building of office suites.

1. Below are three possible titles for this
passage. In each blank, write the letter of
the phrase (A, B or C) which best describes
that title.

_____ Unexplained Sounds in Nick's
Office After Work
_____ Unexplained Sounds and Sights
Reported by People
_____ Nick's Car was Alone in the Park-
ing Lot

   (A) too narrow
   (B) too broad
   (C) comprehensive title

2. How many offices did Nick examine?

   ☐ (A) 2   ☐ (C) 10
   ☐ (B) 5   ☐ (D) 12

3. For about how long had Nick been alone
in the offices?

   ☐ (A) 20 minutes   ☐ (C) 2 hours
   ☐ (B) 1 hour   ☐ (D) 10 hours

4. A "suite," according to the context of line
14, is a

   ☐ (A) jacket and pants or skirt which
match and are worn together
   ☐ (B) group of rooms
   ☐ (C) legal action taken to obtain money
   ☐ (D) fat-based substance used to feed
birds in winter

5. According to the passage,

   ☐ (A) this was the first time that Nick
had heard unexplained sounds
   ☐ (B) Nick had heard unexplained
sounds before
   ☐ (C) Nick was able to figure out who
had made the sounds
   ☐ (D) Nick could not figure out who had
made the sounds this time, but the
last time it had been fellow office
workers

6. According to the passage, the noises were
especially mysterious because

   ☐ (A) Nick worked for the Community
Development Corporation
   ☐ (B) the front door should have been
locked but wasn't
   ☐ (C) the back door had been knocked
down
   ☐ (D) the front and back doors were both
locked

7. The passage seems most likely to be

   ☐ (A) part of a ghost story
   ☐ (B) part of a description on how the
Community Development Corpo-
ration operates
   ☐ (C) part of an article about Browns-
ville, Texas
   ☐ (D) part of a Texas history book

PASSAGE G

¹ This book teaches you how to write programs for the TI 99/4A computer.

² You will learn how to make your own action games, board games and word
³ games. You may entertain your friends with challenging games and provide
⁴ some silly moments at your parties with short games you invent.

⁵ Perhaps your record collection or your paper route needs the organization your
⁶ special programs can provide. If you are working on the school yearbook, maybe
⁷ a program to handle the finances or records would be useful.

⁸ You may help your younger sisters and brothers by writing drill programs for
⁹ arithmetic facts or spelling. Even your own schoolwork in history or foreign
¹⁰ language may be made easier by programs you write.

¹¹ **How to Use This Book:** Do all the examples. Try all the assignments. If you
¹² get stuck, first go back and reread the lesson carefully from the top. You may
¹³ have overlooked some detail. After trying hard to get unstuck by yourself, you
¹⁴ may go ask a parent or teacher for help.

¹⁵ There are review questions for each lesson. Be sure you can answer them before
¹⁶ announcing that you have finished the lesson!

¹⁷ MAY THE BLUEBIRD OF HAPPINESS EAT ALL THE BUGS IN YOUR
¹⁸ PROGRAMS!

1. Below are three possible titles for this passage. In each blank, write the letter of the phrase (A, B or C) which best describes that title.

    _____ The Purpose of This Book and How to Use It
    _____ How to Use This Book
    _____ How to Use and Write Programs For Computers

    (A) too narrow
    (B) too broad
    (C) comprehensive title

2. The passage lists all of the following uses for computer programs EXCEPT

    ☐ (A) to help with school yearbook records
    ☐ (B) to balance a checkbook
    ☐ (C) to create games
    ☐ (D) to help with things learned in school

3. According to the passage, each lesson in the book has

    ☐ (A) examples only
    ☐ (B) examples and assignments only
    ☐ (C) examples, assignments and review questions
    ☐ (D) examples, assignments, review questions, word games and party games

4. As used in line 13, the work "overlooked" means

    ☐ (A) not read or understood
    ☐ (B) watched over someone's shoulder
    ☐ (C) carefully studied

5. When you get stuck in a lesson, the passage tells you to ask for help from a parent or teacher

    ☐ (A) after you finish the review questions
    ☐ (B) as soon as possible (right away)
    ☐ (C) before you reread the lesson
    ☐ (D) after you have tried to help yourself get unstuck

PASSAGE H

Vocabulary preview: **staggering** (verb)—walking crookedly,
unsteadily and with poor balance.

1 Suddenly you look and find the boy staggering
2 down the aisle, peering into the faces of people as he
3 passes them. "Here! Come back here, Roger!" you
4 cry, lurching after him and landing across the knees of
5 the young lady two seats down. Roger takes this as a
6 signal for a game and starts to run, screaming with
7 laughter. After four steps he falls and starts to cry.
8 On being carried kicking back to his seat, he is told
9 that he mustn't run down the aisle again. This strikes
10 even Roger as funny, because it is such a flat thing to
11 say. Of course he is going to run down the aisle again
12 and he knows it as well as you do. In the meantime,
13 however, he is perfectly willing to spend a little time
14 with the lady in the black silk dress.
15 "Here, Roger," you say, "don't bother the lady."
16 "Hello, little boy," the lady says, nervously, and
17 tries to go back to her book. The interview is over as
18 far as she is concerned. Roger, however, thinks that it
19 would be just dandy to get up in her lap. This has to be
20 stopped, and Roger has to be whispered to.

1. Below are three possible titles for this selection. In each blank, write the letter of the phrase (A, B or C) which best describes that title.

_____ Roger Bothers the Lady in the Black Dress
_____ Trying to Keep Roger Close and Out of Trouble
_____ Complete Guide to Raising Children

(A) comprehensive title
(B) too broad
(C) too narrow

2. The action in this passage seems to take place

☐ (A) on a bus, train or plane
☐ (B) when Roger went to the circus
☐ (C) in Roger's home
☐ (D) at a nursery school

3. The writer believes that telling Roger not to run in the aisle again will

☐ (A) make him feel guilty about his behavior
☐ (B) stop him from ever doing it again
☐ (C) hurt his feelings and make him cry
☐ (D) stop him only for a short time

4. When the character "you" in the passage fell over the young lady, Roger

☐ (A) became frightened and immediately began crying
☐ (B) became frightened and ran to his mother
☐ (C) thought that person was playing with him and tried to continue the fun
☐ (D) immediately climbed in the lap of the lady in the black dress

5. One can conclude from the passage that the lady in the black dress

☐ (A) would rather read than play with Roger
☐ (B) loves playing with children
☐ (C) is a friend of Roger
☐ (D) is a friend of the writer

6. The word *lurching* in line 4, according to the context, means

☐ (A) softly whispering
☐ (B) loudly screaming
☐ (C) walking gracefully
☐ (D) staggering

ADDITIONAL ASSIGNMENTS

1. Pick a paragraph or short passage from one of your textbooks, an encyclopedia or a news article. On a separate piece of paper, write three possible titles for this passage. Write one title that is *too narrow*, one that is *too broad*, and one that is a *comprehensive title*. Beneath the titles, list these three descriptions: too broad, too narrow, comprehensive title. (You have now created a question just like the "title" questions in this unit.)

   Ask a classmate or friend to read the passage and decide which description matches each title.

2. *Write your own paragraph or short passage* on a topic that interests you. Then write a "title" question like the one you wrote for Assignment 1. Ask a classmate or friend to read your passage and answer your "title" question.

3. Study the meaning of the word "conservation" on page 90. Write a sentence on the lines below in which the meaning of "conservation" is *given by contrast* (see Unit 2, CASE III).

   _____

   _____

   _____

4. Study the meaning of the word "vegetarian" on page 92. Write a sentence on the lines below in which the meaning of "vegetarian" is *stated without punctuation* (see Unit 2, CASE II).

   _____

   _____

   _____

5. Study the meaning of the word "corridor" on page 95. Write a sentence on the lines below in which the meaning of "corridor" can be *inferred from ideas in the sentence* (see Unit 2, CASE IV).

   _____

   _____

   _____

6. Study the definition of "rotate" you learned from Exercise 7 on page 94. Write a sentence on the lines below in which the meaning of "rotate" is *stated with punctuation* (see Unit 2, CASE I).

   _____

   _____

   _____

UNIT 7

Tools Of Written Thought:
Cause–Effect,
Contrast,
Emphasis,
Grammatical Decisions

OBJECTIVES

When you have completed this unit you will

● be able to write the "cause" and the "effect" stated in a given sentence;

● be able to write the two ideas that are contrasted in a given sentence, and an explanation of the contrast;

● be able to write one statement that is used to emphasize (strengthen) another statement in a given sentence;

● be able to choose a key word or phrase to connect two separate ideas into a single compound sentence;

● be able to use quotation marks and the colon correctly to show ideas in sentences.

INTRODUCTION

This unit will strengthen your skills in reading, understanding and writing certain important types of sentences. These are sentences that state relationships involving *cause and effect, contrast, emphasis* (accentuation) and *speech*. Proper understanding and use of these kinds of sentences requires good grammar skills. Thus, this unit will also stress your ability to use a few important grammar rules.

There are five parts in this unit. The first three parts teach about cause and effect, contrast and emphasis sentences. The fourth part gives practice in using some special words to write those kinds of sentences. The fifth part teaches about sentences containing speech and sentences that use the colon (:) punctuation mark.

PART I: Cause and Effect

Words like "because", "since", "so," and "therefore" are used in sentences to show *cause—effect relationships*. Here is an example:

Because I was hungry, I made myself a sandwich.

CAUSE: I was hungry.
EFFECT: I made myself a sandwich.

In the above sentence the *cause* is stated first and then the *effect* is stated. Sometimes, the effect is stated first, as in this example:

**He was 20 pounds overweight as a result of eating
too much candy.**

CAUSE: He ate too much candy.
EFFECT: He was 20 pounds overweight.

Notice that the original sentence contains the phrase "as a result of eating too much candy." This phrase indicates what the cause is, but does not actually state the cause directly. To state a cause directly, you use a complete sentence such as "He ate too much candy."

Here is a type of sentence which can be tricky to understand. Try to write the cause and the effect.

**We knew it was raining outside because we saw that
Fred was wet.**

CAUSE: _____

EFFECT: _____

That sentence says that we knew a cause (it was raining) *because* we saw its effect (Fred was wet). Think carefully—in this case "seeing an effect" is the *cause*, and "knowing a cause" is the *effect!*

CAUSE: We saw that Fred was wet.

EFFECT: We knew it was raining outside.

You will see some sentences like this last example in the exercises that follow. Read and analyze them carefully to make sure you understand the relationships they state.

EXERCISE INSTRUCTIONS

Each exercise is a sentence. Read it carefully. Then write the CAUSE and the EFFECT stated in the sentence. *Make sure to write complete sentences.* (Do not include words like "because" or "since." These are not part of the cause or effect. They are used to connect the cause with the effect in a single sentence.)

EXERCISE 1

Because I like roses, I bought a dozen of them.

CAUSE: _____

EFFECT: _____

_____

EXERCISE 2

I bought a dozen roses because I like them.

CAUSE: _____

EFFECT: _____

_____

EXERCISE 3

(NOTE: Check to see that your answers to Exercises 1 and 2 are the same. These two sentences have the same meaning. They state the same cause—effect relationship.)

We cannot eat dinner now because the turkey is not ready yet.

CAUSE: _____

EFFECT: _____

_____

EXERCISE 4

Because the turkey is not ready yet, we cannot eat dinner now.

CAUSE: _____

EFFECT: _____

_____

EXERCISE 5

(Check to see that your answers to Exercises 3 and 4 are the same.)

Albie's black slacks were dirty; therefore, he wore his dark blue ones.

CAUSE: _____

EFFECT: _____

EXERCISE 6

CAUTION: The answers to parts A and B are **not** the same.

A. My uncle has a lot of money because he always looks for bargains.

   CAUSE: _____

   EFFECT: _____

B. I figured my uncle had a lot of money since he never looks for bargains.

   CAUSE: _____

   EFFECT: _____

EXERCISE 7

A. Greg was hungry, so he ate quickly.

   CAUSE: _____

   EFFECT: _____

B. We knew Greg was hungry because he ate quickly.

   CAUSE: _____

   EFFECT: _____

EXERCISE 8

A. Julienne's car was broken, so she rode the bus to work.

   CAUSE: _____

   EFFECT: _____

B. Since Julienne rode the bus to work, we knew her car was broken.

   CAUSE: _____

   EFFECT: _____

EXERCISE 9

A. Their TV broke because it was old.

CAUSE: _____

EFFECT: _____

B. Their TV broke, so they called a TV repair technician.

CAUSE: _____

EFFECT: _____

C. We knew their TV was broken because they called a TV repair technician.

CAUSE: _____

EFFECT: _____

EXERCISE 10

The dirtiness of the water was the result of a factory dumping waste in the river.

CAUSE: _____

EFFECT: _____

EXERCISE 11

We stayed home because of rain.

CAUSE: _____

EFFECT: _____

EXERCISE 12

Because of poor sales, the artist quit painting and took a job washing dishes.

CAUSE: _____

EFFECT: _____

EXERCISE 13

Exercise 6B is tricky because it says we knew a cause because we observed its effect.

CAUSE: _____

EFFECT: _____

_____

EXERCISE 14

This computer is called "user-friendly" because it was designed to be easy for the average person to use.

CAUSE: _____

EFFECT: _____

_____

EXERCISE 15

Sugar is made of carbon along with hydrogen and oxygen, so it is called a carbohydrate.

CAUSE: _____

EFFECT: _____

_____

EXERCISE 16

Plants require light because they use it for making food through a process called photosynthesis.

CAUSE: _____

EFFECT: _____

_____

EXERCISE 17

TV waves do not follow the roundness of the Earth but travel in a straight line, so they are bounced off satellites to reach places all around the Earth.

CAUSE: _____

EFFECT: _____

PART II: Contrast

Words and phrases like "but", "although", "however", "nevertheless" and "in spite of" are often used to show a *contrast* between two ideas. They let you know there is an inconsistency (lack of agreement) between two situations. Here is an example:

Although it was still raining, Gilda went swimming.

SITUATION 1: It was raining.
SITUATION 2: Gilda went swimming.

THIS IS A CONTRAST BECAUSE: Usually you don't go swimming in the rain because you might get cold or get struck by lightning.

Here is another example. Try this one yourself. On the lines, write the two situations given in the sentence and the reason they form a contrast.

In spite of being sick, Mr. Shearn went to school and taught his classes.

SITUATION 1: _____

SITUATION 2: _____

THIS IS A CONTRAST BECAUSE: _____

_____

_____

After you have written your answers, compare them with the ones below.

SITUATION 1: _Mr. Shearn was sick._

SITUATION 2: _He went to school and taught his classes._

THIS IS A CONTRAST BECAUSE: _Usually you don't go_

to work when sick because you might get sicker or

spread the sickness to others.

Notice that the original sentence contains the phrase "being sick." These words *do not* by themselves describe a situation. To describe a situation, you use a complete sentence such as "Mr. Shearn was sick."

EXERCISE INSTRUCTIONS

Read each exercise carefully. Then write sentences describing the two situations given and the reason they form a contrast. Write complete sentences, not just phrases like "being sick."

EXERCISE 1

The package was big; however, it was not heavy.

SITUATION 1: _____

SITUATION 2: _____

THIS IS A CONTRAST BECAUSE: _____

_____

_____

EXERCISE 2

My uncle has a lot of money; nevertheless, he is always looking for bargains.

SITUATION 1: _____

SITUATION 2: _____

THIS IS A CONTRAST BECAUSE: _____

_____

_____

EXERCISE 3

Jeremy had saved three lives but refused to be called a hero.

SITUATION 1: _____

SITUATION 2: _____

THIS IS A CONTRAST BECAUSE: _____

_____

_____

EXERCISE 4

In spite of being very hungry, she gave half of her lunch to her friend.

SITUATION 1: _____

SITUATION 2: _____

THIS IS A CONTRAST BECAUSE: _____

_____

_____

_____

EXERCISE 5

Although very poor, the artist was happy.

SITUATION 1: _____

SITUATION 2: _____

THIS IS A CONTRAST BECAUSE: _____

_____

_____

_____

EXERCISE 6

Christine and Jack went to the zoo in spite of the rain.

SITUATION 1: _____

SITUATION 2: _____

THIS IS A CONTRAST BECAUSE: _____

_____

_____

EXERCISE 7

Suffering from a sprained ankle, Pedro nevertheless ran the race.

SITUATION 1: _____

SITUATION 2: _____

THIS IS A CONTRAST BECAUSE: _____

_____

_____

EXERCISE 8

Although the Olympic games are about 3,000 years old, women have only been allowed to compete in them for about 60 years.

SITUATION 1: _____

SITUATION 2: _____

THIS IS A CONTRAST BECAUSE: _____

_____

_____

EXERCISE 9

A computer could be called smart since it can handle a large amount of information quickly; nevertheless, it is stupid in the sense that it can only do exactly what it is told.

SITUATION 1: _____

SITUATION 2: _____

THIS IS A CONTRAST BECAUSE: _____

_____

_____

EXERCISE 10

In spite of a computer breakdown shortly after take-off and a fire during landing, the space flight was considered successful.

SITUATION 1: _____

SITUATION 2: _____

THIS IS A CONTRAST BECAUSE: _____

_____

_____

_____

EXERCISE 11

Animals take in oxygen and expel (give out) carbon dioxide; however, plants take in carbon dioxide and expel oxygen.

SITUATION 1: _____

SITUATION 2: _____

THIS IS A CONTRAST BECAUSE: _____

_____

_____

_____

EXERCISE 12

Historians don't have solid facts about Plato's early education; in spite of this, it is believed that Plato received a fine basic education because his family was part of the upper class in Greece.

SITUATION 1: _____

SITUATION 2: _____

THIS IS A CONTRAST BECAUSE: _____

_____

_____

PART III: Accentuation (Emphasis)

The phrases "in fact" and "on the contrary" are used in sentences to introduce an idea that supports, strengthens or emphasizes a statement that has already been made. Study this example:

He is not clumsy; on the contrary, he is a good athlete.

THE STATEMENT <u>He is a good athlete.</u>

STRENGTHENS THE STATEMENT <u>He is not clumsy.</u>

Notice that the phrase "He is a good athlete" is a contrast to "He *is* clumsy." Therefore, it strengthens what is actually stated: "He *is not* clumsy."

Now study this example:

This play is excellent; in fact, it is the best play I've ever seen.

THE STATEMENT <u>It is the best play I've ever seen.</u>

STRENGTHENS THE STATEMENT <u>This play is excellent.</u>

In this case the phrase "It is the best play I've ever seen" adds direct support to the statement "This play is excellent."

EXERCISE INSTRUCTIONS

Read each of the following sentences carefully. Then complete the blanks to show which statement in the sentence strengthens which other statement.

EXERCISE 1

The water is not safe to drink; on the contrary, a glass of it would kill an elephant.

THE STATEMENT _____

STRENGTHENS THE STATEMENT _____

EXERCISE 2

Prentice is a good writer; in fact, he has won several writing awards.

THE STATEMENT _____

STRENGTHENS THE STATEMENT _____

EXERCISE 3

I am not poor; in fact, I can lend you some money if you need it.

THE STATEMENT _____

STRENGTHENS THE STATEMENT _____

_____

EXERCISE 4

I am not poor; on the contrary, I own this store.

THE STATEMENT _____

STRENGTHENS THE STATEMENT _____

_____

EXERCISE 5

The elevator cable is not too weak; on the contrary, it could support many more people than could possibly fit in the elevator.

THE STATEMENT _____

STRENGTHENS THE STATEMENT _____

_____

EXERCISE 6

Wood is not just used in building houses and furniture; on the contrary, it is used for such varied purposes as making paper and hitting baseballs.

THE STATEMENT _____

STRENGTHENS THE STATEMENT _____

_____

EXERCISE 7

The world's supply of oil is not endless; in fact, at the rate we are now using oil, there will be none left in about 25 years.

THE STATEMENT _____

STRENGTHENS THE STATEMENT _____

_____

EXERCISE 8

Smoking is bad for your health; in fact, it has been linked to lung diseases and cancer.

THE STATEMENT _____

STRENGTHENS THE STATEMENT _____

PART IV: Relations Between Sentences

Words like "therefore" and phrases like "in fact" are sometimes used with a semicolon to connect two closely related sentences into a single sentence. For example:

My car was broken; therefore, I took the bus to work.

This single sentence is made up of two complete sentences which could be written separately:

My car was broken.
I took the bus to work.

Notice the relation between the two sentences. The first sentence gives the *cause* for the action taken in the second sentence (the *effect*). Remember what you learned in PART I of this unit? A cause and an effect can be connected in a sentence by using a word like "therefore":

My car was broken; therefore, I took the bus to work.

The semicolon and "therefore," used together, tell you that the two ideas are separate (the semicolon does this) but connected ("therefore" does this).

Now study how a semicolon and the word "nevertheless" let two sentences be combined into this single sentence:

It was raining; nevertheless, Christine and Jack went to the zoo.

In this case two *contrasting* sentences are connected in a single sentence: (1) It was raining; (2) Christine and Jack went to the zoo.

The following words and phrases are commonly used to connect two sentences into a single sentence. Read the definition of each word or phrase. Then study how it is used in sentences to combine ideas.

1. *furthermore:* also, in addition

   The climate in Daytona Beach is pleasant; *furthermore*, the cost of living is not high.

2. *therefore:* because of that

   There is only one way to do the job well; *therefore*, don't try to use other ways or shortcuts.

3. *consequently:* because of that ("consequently" means the same as "therefore")

   My car was broken; *consequently*, I took the bus to work.

4. *nevertheless:* in spite of that (opposite of "therefore"); used to introduce an un-
expected or somewhat inconsistent
idea

Carla had a bad cold; *nevertheless*, she competed
in the race.

5. *in fact:* in truth, actually; used to introduce a statement which strengthens an earlier statement

Philippe is widely travelled; *in fact*, he has been to
almost every country in the world.

6. *on the contrary:* similar to "in fact," but used
when something is said *not to be
true* and then the true situation is
described; just the opposite of
what is said not to be true

I did not lose the race; *on the contrary,* I finished
in first place.

7. *however:* on the other hand, by contrast, but

The library has a good collection of classic books;
however, they are kept in a special room and few
students get to see them.

8. *for instance:* for example; used to introduce an
example proving or strengthening a
point

New York City has a terrible traffic problem; *for
instance,* it sometimes takes 15 minutes to travel
two blocks by bus.

EXERCISE INSTRUCTIONS

For each exercise, choose and then write the word or phrase that
best fits in the blank (connects the first part of the sentence with
the second part most meaningfully). You will need to read each
sentence carefully to see exactly what the relation is between the
first and second parts. Refer to the definitions of the words and
phrases given above whenever it will help you. The first exercise is
done for you.

EXERCISE 1

The central heating unit is broken; ____therefore____ ,
use the small electric heater.

on the contrary   therefore
for instance

EXERCISE 2

The central heating unit is broken; _____ ,
the small electric heater will keep the room warm enough.

on the contrary   however
for instance

EXERCISE 3

The factory workers decided their salaries were too low;
_____ , they called a strike.

however   consequently
on the contrary   for instance

EXERCISE 4

Melville was a great American writer; _____ ,
he was not honored until after his death.

for instance   however
therefore   consequently

EXERCISE 5

Brett is good in math; _____ , she is a talented
musician.

for example   furthermore
on the contrary

EXERCISE 6

Brett is good in math; _____ , she is weak in
English.

for example   in fact
however

EXERCISE 7

The rain had stopped; _____ , Juanita continued to carry her umbrella open above her head.

therefore   for instance
nevertheless   in fact

EXERCISE 8

Adam is no longer a thief; _____ , he is now a
police officer.

however   therefore
in fact   nevertheless

EXERCISE 9

Adam is no longer a thief; _____ , he is now a
police officer.

however   therefore
on the contrary   nevertheless

EXERCISE 10

Tina is a talented writer; _____ , she won the creative writing award at her school.

nevertheless   in fact
however   on the contrary

EXERCISE 11

Wanda is a serious student; _____ , she spent the entire weekend studying for a history test on Monday.

nevertheless   for instance
on the contrary   however

EXERCISE 12

The weekend was cold; _____ , there were many people at the beach.

therefore   for instance
on the contrary   nevertheless

EXERCISE 13

A regular microscope can magnify objects up to 2,000 times; _____ , an electron microscope can magnify objects up to 1,000,000 times.

therefore   however
for instance   nevertheless

EXERCISE 14

Spiders can be useful to man; _____ , spiders eat flies and other insects which pester man and can spread disease.

nevertheless   for instance
however   on the contrary

EXERCISE 15

The refrigerator broke; _____ , the food spoiled.

on the contrary   however
consequently   nevertheless

EXERCISE 16

The new plane is very large; _____ , it can hold many passengers.

nevertheless   therefore
on the contrary   however

EXERCISE 17

The new plane is very large; _____ , it handles as easily as most smaller planes.

therefore   in fact
on the contrary   nevertheless

EXERCISE 18

The new large plane is not hard to handle; _____ ,
it handles like a small plane.

therefore   however
on the contrary   nevertheless

EXERCISE 19

Charnell's blue dress was dirty; _____ , she wore her green dress.

nevertheless   consequently
on the contrary

EXERCISE 20

Charnell's blue dress was dirty; _____ , she wore it to school.

nevertheless   consequently
on the contrary

EXERCISE 21

Charnell's blue dress was not clean; _____ , it was covered with food stains.

nevertheless   consequently
on the contrary

EXERCISE 22

It is not always true that the further north you go the colder it becomes; _____ , below the equator, the further north you travel the warmer it becomes.

however   nevertheless
in fact   therefore

EXERCISE 23

The building industry is not in a slump; _____ , there was an increase in new houses built last month.

nevertheless   however
in fact

EXERCISE 24

The building industry is not in a slump; _____ , there was an increase in new houses built last month.

however   nevertheless
on the contrary

EXERCISE 25

Several American presidents had been former military leaders; _____ , Grant and Eisenhower were both generals in the army.

however   furthermore
on the contrary   for instance

EXERCISE 26

By observing good health practices one can expect to live past 70; _____ , one's life should be full and lively.

furthermore   on the contrary
nevertheless   however

PART V: Grammatical Decisions— Quotation Marks and Colon

The ability to understand the use of punctuation marks in written material is important for analytical reading. It helps us see the relations between the written ideas. Clearly, this ability is just as important in our own *writing*. It helps us present our ideas in an easy-to-understand way.

In PART IV of this unit you learned about one role of the *semicolon*—to link separate but connected thoughts into a single sentence. In this part of the unit you will learn and practice the use of *quotation marks* (" ") and the *colon* (:).

Below are explanations and examples of some of the uses of quotation marks and the colon. (There are other uses of each that will not be covered here.) As you review these lists, study how the *thought* behind the punctuation mark is expressed through its use in a sentence.

QUOTATION MARKS (" ")

1. **used to enclose direct speech** (thought—these words are actually spoken)

   "Go to the store," Mom said, "and buy some tacos."

2. **used to enclose words or phrases which need special attention or which are used in a special way;** (thought—these words have a special meaning)

   In math class we can always count on "the brain" to have the correct homework answers.

3. **used to enclose titles of magazine articles, book chapters, short poems, short stories, songs, lectures, and radio and TV programs** (thought—this is the title of something)

   Important Note: The titles of books, magazines, plays and newspapers **are not** enclosed in quotation marks. These longer works are instead underlined when typed, or put in italics when printed.

   The third chapter of the book <u>American History</u> is called "The American Revolution."

COLON (:)

1. **used to introduce a phrase or clause that explains or illustrates (gives an example of) what has just been said** (thought—this explains what has just been said)

   It was a poor quality radio: the sound was weak and fuzzy.

2. **used to introduce a list or series of things** (thought—all of these things are items of the list mentioned)

Angelo's record collection included the finest rock groups: Beatles, Rolling Stones, Pink Floyd, Who and Police.

3. **used to separate a title from a subtitle** (thought—the title of this work contains a subtitle)

Europe and America: A History of Western Civilization was written in 1983.

4. **used to separate the hour from the minutes in telling time** (thought—it was this many minutes past the hour)

We guessed the murder was committed at 3:40 because the broken clock on the floor had stopped at that time.

5. **used after the salutation in a formal letter** (thought—here is the body of the letter)

Dear Mrs. Wang:

Thank you for your order. We will ship immediately.

Sincerely,
Mrs. Ina Lopez
Sales Manager

Knowing when and how to add punctuation marks to written material requires careful thinking. For example, try to add quotation marks correctly to the following two sentences.

1. After we finished dinner, Tom asked, Can I go to a movie?
2. After we finish dinner, Tom asked, can I go to a movie?

You should have thought about these three things as you tried to add your quotation marks:

(A) Sentence 1 contains the word *finished*, whereas Sentence 2 contains *finish*.

(B) In Sentence 1 the letter *C* is capitalized in *Can*, telling you that this is the beginning of a direct quote.

(C) The words *Tom asked* are contained in both sentences. These words would not be part of a direct quote in either sentence. So, *Tom asked* should not be enclosed in quotation marks in either sentence.

Based on this thinking, you can understand that in Sentence 1 dinner was finished and Tom asked: "Can I go to a movie?" In Sentence 2 Tom was still eating dinner and asked: "After we finish dinner, can I go to a movie?" Therefore, you should have added quotation marks as shown at the top of the next page.

1. After we finished dinner, Tom asked, "Can I go to a movie?"

2. "After we finish dinner," Tom asked, "can I go to a movie?"

These examples show that in adding quotation marks you must think about *exactly* what a person said, and what he or she did not say. (In other cases, you must think about exactly what the title, slang words or other words are that need to be enclosed in quotation marks.)

Now try to add a colon to the following sentence. Again, think carefully.

Marlene likes several sports baseball, football, soccer and golf.

Careful thinking shows that this sentence *lists* four sports that Marlene likes. The four sports are baseball, football, soccer and swimming. Again, thinking carefully about *exactly* what the sentence is saying makes it possible to correctly add the colon.

Marlene likes several sports: baseball, football, soccer and golf.

EXERCISE INSTRUCTIONS

Each of the following exercises contains a sentence that is missing *one or more* quotation marks or a colon. Think carefully about exactly what the sentence is saying, then add the missing quotation marks and/or colons. The first one has the answer shown to demonstrate the procedure.

EXERCISE 1

The general said, "Don't forget to take these things your helmet, your shovel, your rifle and your backpack.

Answer

The general said, "Don't forget to take these things: your helmet, your shovel, your rifle and your backpack."

EXERCISE 2

(HINT: Add one quotation mark.)

The child said, Our teacher is funny."

EXERCISE 3

The waiter said, "Good evening, as he pulled out the chair.

EXERCISE 4

(HINT: Add a colon.)

The following cars are produced in Japan Toyota, Datsun, Honda and Isuzu.

EXERCISE 5

It is raining very hard; therefore, take your umbrella," insisted Uncle Jake.

EXERCISE 6

"After dinner, Mom said, "we'll go to a movie."

EXERCISE 7

Can you tell me, Mr. Soo, what the capital of South Dakota is?" asked the teacher.

EXERCISE 8

The article entitled "Getting Rich was full of good money-making advice.

EXERCISE 9

(HINT: Add three quotation marks.)

Improving your grades, Mrs. Higgins advised, requires spending more time studying."

EXERCISE 10

"I will arrive in St. Paul at 6 00 on Thursday," said Isaac.

EXERCISE 11

"Your test performance was poor; therefore, you should go for tutoring, suggested the instructor.

EXERCISE 12

Lucille queried, Where is my notebook?"

EXERCISE 13

After studying herself in the mirror for ten minutes, Karen exclaimed, Brooke Shields, eat your heart out!"

EXERCISE 14

I don't like spinach, complained Cleo, so stop cooking it."

EXERCISE 15

The "underground railroad was not really a railroad but a series of routes and secret rest stops for slaves escaping from the South.

EXERCISE 16

(HINT: Add four quotation marks.)

He always referred to money as "lettuce or cabbage, and dollars he called bucks".

EXERCISE 17

(HINT: Add a colon to separate a main title from a subtitle.)

While studying about Germany I read an interesting and funny book with the amusing title *Science and Sauerkraut A View of the German National Character.*

EXERCISE 18

Life Patterns in Arid Lands is the title of the first chapter in the text *The Desert.*

EXERCISE 19

On his latest trip the diplomat visited several European cities Rome, Paris, London and Madrid.

EXERCISE 20

(HINT: Add a colon to introduce the illustration of what is said.)

Conditions in the country were bad many people were out of work and a large number had lost their homes.

EXERCISE 21

"What other jobs need to be done, Charlie asked, after we finish mowing the lawn?

EXERCISE 22

"What other jobs need to be done? Charlie asked, as we finished mowing the lawn.

EXERCISE 23

NOTE: Exercise 21 required **three** quotation marks.
       Exercise 22 required **one** quotation mark.

As we walked to the library, Leroy suggested, Let's stop for something to eat."

EXERCISE 24

As we walk to the library, Leroy suggested, let's stop for something to eat."

EXERCISE 25

Let's stop for something to eat, Leroy suggested, before we get to the library.

EXERCISE 26

NOTE: For Exercises 23-25, check to see that one exercise needed **four** quotation marks, one exercise needed **three** quotation marks, and one exercise needed just **one** quotation mark.

The gang claimed their mission was to "share" the country's wealth, but by share" they meant steal from others and spend the money themselves.

EXERCISE 27

The teacher passed out copies of the encyclopedia article "The Color Spectrum and said, Study it; don't just skim it!"

EXERCISE 28

Three outstanding automobiles are produced in Germany Mercedes, Porsche and Audi.

EXERCISE 29

Read the chapter New Nations in the book *History in the Making* by next Monday.

EXERCISE 30

Michelle had only one goal winning an Olympic gold medal.

EXERCISE 31

"General Sanchez, said Aurelio, was our best military planner.

EXERCISE 32

General Sanchez said, Aurelio was our best military planner."

EXERCISE 33

At one time the United States had an open door" policy and welcomed immigrants from other countries.

EXERCISE 34

The poem Trees is a tribute to the beauty of nature.

EXERCISE 35

Exercise is terrific for you it strengthens the heart, muscles and lungs.

EXERCISE 36

The title of our textbook is *Problem Solving and Comprehension A Short Course in Analytical Reasoning.*

EXERCISE 37

I have no excuse for being late, mumbled Tony, looking nervously out the window, but it won't happen again."

EXERCISE 38

The watch was described as "waterproof in the ad, but when it stopped running after becoming wet, rip off" seemed like a better description!

EXERCISE 39

Three countries make up North America Canada, Mexico and the United States, answered Theresa proudly.

EXERCISE 40

After the committee had met for several hours, the mayor came out saying, We agreed not to give information to the press at this time, but the reporters continued to follow her and ask questions.

ADDITIONAL ASSIGNMENTS

1. On the lines below, write a sentence that states a cause—effect relationship. (Your sentence should be like the exercise sentences in PART I of this unit.)

_____

_____

Now, ask a classmate or friend to read your sentence and then to write the CAUSE and the EFFECT stated in the sentence.

CAUSE: _____

EFFECT: _____

> In PART IV of this unit you learned how two sentences can be combined into a single sentence. This can be done by using a word or phrase such as "therefore", "however", "on the contrary," and so on. Use what you learned to complete the following assignments. Reread pages 113 and 114 if you need help.

2. _Use a semicolon and the word "therefore"_ to combine these two sentences into a single sentence. Write your sentence on the lines below.

> John's bicycle had a flat tire.
> He could not finish his paper route.

_____

_____

3. _Use a semicolon and the word "nevertheless"_ to combine these two sentences into a single sentence. Write your sentence on the lines below.

> Linda and Darwin are going to the movies.
> Darwin is not feeling well.

_____

_____

ADDITIONAL ASSIGNMENTS

4. *Use a semicolon and the phrase "on the contrary"* to combine these two sentences into a single sentence. Write your sentence on the lines below.

> A long and deep sleep will help your mind stay alert during an exam.
>
> It is not smart to stay up all night before an exam.

_____

_____

_____

NOTE: Use what you learned in PART V of this unit to complete the following exercises. Review pages 118-124 if you need help.

5. Write a sentence on the lines below that is *missing one or more quotation marks*. Ask a classmate or friend to correct your sentence by writing in the missing quotation mark(s).

_____

_____

6. Write a sentence on the lines below that is *missing a colon*. Ask a classmate or friend to correct your sentence by writing in the missing colon where it belongs.

_____

_____

7. Write a sentence on the lines below that is *missing* both *a colon and one or more quotation marks*. Ask a classmate or friend to correct your sentence by writing in the missing colon and quotation mark(s).

_____

_____

_____

UNIT

8

Synthesizing Sentences To Master Complexity

OBJECTIVES

When you have completed this unit you will

- understand how a complex sentence is made of two simple sentences;

- be able to choose a key word to combine two simple sentences into one complex sentence;

- be able to re-write two simple sentences into one complex sentence by using a conjunction;

- be able to use commas correctly to show nonessential (extra) information in a complex sentence;

- be able to re-write two simple sentences into one complex sentence by using the pronouns "which" or "who".

INTRODUCTION

This unit will give you more practice in understanding how individual ideas can be linked in complex sentences.

Research studies have found that many students experience difficulty comprehending certain types of complex sentences. Studies have also shown that when students practice constructing complex sentences of their own, their ability to comprehend such sentences when they read them improves dramatically. In other words, students who have synthesized (built) complex sentences from simple ones are better equipped to analyze complex sentences into their basic ideas and thus understand them.

This unit teaches several patterns used in complex sentences. You will find that practicing these sentence patterns will help you to express your ideas more effectively in the papers and reports you write. The exercises will also strengthen your reading skill. The sentence patterns discussed here are used widely in academic and professional writing. Practice in creating and writing these sentences will help you to recognize and comprehend them when you encounter them in your reading.

PART I: Combining Sentences Using Subordinating Conjunctions

PATTERN A

Consider these two sentences:

Eighteen inches of snow had fallen during the night.
We could not get the car out of the garage.

The conjunction *because* can be used to combine the two sentences and show that one sentence describes the cause for the situation depicted in the other sentence.

Because **eighteen inches of snow had fallen during the night, we could not get the car out of the garage.** ← *comma*

Notice that when a conjunction like *because* is placed in front of the first sentence, a comma is placed between the sentences.

Here are the definitions of several common conjunctions used in the exercises that follow:

because	Used to indicate that one event caused another.
since	One meaning of "since" is *because*.
before	Used to indicate that one event preceded another.
after	Used to indicate that one event followed another.
when	Used to indicate that one event occurred at (or close to) the time of another event.
although	Used to indicate a contrast between ideas.
if	Used to indicate that when one statement is true, another statement is true.
unless	Used to indicate that when one statement is false, another statement is true.

Conjunctions such as these are used to combine sentences for two reasons. First, they allow a writer to show the relationship between two events, situations, or ideas. And second, they provide a writer with the power to create sentences which are richer and more informative, rather than just simple and immature. In the exercises which follow, you will transform simple, unconnected sentences into richer sentences showing relationships between ideas. The early exercises are relatively easy. But as you progress through the unit, you will learn sentence patterns that increase your understanding of how writers can express ideas.

EXERCISE INSTRUCTIONS

Each exercise presents two conjunctions and two sentences. Read the sentences carefully and decide which conjunction to place in front of the first sentence in combining the sentences. Choose the conjunction which shows the logical relationship between the sentences. Then write the combined sentence, using the conjunction in front of the first sentence and a comma between the original sentences.

Try this sample exercise:

Combine these sentences using *unless* or *after*.

> **They had drifted for four days in their rubber raft.**
> **The crew of the wrecked plane finally sighted land.**

COMBINED: _____

_____

_____

The conjunction *after* shows the time relationship implied by the two sentences. The conjunction *unless* does not make sense with these sentences. Therefore, *after* is used in combining the sentences.

COMBINED: **After they had drifted for four days in their**

rubber raft, the crew of the wrecked plane finally sighted land.

Use the same procedure in doing the exercises below.

EXERCISE 1

Combine these sentences using *if* or *when*.

> Bob stepped on his brake pedal.
> He realized that his driveway was a sheet of ice and that his car would not stop before reaching the closed garage door.

COMBINED: _____

_____

_____

EXERCISE 2

Combine these sentences using *because* or *before*.

> I cannot understand the directions for programming my VCR.
> It sits in my living room continuously blinking 12:00 a.m.

COMBINED: _____

_____

_____

EXERCISE 3

Combine these sentences using *before* or *although*.

Some people claim to read very rapidly.
Their comprehension of difficult material may be poor.

COMBINED: _____

_____

_____

EXERCISE 4

Combine these sentences using *because* or *before*.

Comedians help people laugh at common problems.
They reduce and relieve many of society's tensions.

COMBINED: _____

_____

_____

EXERCISE 5

Combine these sentences using *before* or *if*.

The United States helped the Cuban government institute a sanitation program in 1902.
Cuba had been ravaged by yellow fever for years.

COMBINED: _____

_____

_____

EXERCISE 6

Combine these sentences using *before* or *since*.

Voting participation tends to be related to income level.
A candidate with many affluent supporters has an advantage at the polls.

COMBINED: _____

_____

_____

PATTERN B

There is another pattern which can be used for combining simple sentences with a subordinating conjunction — the conjunction can be placed between the sentences. With this pattern, a comma is generally not needed. Here is an example:

**President Clinton had clapped enthusiastically.
A comedian imitated him playing the saxophone.**

COMBINED: President Clinton had clapped enthusiastically *when* a comedian imitated him playing the saxophone.

EXERCISE INSTRUCTIONS

Each exercise presents two conjunctions and two sentences. Decide which conjunction could be placed between the two sentences to join them logically. Then write the combined sentence.

Try this sample exercise first:

Combine these sentences using *if* or *after*.

**You can get Indian jewelry at bargain prices in Sante Fe.
You buy from the Native Americans displaying their products at the central plaza instead of buying from the tourist shops.**

COMBINED: _____

_____

_____

_____

The conjunction *if* shows the logical relationship implied by the two sentences because the first sentence is true under the condition described in the second sentence. The conjunction *after* does not make sense with these sentences. Therefore, *if* is used in combining the sentences.

COMBINED: **You can get Indian jewelry at bargain prices in Santa Fe if you buy from the Native Americans displaying their products at the central plaza instead of buying from the tourist shops.**

Use the same type of reasoning to complete the exercises that begin on the next page.

EXERCISE 1

Combine these sentences using *because* or *before*.

John was late for his medical examination.
A sudden storm flooded the streets and delayed traffic.

COMBINED: _____

_____

_____

EXERCISE 2

Combine these sentences using *before* or *unless*.

Our company will have a picnic at the beach this Saturday.
The Friday evening weather report predicts rain for Saturday.

COMBINED: _____

_____

_____

EXERCISE 3

Combine these sentences using *before* or *if*.

Only men had the right to vote in national elections.
The Nineteenth Amendment was enacted into law in 1920.

COMBINED: _____

_____

_____

EXERCISE 4

Combine these sentences using *although* or *if*.

The history of a nation can be fully understood.
The basic conditions that effect both the social lives of common people and the decisions of political leaders are investigated.

COMBINED: _____

_____

_____

EXERCISE 5

Combine these sentences using *when* or *unless*.

Many people think of verbs as action words and then become confused.
Textbooks or teachers call other types of words verbs.

COMBINED: _____

_____

_____

EXERCISE 6

Combine these sentences using *before* or *if*.

You will avoid confusion and find it easier to identify verbs in sentences.
You remember that there are several types of verbs, including action verbs such as
"kick" and linking verbs such as "is."

COMBINED: _____

_____

_____

EXERCISE 7

Combine these sentences using *although* or *since*.

You can ski six months of the year in the northeast United States.
There is usually snow on the mountains from November through April.

COMBINED: _____

_____

_____

EXERCISE 8

Combine these sentences using *although* or *unless*.

The United States' space program may be reduced to only small-scale missions.
More money can be spent on new equipment and more human resources.

COMBINED: _____

_____

_____

PART II: Combining Sentences Using Relative Pronouns

This part of the unit illustrates another family of patterns for combining simple sentences into complex sentences — patterns that use the relative pronouns *who* and *which*.

PATTERN C

Consider these sentences:

Our apple tree provides fruit all fall.
The tree is 10 years old.

The second sentence gives additional information about the tree. If the first sentence is considered to be the main sentence, then the information from the second sentence can be added to it by using the pronoun *which* in this way:

Our apple tree, *which* is ten years old, provides fruit all fall.
        ⟵   commas   ⟶

Notice the role that *which* plays in the complex sentence. *Which* represents "The tree."

Our apple tree, which is 10 years old . . .
         ⋀
The tree is 10 years old . . .

Notice also that *which* is placed right after "tree" in the combined sentence because it adds information about the tree.

Finally, notice that the information added to the main sentence is enclosed with commas. It stands apart from the rest of the sentence.

EXERCISE INSTRUCTIONS

Each exercise presents two sentences. Combine the sentences using *which* and commas as shown in the above example.

Try this sample exercise on your own before checking the answer on the next page.

Add the information from the second sentence to the first sentence using *which* and commas.

    A large wooden box forced cars to swerve sharply and several nearly collided.
    The box had fallen onto the highway from a truck.

COMBINED: _____

_____

_____

To combine those sentences, *which* is substituted for "box" in the second sentence. Then the second sentence is added right after "box" in the first sentence — because it provides additional information about the box.

COMBINED: **A large wooden box, which had fallen onto the highway from a truck, forced cars to swerve sharply and several nearly collided.**

Complete the following exercises in the same way.

EXERCISE 1

Two large dogs tipped over our garbage can and scattered the contents.
The dogs had escaped from their backyard.

COMBINED: _____

_____

_____

EXERCISE 2

Vegetarian hot dogs are made from low-cholesterol soy flour and wheat protein.
The hot dogs taste enough like meat to fool even a restaurant critic.

COMBINED: _____

_____

_____

EXERCISE 3

The university library is closed because a water pipe burst and flooded several floors.
The library is where we intended to spend the afternoon.

COMBINED: _____

_____

_____

EXERCISE 4

Fred's customized Chevy has a twenty-speaker sound system.
The Chevy has won prizes in numerous car shows.

COMBINED: _____

_____

_____

PATTERN D

Compare the sentences below. They both contain *which*, but only one has commas.

Breakfast cereals, *which* are made from grains, **provide protein and energy.**
Breakfast cereals *which* contain excessive sugar **should be avoided.**

Why does the first sentence contain commas but not the second? Try deleting the lightface (light type) portion from the first sentence.

Breakfast cereals provide protein and energy.

This sentence still has the same basic meaning. The information that was deleted was *not essential*. It was extra information.
Now try deleting the lightface portion from the second sentence.

Breakfast cereals should be avoided.

Clearly, the basic meaning of this sentence has been changed. It now says that all breakfast cereals should be avoided, whereas the original sentence only said that people should avoid breakfast cereals that contain excessive sugar. The lightface portion — the portion using *which* — is essential to the meaning of the sentence. Therefore, it is NOT enclosed in commas (it is not set apart from the rest of the sentence). Only extra or nonessential information is enclosed in commas.
See the difference?

```
extra (nonessential) information  ⟶  enclosed in commas

      essential information  ⟶  no commas
```

In the following exercise set, you will use *which* to add information from one sentence to another. The information you add should be considered *essential* information, so you will *not* use commas.

EXERCISE INSTRUCTIONS

Each exercise presents two sentences. Combine the sentences using *which* but without commas.
Here's a sample exercise to try:

Add the information from the second sentence to the first sentence using *which* but without commas.

The books should be returned to the library today.
The books are piled on the coffee table.

COMBINED: _____

_____

_____

To combine the sentences, *which* is substituted for "books" in the second sentence. Then the second sentence is added right after "books" in the first sentence.

COMBINED: **The books which are piled on the coffee table should be returned to the library today.**

Use the same procedure in doing the following exercises.

EXERCISE 1

Food additives are no longer on the market.
The additives have been found to cause cancer.

COMBINED: _____

_____

_____

EXERCISE 2

Buyers of new cars must pay a luxury tax.
The cars cost more than $30,000.

COMBINED: _____

_____

_____

EXERCISE 3

A herring may be called a sardine.
The herring is not yet fully grown.

COMBINED: _____

_____

_____

EXERCISE 4

Medium-priced automobiles bear witness to the wonders of modern technology.
The automobiles can be driven for over 100,000 miles with only minor repairs.

COMBINED: _____

_____

_____

PATTERN E

The word *who* can be used much like *which* for combining sentences — but *who* is used to add information about humans, whereas *which* is used for nonhumans. Here is an example of how extra information can be added to a sentence using *who* and commas:

My oldest brother is a marathon runner.
This brother lives in Texas.

COMBINED: My oldest brother, *who* lives in Texas, is a marathon runner.

Notice that *who* is placed right after "brother" because it introduces additional information about the brother. Since the added information in this example is extra or nonessential, commas are used just as they are when using *which* with extra information.

EXERCISE INSTRUCTIONS

Add the information from the second sentence to the first sentence by using *who* and commas.

EXERCISE 1

Abraham Lincoln was assassinated while attending a play at Ford's Theater.
Lincoln served as America's president from 1861 to 1865.

COMBINED: _____

_____

_____

EXERCISE 2

My uncle Jack often has difficulty maintaining friendships.
Jack is cursed with a violent temper.

COMBINED: _____

_____

_____

EXERCISE 3

The ship's captain was determined to capture the beast on this trip.
The captain had lost a leg in a previous encounter with the white whale.

COMBINED: _____

_____

_____

EXERCISE 4

Charles Lindbergh helped Nobel Prize winner Alexis Carrel invent an early artificial heart.
Charles Lindbergh made the first nonstop, solo transatlantic flight.

COMBINED: _____

_____

_____

PATTERN F

Just as when using *which*, when the information added to a sentence by using *who* is essential to the basic meaning of the sentence — or is essential in identifying the person being discussed — commas are not used. Read this example:

The person must remove the car immediately.
The person parked a red Mustang in a reserved space in the parking lot.

COMBINED: The person *who* parked a red Mustang in a reserved space in the parking lot must remove the car immediately.

In this sentence the information added using *who* is considered essential because it identifies the person specifically as the one who parked the Mustang. Therefore, commas are not employed.
Use this pattern in doing the following exercises.

EXERCISE INSTRUCTIONS

In each exercise, add the information from the second sentence to the first sentence using *who* but without commas.

EXERCISE 1

The student was given a reward.
The student found the teacher's purse.

COMBINED: _____

_____

_____

EXERCISE 2

Any tourist should visit the Henry Ford Museum.
The tourist will spend time in the Detroit area.

COMBINED: _____

_____

_____

EXERCISE 3

Married couples overlook many flaws and weaknesses in their partners.
The couples are deeply in love.

COMBINED: _____

_____

_____

EXERCISE 4

Most progressive politicians supported democratic ideals rather than the interests of
the aristocratic rich.
The politicians came to power in the first decade of the 20th century.

COMBINED: _____

_____

_____

ADDITIONAL ASSIGNMENTS

> For these exercises, you will be doing the reverse of what you did in this unit. Here, you will start with a complex sentence and then break it down into two simple sentences that make up the complex sentence. The first exercise has been completed as an example.

1. Read the complex sentence. Then write two simple sentences that make up that sentence.

   Complex Sentence: William Shakespeare, who was born in 1564, wrote the play *Macbeth*.

   Simple Sentence: __**William Shakespeare wrote the play *Macbeth*.**__

   Simple Sentence: __**William Shakespeare was born in 1564.**__

2. Read the complex sentence. Then write two simple sentences that make up that sentence.

   Complex Sentence: The Nineteenth Amendment, which became law in 1920, gave women the right to vote in national elections.

   Simple Sentence: _____

   Simple Sentence: _____

4. Read the complex sentence. Then write two simple sentences that make up that sentence.

   Complex Sentence: The screwdriver which was used for the very smallest screws could not be found.

   Simple Sentence: _____

   Simple Sentence: _____

5. Read the complex sentence. Then write two simple sentences that make up that sentence. [HINT: This one is a bit different, but think carefully and you can figure it out.]

   Complex Sentence: Sarah gazed at the old photo, which had been taken by her father, and smiled.

   Simple Sentence: _____

   Simple Sentence: _____

UNIT 9

Arranging Sentences
In Logical Order

INTRODUCTION

The ability to understand the logical order (sequence) of several ideas is a major language skill. It is important for understanding the flow of ideas stated in a lengthy paragraph. It is also important for arranging your own ideas clearly in paragraphs you write.

This unit will improve your ability to analyze written ideas and arrange them in their most logical (their clearest) order. You cannot put statements into their best logical order unless you think about their meaning carefully. Further, you must think about the wording of the statements so that the ideas are properly connected as you go from one sentence to the next. (In Units 7 and 8, you learned about the role that words such as "however", "therefore", "before" and so on play in connecting the ideas in sentences.) So, this unit will add to your skill in analyzing facts and relationships so that you learn to read and write with the flow of ideas in mind.

EXERCISE INSTRUCTIONS

Each exercise is a listing of several sentences that can be put into an order that makes a clear paragraph. First, you should carefully read all of the sentences. Then number the sentences to show the correct order they should have in a paragraph. Write "1" next to the sentence you think comes *first* in the paragraph. Write "2" next to the sentence you think comes *second*—continue numbering the rest of the sentences until they have all been numbered in their best order.

You should write your numbers in pencil so that you can erase and re-number the sentences if you need to. You may often find that you need to erase and re-number the sentences. This is fine. When you work a jigsaw puzzle, it sometimes takes a while to figure out where all the pieces go. Work these exercises as if they are puzzles. Take the time to read the sentences over and over again until you are sure you know exactly how they fit together (their correct order). To practice this procedure, review the example below.

EXAMPLE: Read all four sentences. Then number the sentences to show their most logical order.

———— **A. But the city has been rebuilt.**

———— **B. However, during World War II large parts of Munich were destroyed.**

———— **C. Today, Munich is again a center for German art, architecture and education.**

———— **D. For many years before World War II the city of Munich was one of Germany's great cultural centers.**

Answer:

    __3__ A. But the city has been rebuilt.

    __2__ B. However, during World War II large parts of Munich were destroyed.

    __4__ C. Today, Munich is again a center for German art, architecture and education.

    __1__ D. For many years before World War II the city of Munich was one of Germany's great cultural centers.

In this numbered order, the four sentences make a clear paragraph. It can be summarized like this:

> Munich was a cultural center *before* World War II.
> It was partly destroyed *during* World War II.
> It has been rebuilt.
> It is again a cultural center *today*.

If you numbered the sentences differently than shown in this answer, try reading the four sentences aloud in your order and then in the answer's order. Listen for the flow of ideas from one sentence to the next. In the answer's order, the sentences flow smoothly from one to the next.

You learned in earlier units that words and phrases such as "but", "in addition", "furthermore" and "because" can help you see the order of ideas in sentences. In the EXAMPLE, the word "however" should have told you that there was a *contrast* between sentence B and some other sentence. Therefore, sentence B must follow another sentence. (Munich was one of Germany's great cultural centers. *However,* large parts of it were destroyed.)

Also, the word "but" in sentence A should have told you there was another contrast. Sentence A must also follow some other sentence. (Large parts of Munich were destroyed. *But* the city has been rebuilt.)

Words and phrases like "however", "but" and "in addition" are called *transition* words or phrases. They indicate a transition (connection) between two sentences. These words and phrases can be very helpful in ordering sentences logically. Look for them when you read sentences. (Also, use them to link sentences in your own writing.)

However (here comes a contrast to the last paragraph), you will *not always* find transition words or phrases in sentences. So, you need to read sentences carefully for their *meaning* as well as *wording.* Together, meaning and wording will indicate the best logical order for sentences.

One additional step is useful in improving your verbal or language competency. In each exercise, after you are sure you numbered the sentences in the best logical order, copy the sentences in the order you numbered them onto a piece of paper. Read over the paragraph to double-check your order of the sentences. Do you have a logical paragraph? (Rewriting the vocabulary and sentences used in well-written paragraphs will improve your writing skills, too, making you more familiar with effective types of writing.)

Begin working now on the exercises that follow.

EXERCISE 1

_____ A. It was the first flight to have five crew members.

_____ B. The Space Shuttle's seventh flight set two special records.

_____ C. Her name was Sally Ride.

_____ D. In addition, one of these five was a woman—the first American woman in space!

EXERCISE 2

_____ A. These Pilgrims had to build their own houses because America was still undeveloped.

_____ B. Columbus discovered America in 1492.

_____ C. They also had to hunt or grow most of their own food.

_____ D. But it was not until many years later, in 1621, that the Pilgrims landed at Plymouth, Massachusetts.

EXERCISE 3

_____ A. After he arrived, he had a try-out with the New York Giants' minor league baseball team.

_____ B. Orlando was hired by this minor league team.

_____ C. Orlando Cepada left Puerto Rico and came to the United States in 1955.

_____ D. Two years later he was moved up from the minor leagues to the Giants' major league team.

EXERCISE 4

_____ A. For example, a black scientist named Charles Drew developed a method which allowed blood to be stored.

_____ B. The work of scientists has helped people stay alive and healthy.

_____ C. If you were such an accident victim and the blood you received saved your life, you would be very thankful to Charles Drew and science.

_____ D. This meant that blood given to a hospital could be saved until it was needed by an accident victim.

EXERCISE 5

_____ A. Alaska is important as a source of furs, fish, oil and gold.

_____ B. Because of this location, several airports have been built where planes traveling to Japan or China can stop for fuel.

_____ C. But in this age of airplanes, it is important for another reason also.

_____ D. It is located at a good stopping place on the shortest air route from Seattle, Washington, to China or Japan.

EXERCISE 6

_____ A. Simple, quick checks of a car battery's water level and wire condition can save expensive towing and service costs.

_____ B. That is, they forget it until one cold morning when their battery won't do its job and the engine won't start.

_____ C. However, most people tend to forget about their car battery.

_____ D. On such a morning, people are coldly reminded of the need for proper battery maintenance.

EXERCISE 7

_____ A. Drake fought his way to safety, but many of his crew were killed.

_____ B. In the middle of the night, while Drake's small ships were anchored, they were attacked by a large Spanish fleet.

_____ C. After reaching safety, he swore he would get revenge or die trying.

_____ D. In 1567 an English trader named Francis Drake sailed to the West Indies with a cargo of woolen goods and slaves from Africa.

EXERCISE 8

_____ A. Then write every step in a language your computer understands.

_____ B. First break the task down into every single step the computer must do.

_____ C. Here is how to write a computer program to perform some task like keeping a record of sales in a store.

_____ D. Some of these computer languages are called LOGO, BASIC, FORTRAN and COBOL.

EXERCISE 9

_____ A. He wasn't.

_____ B. This building and the Capitol were in quite different places in the city.

_____ C. Almost everybody, including William Shakespeare, seems to think that Julius Caesar was killed in the Capitol in ancient Rome.

_____ D. He was assassinated near the statue of Pompey, which was in the Senate House.

EXERCISE 10

_____ A. Therefore, when lightning occurs, the light flash reaches your eye almost immediately, but the thunder reaches your ear somewhat later.

_____ B. The flash of lightning is always seen before the thunder is heard for a simple reason based on two facts.

_____ C. First, light travels at the fantastic speed of 186,282 miles per second.

_____ D. Sound, on the other hand, travels much more slowly—about five miles per second.

EXERCISE 11

_____ A. Suddenly Tony tired, and Rollo pinned Tony's arm on the desk.

_____ B. Each time that Tony would bring Rollo's knuckles down close to the desk, Rollo was able to bring his arm up straight again.

_____ C. Tony and Rollo were arm wrestling while waiting for the end of study hall.

_____ D. They both laughed, and Rollo said, "Wanna try again?"

EXERCISE 12

_____ A. Computer artists think of the computer screen as a piece of graph paper.

_____ B. By coloring in each pixel with the right color, computer artists can make almost any picture appear on the screen.

_____ C. These squares, called pixels, are the building blocks for computer pictures.

_____ D. When they look at the screen, they imagine that they are looking at a full page of small, equal-sized squares.

EXERCISE 13

_____ A. To perform math with numbers such as these, scientists often use a "language" called scientific notation.

_____ B. In scientific notation, the number 800,000 is written as 8×10^5 and 6,000,000 is 6×10^6.

_____ C. For example, they use numbers like 800,000 (round trip kilometers to the moon) and 6,000,000 (mass of the Apollo II rocket).

_____ D. Astronomers, astronauts and other scientists often work with very large numbers.

EXERCISE 14

_____ A. However, the Wright brothers benefited from the efforts of others, such as the kite-flying experiments of A. Lawrence Roth and Alexander Graham Bell.

_____ B. They also used ideas discovered by Otto Lilienthal in his experiments with gliders, which eventually took his life.

_____ C. The names Wilbur and Orville Wright are commonly linked with the development of the airplane because they successfully flew the first airplane at Kitty Hawk, North Carolina, in 1903.

_____ D. These facts together illustrate that a new invention may often be the result of work by many pioneering thinkers.

EXERCISE 15

(Notice that there are only _three_ sentences to be ordered.)

_____ A. The ships brought goods from the East to the Mediterranean ports of Italy, the goods went from there to northern nations like France, and the Italian cities grew rich from the shipping profits.

_____ B. After hearing about these luxuries, Europeans wanted them, so Italian cities sent fleets of merchant ships to the East.

_____ C. The European crusaders who went to the East to defend Christianity came back to Europe and told people about the luxuries (such as spices, silk and jewels) they had seen in the East.

NOTE: The next five exercises have five or six sentences to be ordered. Use the same careful reading and thinking you have used so far.

EXERCISE 16

_____ A. For example, one language is called COBOL, which stands for Common Business Oriented Language.

_____ B. This language is especially suited for solving problems in math and science rather than in business.

_____ C. As you learn about computers, you will see that there are several different languages for programming a computer.

_____ D. Another language, called FORTRAN (from Formula Transformation), was designed for work with mathematical equations.

_____ E. This language is best for writing a program to help a business carry out tasks like computing salaries for employees.

EXERCISE 17

_____ A. He also arrested nobles and put them in jail without a trial.

_____ B. This document led to the modern concepts of "trial by jury" and "no taxation without representation."

_____ C. King John of England was unjust.

_____ D. In 1215 they forced John to sign the Magna Carta (Great Charter), which controlled how the king could arrest or tax them.

_____ E. After about 15 years of such unjust treatment the nobles rebelled.

_____ F. For example, he seized the property of his nobelmen and forced them to pay large sums of money.

EXERCISE 18

_____ A. Therefore, only monks and a few scholars learned to read and write.

_____ B. Soon many people learned to read and it became easier for new ideas to spread and gain support.

_____ C. However, around 1470 John Gutenberg invented a printing press with movable type.

_____ D. In the Middle Ages (500-1450) every book had to be printed by hand.

_____ E. This made books cheaper and more common.

_____ F. This method of printing meant it took months or even years to make a book, so books were rare and expensive.

EXERCISE 19

_____ A. This is because the muscles and organs of your body are built out of protein.

_____ B. For these reasons, too little protein in the diet is extremely dangerous.

_____ C. The human body requires that protein be a major part of the diet.

_____ D. But too much can be a danger, as well.

_____ E. Therefore, a moderate (middle-of-the-road) amount is best.

_____ F. Further, every reaction—nervous, circulatory, digestive, muscular, mental—depends on these muscles and organs.

EXERCISE 20

Vocabulary preview: **heir** (noun)—a person who receives the property, rights or in the case of a king, the throne of a person that dies.

_____ A. At first the English were successful in their invasion and it appeared the English would conquer the French.

_____ B. In 1328 the French king died without leaving a direct male heir and King Edward III of England, who had been related to the dead French king, claimed that he was now king of both England and France.

_____ C. This peasant girl so inspired the French troops that they began to win one victory after another.

_____ D. He invaded France with an English army to take the French throne, thus starting the Hundred Years' War.

_____ E. However, before the English were completely driven out of France, they captured Joan and she was burned at the stake as a witch.

_____ F. But a peasant girl, Joan of Arc, believed the saints had called upon her to rid France of the English.

NOTE: The next few exercises have long, complex sentences and high-level vocabulary. Take your time, read carefully, look for transition words—and you will be successful.

EXERCISE 21

_____ A. Among other things, his promotion took the form of establishing a naval school, and hiring the best map-makers and captains of Europe.

_____ B. Prince Henry of Portugal, born in 1394, was called Henry the Navigator and is said to have begun the "Age of Discovery."

_____ C. Henry never went on any of these exploratory trips himself, but he used his money and influence to promote exploration.

_____ D. This "Age" was the period when European explorers sailed on daring adventures to find new routes to the riches of India and China.

EXERCISE 22

_____ A. A scientist wanted to find out if the song of a certain bird species was learned or instinctive (inborn).

_____ B. To study this question, she put many eggs into an incubator to hatch, and then divided the newly hatched birds into two groups.

_____ C. One group was raised separately from all singing adult birds; the other group was raised with singing adult birds.

_____ D. Comparing these two groups, she found that both groups started to sing at the same time and sang the same song.

EXERCISE 23

_____ A. After reaching the Cape of Good Hope, they turned north and took another seven months to reach India.

_____ B. In 1498 Vasco da Gama was given four ships by the government of Portugal to try to sail around Africa and reach India.

_____ C. Da Gama returned to the city of Lisbon in Portugal the following year and sold the cargo he had gotten from India for six times the cost of the expedition.

_____ D. Da Gama's four ships began by sailing south from Portugal and took ninety-three days to reach the Cape of Good Hope at the southern tip of Africa.

EXERCISE 24

_____ A. In contrast to these ideas, Boyle proved that air was a mixture of gases not a basic substance, and that a metal like copper could not be changed into gold.

_____ B. Robert Boyle, born in 1627 and called the father of modern chemistry, helped eliminate the following two false beliefs.

_____ C. Second, before Boyle people believed in alchemy—the notion that cheap metals could be changed into gold.

_____ D. First, before Boyle's work, people believed Aristotle's theory that all the world was made of four substances: air, water, fire and earth.

EXERCISE 25

_____ A. He named the gas oxygen, and he demonstrated that burning was really rapid "oxidation"—the combining of oxygen with other substances.

_____ B. After Lavoisier was beheaded, a fellow scientist made the following remark: "It took but a moment to cut off that head, though a hundred years perhaps will be required to produce another like it."

_____ C. In spite of these scientific contributions, Lavoisier was beheaded during the French Revolution because he was connected with the French royal government.

_____ D. Lavoisier was an early chemist who showed that when something is burned a gas is taken from the air.

EXERCISE 26

_____ A. One reason was the growing number of poor people in Rome, many of whom were small farmers who had lost their farms to more efficient large farmers and had moved to the city to get free food, becoming a financial burden on the government.

_____ B. As a result, when an emperor died, there was a violent fight between the leaders for the throne—although the winner's success was often short-lived since 20 of the 22 emperors between 235 and 284 A.D. were murdered.

_____ C. Another reason was that Rome had no rules stating who would be the next emperor when one died.

_____ D. The Roman Empire fell for a variety of reasons.

NOTE: In the following exercises transition words are kept to a minimum. The focus of the exercise is on your skill in arranging the **ideas** of the sentences into an order that makes sense. Read carefully and make sure you clearly understand what each sentence says. Then write the correct order for the sentences.

EXERCISE 27

_____ A. When the trees started growing, they were taken to Malaysia and planted on plantations.

_____ B. He planted them in a greenhouse in England.

_____ C. Soon rubber production became a major source of Malaysian income.

_____ D. But around 1900 an Englishman smuggled some rubber tree seeds out of Brazil.

_____ E. Once the wild rubber trees grew only in the Amazon Valley of Brazil.

EXERCISE 28

_____ A. During this period one of Athen's greatest leaders was a man named Pericles.

_____ B. It was called "The Golden Age of Athens" and occurred between 460 and 430 B.C.

_____ C. Although not all people could vote in Athens, Pericles worked to give this right to more people.

_____ D. The high point of ancient Greek civilization was found in the city of Athens.

EXERCISE 29

_____ A. Some of the water goes off into the air (evaporates), but the calcite does not, so it is left on the ceiling.

_____ B. Water runs along the ceiling of a limestone cave, picking up bits of a mineral called calcite that is in the limestone.

_____ C. As more water evaporates, more calcite is left on the ceiling.

_____ D. Over the years, this evaporation forms a bump which grows down from the ceiling as calcite is added—a stalactite.

EXERCISE 30

_____ A. This did not provide enough thread for all the cloth the merchants could sell.

_____ B. Soon a bigger, water-powered spinning machine was built.

_____ C. But thread for making cloth was produced on simple spinning wheels run by women working at home.

_____ D. The water-powered machine was too large for a home, so cloth factories came into being.

_____ E. English merchants wanted to sell cloth in English colonies all over the world.

_____ F. This problem was partly solved about 1760 when a machine called a spinning jenny was invented, which could spin sixteen or more threads at once, although this machine was still operated by a woman working at home.

EXERCISE 31

_____ A. Finally, the smoke from the explosion is forced out of the engine so the cycle can start again.

_____ B. The mixture is ignited (lit up) by the spark plug and explodes.

_____ C. Most automobile engines operate by going through the following four-stage cycle.

_____ D. This explosion pushes down an engine part called a piston, which turns the crankshaft and can make the car move.

_____ E. Gasoline mixed with air is squirted into the engine by the carburetor.

EXERCISE 32

_____ A. In the spring they started their trip back to St. Louis.

_____ B. They began by heading west along the Missouri River with an Indian squaw named Sacajawea as their guide, and eventually reached the foothills of the Rocky Mountains, which was the land of the Shoshone Indians.

_____ C. Leaving the Shoshone, the explorers crossed the Rockies and floated down the Columbia River to the Pacific Ocean.

_____ D. In 1804 Lewis and Clark set out from St. Louis to explore the Louisiana Territory.

_____ E. These Indians were Sacajawea's people and they gave the expedition fresh horses and supplies.

_____ F. They built Fort Clatsop on the Pacific coast and spent the winter.

ADDITIONAL ASSIGNMENTS

1. Find a paragraph that consists of four sentences in one of your textbooks (but not a literature book). On a separate piece of paper, create an exercise like the ones in this unit by listing the four sentences *out of order*.

    Have a classmate or friend read the four sentences and number them in their correct order. Discuss with that person the *meaning* or *wording* clues that they used to find the correct order.

2. Find a paragraph that consists of four sentences in a literature book, novel or fiction magazine article. On a separate piece of paper, create an exercise like the ones in this unit by listing the four sentences out of order.

    Have a classmate or friend read the four sentences and number them in their correct order. Discuss with that person how he or she decided on the answer.

3. On a piece of scrap paper, write a factual (non-fiction) paragraph consisting of four sentences. Write the paragraph about any topic in which you are interested. On the lines below, write the four sentences out of order. Have a classmate or friend read the four sentences and number them in their correct order.

    _____ A. _____

    _____

    _____ B. _____

    _____

    _____ C. _____

    _____

    _____ D. _____

    _____

4. Study the meaning of the word "heir" on page 151. Write a sentence on the lines below in which the meaning of "heir" is *stated without punctuation* (see Unit 2, CASE II).

    _____

    _____

    _____

UNIT 10

Following Written Directions, Diagrams And Computer Flowcharts

INTRODUCTION

A major portion of our everyday reading involves reading instructions and directions so that we know how to do something. This includes reading the directions for cooking a meal, for playing games, for putting together toys or stereos, for filling out forms, for using a computer or calculator, and so on.

Reading and following directions is also an important part of schoolwork. We read the directions for completing a workbook, for doing homework, for taking a test, for doing an experiment and for using the library.

To fully understand and properly follow directions, you must read the directions carefully. Each step of the directions must be clearly understood. You must also have a total "picture" of what you are doing so that you know what the complete task is. Sometimes written directions come with drawings or diagrams to help you "picture" the complete task. But other times you read just a written set of directions and must create your own mental "picture" of the task. In this case, making your own drawing or diagram can greatly help you comprehend the directions. Flowcharts—diagrams of what step to do at which point in time—are one way of making a "picture" of a set of directions.

The ability to read and carry out directions improves with practice. In this unit, you will strengthen your skill in carefully reading written directions and diagrams. This is a very valuable skill: Have you ever been embarrassed or made a serious mistake because you failed to *follow the directions*?

EXERCISE INSTRUCTIONS

Each exercise is a set of directions for doing something. *For Exercises 1 through 7*, do what the directions say to do.

Exercises 8 through 14 give directions for a task like baking a cake. Read the directions and then answer the questions that come after the directions. Read the directions and study any diagrams carefully. Try to "carry out" the directions in your head so that you fully understand them. Then read and answer the questions so that you score 100% correct. Take your time. Remember, not following directions can lead to major mistakes.

EXERCISE 1: In the box below, print your full name, last name first.

_____

```
┌──────────────────────────────────────────────────────────────┐
│                                                              │
│                                                              │
└──────────────────────────────────────────────────────────────┘
```

EXERCISE 2: On line 3 below, print your full first name. On line 1, print your last name. Print your first name backwards on line 2. On line 4, if you have a middle name, print your middle initial. Draw a circle around the second word you wrote in this exercise.

1. _____   3. _____

2. _____   4. _____

EXERCISE 3: Look at your answers to Exercise 2. Print the answer you wrote for Exercise 2 line 1 on line 4 below, but print it backwards. Also, on line 2 below, print the answer you wrote for Exercise 2 line 2, but print it backwards from the way you wrote it in Exercise 2.

1. _____   3. _____

2. _____   4. _____

EXERCISE 4: If the word _tortilla_ has eight letters, circle the first _t_ in that word.

EXERCISE 5: If the first word in this sentence has fewer than four letters, circle the last letter in that word.

EXERCISE 6: Look at your answers to Exercise 2. If the answer on line 4 has more than three letters, put an X in box C below. But if that answer has less than three letters, put a W in box A below.

A. ☐   B. ☐   C. ☐   D. ☐

EXERCISE 7: If the word _exclaim_ has three vowels and four consonants, circle the _x_ in that word. If, in addition to having three vowels and four consonants, one of the consonants is an _m_, circle the _l_ as well as the _x_ in that word.

EXERCISE 8: Read the directions for this puzzle carefully. Then answer the five questions.

CHERRY PUZZLE

Fig. 1. Take an oblong piece of fairly stiff paper (a post card will do). On this draw and then cut two lines and a little circle. The round hole must be smaller than a cherry.

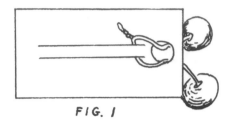

FIG. 1

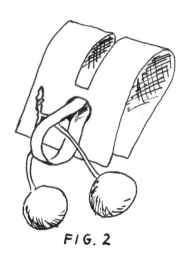

FIG. 2

Fig. 2. Bend the ends of the card nearly together, and pull the strip made by the two lines through the hole, so that you get a little loop, as shown here. Next, put one of your two cherries through the loop. You must, of course, have two cherries on one stalk.

Now get the loop and cherry stalks back into place, as in Fig. 1, and show it to your friends. Ask them if they can undo the cherries without damaging the card or the stalks. It will puzzle them, you can be sure of that.

1. Which would you *not* need to carry out the instructions?

    ☐ (A) a piece of cardboard
    ☐ (B) some tool for cutting the cardboard
    ☐ (C) a string for pulling the cherries through the hole
    ☐ (D) a writing instrument to draw the lines and the circle on the cardboard

2. Which *Figure* shows the Cherry Puzzle as you will give it to friends to solve?

    ☐ (A) *Figure 1*
    ☐ (B) *Figure 2*
    ☐ (C) Neither *Figure 1* nor *Figure 2*

3. Number the steps below in the order in which they would be done.

_____ (A) Unbend the cardboard so the puzzle looks like *Fig. 1*.
_____ (B) Pull the strip through the hole to form a loop.
_____ (C) Bend the cardboard.
_____ (D) Draw two lines and a little circle on the cardboard.
_____ (E) Put one of the cherries through the loop.
_____ (F) Cut along the two lines and the little circle.

4. Which statement is correct?

☐ (A) The strip which is cut must be shorter than the size of a cherry.
☐ (B) The hole must be smaller than the thickness of the strip and also smaller than a cherry.
☐ (C) The hole must be larger than the thickness of the strip but smaller than a cherry.
☐ (D) The hole must be smaller than the thickness of the strip but larger than a cherry.

5. The Cherry Puzzle is puzzling because people are fooled into thinking that

☐ (A) the card was folded and the loop passed through the hole, but they don't see how this could have been done
☐ (B) a cherry was passed through the hole, but they don't see how this could have been done
☐ (C) the loop was passed around the cherry, but they don't see how this could have been done

EXERCISE 9: Study these directions carefully. Then answer the questions on the next page.

THE PUZZLE OF THE WELLINGTON BOOTS

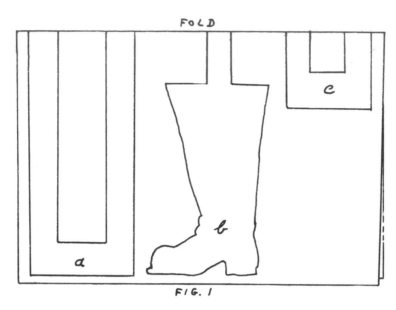

Fig. 1. Fold a piece of strong paper in two, with the crease at the top. Draw and cut out the three parts of the puzzle, as shown. Keep part *c* fairly small.

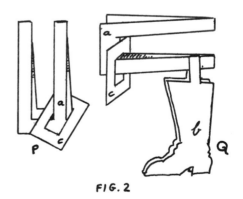

Fig. 2. Unfold part *c* and place it over part *a* (still folded) as in P. Now, holding both sideways, as in Q tuck one boot inside the strip so that both boots hang down, as shown in drawing.

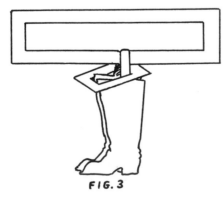

Fig. 3. Now slide part *c* on top of the boots, like this. Unfold part *a* entirely. Ask your friends to try and get the Wellingtons off, without breaking the paper. This will make them scratch their heads.

1. Which is *not* used in making the boots puzzle?

   ☐ (A) a writing instrument for drawing the parts of the puzzle
   ☐ (B) strong paper
   ☐ (C) leather for the boots
   ☐ (D) a cutting tool for cutting out the parts

2. Which step is *not* done in making the boots puzzle?

   ☐ (A) Place part *c* over one folded side of part *a*.
   ☐ (B) Hang the boots over one strip of part *a*.
   ☐ (C) Unfold and flatten the boots.
   ☐ (D) Unfold and flatten part *c*.

3. Which *Figure* shows the following description?: The boots are hung over a strip of part *a*, which already has part *c* on it.

   ☐ (A) *Figure 1*   ☐ (C) *Figure 2Q*
   ☐ (B) *Figure 2P*   ☐ (D) *Figure 3*

4. Number the steps below in the order in which they would be done. (Write "1" for first, "2" for second, etc.)

   _____ (A) Hang the boots over one strip of part *a*.
   _____ (B) Place part *c* over one side of part *a*.
   _____ (C) Unfold and flatten part *a*.
   _____ (D) Unfold and flatten part *c*.
   _____ (E) Draw and cut pieces *a*, *b* and *c*.
   _____ (F) Place part *c* over the strip that connects the boots.

5. Which statement is correct?

   ☐ (A) The hole in part *c* must be bigger than the top of the boots and bigger than the width of the strip of part *a*.
   ☐ (B) The hole in part *c* must be smaller than the top of the boots and smaller than the width of the strip of part *a*.
   ☐ (C) The hole in part *c* must be smaller than the top of the boots, but bigger than the width of the strip of part *a*.
   ☐ (D) The hole in part *c* must be bigger than the top of the boots, but smaller than the width of the strip of part *a*.

6. The boots puzzle is puzzling because people are fooled into thinking that

   ☐ (A) the boots were hung over the strip of part *a* while part *a* was folded
   ☐ (B) part *c* was slipped over part *a* while part *a* was folded
   ☐ (C) part *c* is on the strip connecting the two boots
   ☐ (D) part *c* was slipped over the entire length of the boots

EXERCISE 10:

SIMPLE CHOCOLATE FUDGE

4 squares unsweetened chocolate, 1-ounce size
1½ cups milk
4 cups sugar
⅛ teaspoon salt
¼ cup butter
2 teaspoons vanilla

Butter an 8-inch square pan. Place chocolate and milk in a heavy saucepan. Cook and stir over very low heat until mixture is smooth, well blended, and slightly thickened. Add sugar and salt; stir over medium heat until sugar is dissolved and mixture boils. Continue boiling over medium heat, without stirring, until small amount of mixture forms a soft ball that can be rolled with the fingers into a definite shape in cold water—a temperature of 234°F. on the candy thermometer. Remove from heat; add butter and vanilla. Do not stir. Cool to lukewarm, 110°F. Then beat until mixture begins to lose its gloss and holds its shape. Pour at once into pan. Cool until set; then cut into squares. Let stand in pan until firm. Makes about 36 pieces.

1. If *1-ounce size* in the recipe refers to each chocolate square, how much total chocolate is needed for this recipe?

   ☐ (A) 1 ounce   ☐ (C) 4 ounces
   ☐ (B) 3 ounces   ☐ (D) 5 ounces

2. The ingredients are cooked in

   ☐ (A) a square pan
   ☐ (B) a saucepan
   ☐ (C) a square pan and then a saucepan

3. The ingredients are cooked

   ☐ (A) at a very low heat only
   ☐ (B) first at a medium heat, then at a very low heat
   ☐ (C) first at a very low heat, then at a medium heat
   ☐ (D) at a medium heat only

4. The butter is added to the other ingredients

   ☐ (A) over very low heat
   ☐ (B) after the ingredients have been removed from the heat
   ☐ (C) over medium heat
   ☐ (D) when the mixture is boiling

5. How much vanilla would be needed to make 72 pieces of fudge?

   ☐ (A) 2 teaspoons   ☐ (C) 4 teaspoons
   ☐ (B) 1 teaspoon   ☐ (D) 3 teaspoons

6. What shape are the pieces of fudge?

   ☐ (A) rolled into a soft ball
   ☐ (B) cone-shaped
   ☐ (C) square
   ☐ (D) circular

7. Once the mixture has been removed from the heat,

   ☐ (A) the butter and vanilla are added and the mixture is
          stirred so it will blend together
   ☐ (B) the mixture is never stirred again, but it is beaten after
          it has cooled somewhat
   ☐ (C) the mixture is never beaten, but it is stirred again
          when it has cooled to lukewarm
   ☐ (D) the butter and vanilla are added and the mixture is
          cooled to lukewarm, but it is never stirred or beaten
          again

8. What is the boiling temperature of the ingredients before the
   butter and vanilla are added?

   ☐ (A) the candy thermometer
   ☐ (B) 110°F.
   ☐ (C) 234°F.
   ☐ (D) 100°C.

EXERCISE 11: Read these directions, then answer the questions on the next page.

Vocabulary preview: **invert** (verb)—turn upside down.

CHOCOLATE CHIP NOUGAT

Part 1:
1 cup sugar
2/3 cup light corn syrup
2 tablespoons water
1/4 cup egg whites, at room temperature
Part 2:
2 cups sugar
1-1/4 cups light corn syrup
1/4 cup butter, melted
2 teaspoons vanilla
2 cups chopped nuts
1 cup semi-sweet chocolate mini-chips
2 to 3 drops red food coloring

Line the bottom and sides of a 9-inch square pan with aluminum foil and butter well. Combine 1 cup sugar with 2/3 cup corn syrup and 2 tablespoons water in a small heavy saucepan. Place over medium heat, stirring constantly, until sugar dissolves; then cook without stirring. When candy thermometer reaches 230°F., start beating egg whites until stiff, but not dry. When syrup reaches 238°F. (soft ball stage), add syrup in a thin stream to the beaten egg whites, beating constantly with the mixer at high speed. Continue beating for about 4 to 5 minutes or until mixture becomes very thick. Cover and set aside.

Using ingredients for Part 2, combine sugar and corn syrup in a heavy 2-quart saucepan. Place over medium heat, stirring constantly until sugar dissolves. Cook without stirring to 275°F. on the candy thermometer (soft crack stage). Pour hot syrup all at once over the reserved ingredients of Part 1; blend with a wooden spoon. Stir in butter and vanilla; add nuts and blend thoroughly. Turn one-half of the mixture into the prepared pan; press evenly in pan. Sprinkle chocolate mini-chips evenly over candy in pan. Add red food coloring to remaining one-half candy in the bowl; blend quickly and turn into pan. With buttered fingers, carefully spread this top layer of candy over the chocolate mini-chips. Let candy stand several hours or overnight. Invert the pan and remove the aluminum foil from the nougat. Cut nougat into 1 by 3/4-inch pieces. Wrap individually in waxed paper. Makes about 84 candies.

1. How much total sugar is used in the recipe?
   - ☐ (A) 1 cup
   - ☐ (B) 2 cups
   - ☐ (C) 3 cups
   - ☐ (D) 4 cups

2. How much *corn syrup* is added at 238°F. to the egg whites?
   - ☐ (A) 1-1/4 cups
   - ☐ (B) 2/3 cup
   - ☐ (C) almost 2 cups
   - ☐ (D) 1-11/12 cups

3. The egg whites are
   - ☐ (A) heated to 230°F.
   - ☐ (B) heated to 238°F.
   - ☐ (C) not heated
   - ☐ (D) heated to 275°F.

4. Which statement is correct?
   - ☐ (A) The ingredients from Part 1 are poured over those from Part 2.
   - ☐ (B) The ingredients from Part 2 are poured over those from Part 1.
   - ☐ (C) No ingredients are poured over any other ingredients.

5. Which statement is correct?
   - ☐ (A) The sugar and corn syrup mixture is continually stirred while it is cooking.
   - ☐ (B) The mixture of sugar and corn syrup is stirred only until the sugar melts, and then it is allowed to cool at once.
   - ☐ (C) The mixture of sugar and corn syrup from Part 1 is continually stirred while cooking, but this is not true for Part 2.
   - ☐ (D) The mixture of sugar and corn syrup is stirred only until the sugar melts and it is then cooked more without stirring.

6. Which statement is correct?
   - ☐ (A) Red food coloring is added only to the ingredients of Part 1.
   - ☐ (B) Red food coloring is added to one-half of the ingredients from just Part 2 (excluding the mini-chips)
   - ☐ (C) Red food coloring is added to one-half of a mixture of the ingredients from Parts 1 and 2 (excluding the mini-chips)
   - ☐ (D) Red food coloring is added to the entire mixture of the ingredients from Parts 1 and 2 (excluding the mini-chips)

7. When the nougat is cut, the red portion is
   - ☐ (A) above the mini-chips
   - ☐ (B) below the mini-chips
   - ☐ (C) above and below the mini-chips
   - ☐ (D) inside the mini-chips

EXERCISE 12: Read these dance directions carefully, then answer the questions.

LIGHTLY STEPPING

Rhythm Count: ONE, Two, Three
ONE, Two, Three

MAN'S PART: *Follow these steps.*
Step 1. Left foot forward
Step 2. Right foot forward and to side (point toe slightly inward)
Step 3. Close with left foot
Step 4. Right foot forward (point toe slightly outward)
Step 5. Left foot forward and to side (point toe inward)
Step 6. Close with right foot

RULES FOR WOMAN'S PART:
A. Always move the opposite foot as the man.
B. Move in the opposite direction as the man. When the man moves forward, the woman moves backward. When man points inward, woman points outward.
C. Move foot to side whenever the man does, but use opposite foot.
D. Close when man does, but use opposite foot.

---

1. For the first step, the man should move his

   ☐ (A) left foot forward   ☐ (C) right foot forward
   ☐ (B) left foot backward   ☐ (D) right foot backward

2. For the first step, the woman should move her

   ☐ (A) left foot forward   ☐ (C) right foot forward
   ☐ (B) left foot backward   ☐ (D) right foot backward

3. For the second step, the woman should move her

   ☐ (A) right foot forward and to side (point toe slightly inward)
   ☐ (B) left foot forward and to side (point toe slightly inward)
   ☐ (C) left foot backward and to side (point toe slightly inward)
   ☐ (D) left foot backward and to side (point toe slightly outward)

4. If "close" means to bring the feet together, in which step does the man move his right foot to bring his feet together?

   ☐ (A) Step 1   ☐ (C) Step 4
   ☐ (B) Step 3   ☐ (D) Step 6

5. In which step does the woman move her right foot to bring her feet together?

   ☐ (A) Step 1   ☐ (C) Step 4
   ☐ (B) Step 3   ☐ (D) Step 6

FLOWCHARTS—The final two exercises are directions given in *flowchart* form. A flowchart is a diagram made up of lines, arrows and geometric figures that shows the series of steps someone would do to complete a task.

When directions are given in flowchart form they are often called a *program*. In this sense, *program* means "a series of instructions for completing a task."

Computer programs are one example of directions often given in flowchart form. A computer *programmer* will first write the directions for a computer to follow in flowchart form. Then he or she will translate the flowchart program into a "language" the computer understands (such as BASIC). The flowchart helps the programmer make a mental "picture" of the program.

Flowchart programs are also often used in science or business to give directions for doing an experiment or solving a problem.

To read a flowchart, you simply follow the line path shown by arrows. In addition, flowcharts use *symbols* (geometric figures) to help explain the directions of the program. In the next two exercises the flowcharts have four special symbols. Study the symbols and their meanings:

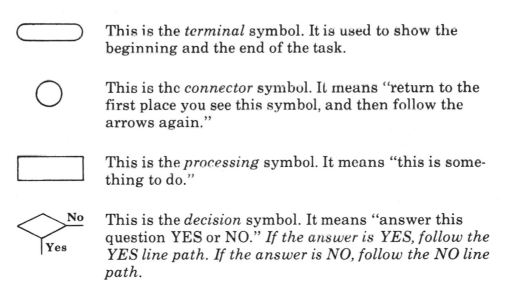

This is the *terminal* symbol. It is used to show the beginning and the end of the task.

This is the *connector* symbol. It means "return to the first place you see this symbol, and then follow the arrows again."

This is the *processing* symbol. It means "this is something to do."

This is the *decision* symbol. It means "answer this question YES or NO." *If the answer is YES, follow the YES line path. If the answer is NO, follow the NO line path.*

Study these symbols and their meanings until you are sure you understand each one. Then do the next two exercises. Each exercise gives a program for a task someone might want to do. Read the entire program until you understand *all* of its steps. Then answer the questions that follow the flowchart.

EXERCISE 13: Study this flowchart. Then answer the questions on the next page. HINT: Follow the arrows. Look back at the symbol meanings whenever you need to.

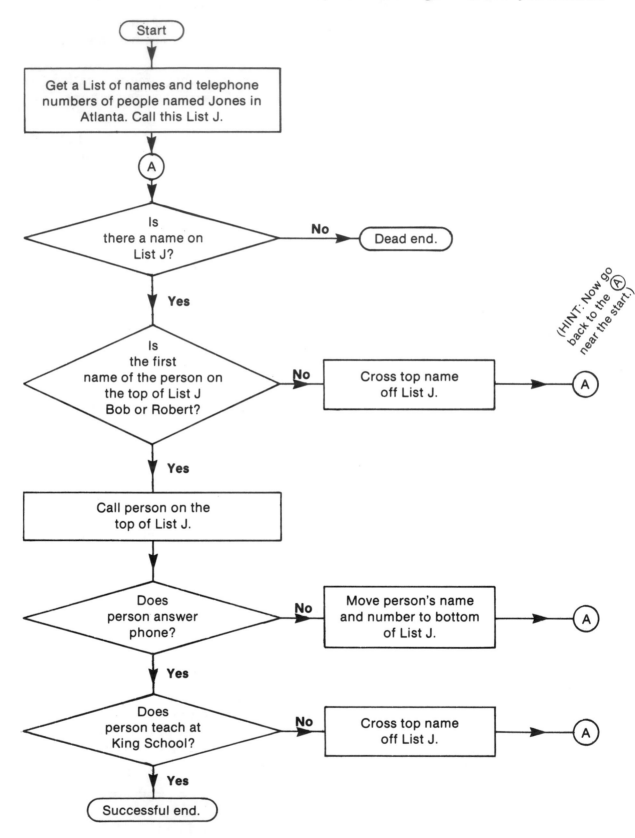

1. What is the first step in the flowchart?

   ☐ (A) Call the person on the top of List J.
   ☐ (B) Ask if the person teaches at King School.
   ☐ (C) Obtain a list of the names and telephone numbers for Joneses in Atlanta.
   ☐ (D) Cross the top name off List J.

2. What is the main purpose of this program?

   ☐ (A) To obtain the names and telephone numbers of people named Jones in Atlanta.
   ☐ (B) To find the people named Bob or Robert Jones in Atlanta.
   ☐ (C) To find out who teaches at King School in Atlanta.
   ☐ (D) To locate the Bob or Robert Jones who teaches at King School in Atlanta.

3. What does the program do when it hits a Jones whose first name is not Bob or Robert?

   ☐ (A) It puts that name at the bottom of the List.
   ☐ (B) It crosses that name off the List.
   ☐ (C) It asks if the person teaches at King School.
   ☐ (D) It calls that person.

4. What does it mean if the "dead end" is reached?

   ☐ (A) The Bob Jones who teaches at King School wasn't home when called.
   ☐ (B) There are only Bob and Robert Joneses left on the List.
   ☐ (C) The Bob or Robert Jones who teaches at King School has not been found, and there are no names left on the List to call.
   ☐ (D) The program is successfully completed.

5. What is the purpose of the first decision in the flowchart ("Is there a name on List J?")?

   ☐ (A) To find out the first name of the person on the top of List J.
   ☐ (B) To stop the program when there are no names left on List J.
   ☐ (C) To cross the top name off List J.

6. What is the purpose of the second decision in the flowchart ("Is the first name of the person on the top of List J Bob or Robert?")?

   ☐ (A) It causes the program to only call Joneses whose first names are Bob or Robert.
   ☐ (B) It determines how many Joneses in Atlanta are named Bob or Robert.
   ☐ (C) It has the program call all the Joneses in Atlanta.

EXERCISE 14: Study this flowchart, then answer the questions on the next **two** pages.

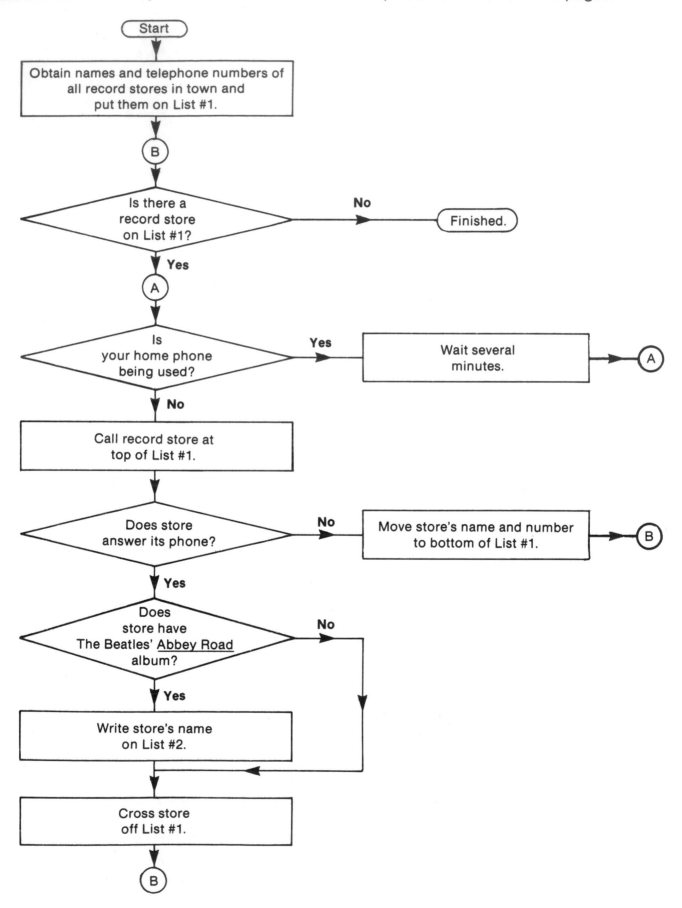

1. After you discover your home phone is being used and you wait a few minutes, connector "A" leads you to which action?

   ☐ (A) To call the record store at the top of List #1.
   ☐ (B) To check again to see if your home phone is being used.
   ☐ (C) To write the store's name on List #2.
   ☐ (D) To move the store's name and number to the bottom of List #1.

2. If a store does *not* answer the phone, the next action is to

   ☐ (A) wait a few minutes
   ☐ (B) write the store's name on List #2
   ☐ (C) move the store's name and number to the bottom of List #1
   ☐ (D) ask if it has The Beatles' *Abbey Road* album

3. If a store answers "no" to the question you ask it, what is the next step?

   ☐ (A) Write the store's name on List #2.
   ☐ (B) Determine if there is another store on List #1.
   ☐ (C) Cross that store off List #1.
   ☐ (D) Call the record store at the top of List #1.

4. If a store has just been crossed off List #1, what is the next step?

   ☐ (A) Write the store's name on List #2.
   ☐ (B) Determine if there is another store on List #1.
   ☐ (C) Call the record store at the top of List #1.
   ☐ (D) Move the store's name and number to the bottom of List #1.

5. When is the program finished?

   ☐ (A) When a store is found that has The Beatles' *Abbey Road* album.
   ☐ (B) When *all* the stores that were on List #1 have been moved to List #2.
   ☐ (C) When a store doesn't answer its telephone.
   ☐ (D) When there are no more stores left on List #1.

6. If there was only one store left on List #1 and it didn't answer its phone, what does the program say to do?

   ☐ (A) Move the name of the store to List #2.
   ☐ (B) Keep calling that store until it does answer.
   ☐ (C) Call another store and ask if the last store has The Beatles' *Abbey Road* album.
   ☐ (D) Try calling three more times and then stop trying.

7. After several calls have been made, the stores still left on List #1

   ☐ (A) definitely have The Beatles' *Abbey Road* album
   ☐ (B) definitely do not have The Beatles' *Abbey Road* album
   ☐ (C) have not yet been asked if they have The Beatles' *Abbey Road* album

8. After several calls have been made, the stores on List #2

   ☐ (A) definitely have The Beatles' *Abbey Road* album
   ☐ (B) definitely do not have The Beatles' *Abbey Road* album
   ☐ (C) have not yet been asked if they have The Beatles' *Abbey Road* album

9. When there are no stores left on List #1, the stores which were on List #1 but were *not* put on List #2

   ☐ (A) definitely have The Beatles' *Abbey Road* album
   ☐ (B) definitely do not have The Beatles' *Abbey Road* album
   ☐ (C) have not yet been asked if they have The Beatles' *Abbey Road* album

10. The main purpose of this program is to

    ☐ (A) find *one* store that has The Beatles' *Abbey Road* album
    ☐ (B) obtain the names and telephone numbers of all record stores in town
    ☐ (C) find *all* the record stores in town that have The Beatles' *Abbey Road* album
    ☐ (D) call all the record stores in town

11. If you wanted this program to just find *one* store that has The Beatles' *Abbey Road* album, how would you change the flow-chart?

    ☐ (A) After the question "Does store have The Beatles' *Abbey Road* album?", put a *terminal* symbol that says "finished" on the NO line and erase the step that says "Write store's name on List #2."
    ☐ (B) After the question "Does store have The Beatles' *Abbey Road* album?", put a *terminal* symbol that says "finished" on the YES line and erase the step that says "Write store's name on List #2."
    ☐ (C) After the question "Does store answer its phone?", put a *terminal* symbol that says "finished" on the NO line.
    ☐ (D) After the question "Does store answer its phone?", put a *terminal* symbol that says "finished" on the YES line.

ADDITIONAL ASSIGNMENTS

1. On a separate piece of paper, write a set of directions like those in Exercise 2 on page 159. Write your directions clearly, so that you are certain that someone reading them will be able to follow them without error.

   Ask a classmate or friend to read your directions and do what they say. Check that person's work to see if there are any mistakes. If there is a mistake, review the directions with the person. Find the part of your directions that caused the mistake. Was it the person's error in thinking, or are your directions unclear? Rewrite your directions, if necessary, so they are crystal clear.

2. On the lines below, write a set of directions like those in Exercise 7 on page 159. *Write your directions so that a reader will have to choose between doing one thing or doing another.* (For example, Exercise 7 made you choose between circling just the *x*, or circling both the *x* and the *l*.)

   Ask a classmate or friend to read your directions and do what they say. Check that person's work. Discuss his or her answers, and rewrite your directions if necessary.

   _____

   _____

   _____

   _____

   _____

   _____

3. On a separate piece of paper, copy a recipe from a cookbook. Then write five questions about the recipe, such as the questions in Exercise 10 on pages 164 and 165. Write your questions so that they would test how well a reader understood the recipe.

   Ask someone to read the recipe and answer your questions. Check that person's work. If he or she made any errors, check to see if the recipe is unclear. Rewrite any parts of the recipe that need to be made more clear. (If the recipe is unclear, you may want to send a letter to the cookbook's author!)

4. On a separate piece of paper, write a set of instructions for making a toy, a piece of clothing or an item of furniture. Draw a diagram if you think one is helpful. Then write five questions about your instructions (like those in Exercise 8 on pages 160 and 161).

   Ask someone to read your instructions and answer your questions. Review that person's work. Rewrite your instructions or re-draw your diagram, if necessary.

ADDITIONAL ASSIGNMENTS

5. Obtain a *form* used for a club membership application, a magazine subscription, a job application or some similar purpose. Then write five questions about the form. Write your questions so that they test how well someone understands how to fill out the form. (Your questions should be like the ones you wrote for Assignments 3 and 4.)

   Ask a classmate or friend to study the form and then answer your questions. Review that person's work. Discuss with him or her how clear, or unclear, the form is. Make up your own sections of the form to replace any sections you feel are unclear.

6. Think of a task such as those in Exercises 13 (page 170) and 14 (page 172). Make a list of the steps someone would need to go through to complete your task. Then create a flowchart for your task. Use the symbols described on page 169 to help you show your steps in flowchart style.

   When you have finished your flowchart, write five questions about it (like the questions on pages 171 and 173). Write your questions so that they test how well someone understands how to complete your task.

   Ask someone to study your flowchart and answer the questions. Check that person's work to see how clear your flowchart was designed. Re-design your flowchart, if necessary.

UNIT 11

Reading For Full Comprehension II: Identifying The Main Idea And Understanding Details

OBJECTIVES

When you have completed this unit you will

- understand what a "main idea" of a reading passage describes;

- understand how a "main idea" is similar to a "comprehensive title";

- be able to select a statement that best describes the main idea of a reading passage;

- be able to answer questions that ask you to interpret details presented in a reading passage;

- be able to use context clues to figure out the meaning of a word as it is used in a certain reading passage.

INTRODUCTION

This unit is similar to Unit 6. As in Unit 6, you will perform *analysis* in reading a passage and answering questions about that passage. (Review page 86 if you don't remember what *analysis* means.)

In this unit you will see a new type of question. This question asks you to identify the MAIN IDEA of the passage. The main idea of a passage is a statement that clearly explains what the passage is about. A correct main idea is like a "comprehensive title." It completely explains *what a passage is about, and only what a passage is about.* It is neither "too broad," nor "too narrow." To pick a correct main idea you should use the same kind of thinking you use to find a "comprehensive title" for a passage. (Review pages 87-89 if you want to refresh yourself on how to find a "comprehensive title.")

EXERCISE INSTRUCTIONS

As always, read each passage carefully. Read so that you understand the ideas, not just "see the words." Study the Vocabulary Preview if there is one before the passage. Use what you have learned about *context clues* to help you figure out the meaning of unfamiliar words. Also, use a dictionary whenever one will help you better understand the material.

To practice answering a "main idea" question, study the example below.

EXAMPLE: Read this passage and then answer the question at the top of the next page.

In 1664 the king of England sent four ships to capture New Amsterdam (now New York City) from the Dutch. Because of the explorations of John Cabot, England claimed the whole area on which the colony of New Netherland was built. Serving as the Dutch governor of New Netherland was one-legged, vigorous Peter Stuyvesant. He was to be the last Dutch governor of the colony. Stuyvesant tried to resist the invading English and their demands to surrender. He failed because the rich merchants of New Amsterdam were tired of his rule. He could not enlist their help or their loyalty. New Amsterdam and New Netherland thus fell to the English without a single shot being fired. New Amsterdam was renamed New York, in honor of the Duke of York, the brother of the king of England.

The main idea of this selection is:

- ☐ (A) Peter Stuyvesant was the one-legged, vigorous governor of New Netherland, the colony including what is now New York City.
- ☐ (B) England sent four ships to capture New Amsterdam (now New York City).
- ☐ (C) England took New Amsterdam from the Dutch in 1664 without a fight because the people there were glad to be rid of Peter Stuyvesant, the Dutch governor.
- ☐ (D) New Amsterdam was renamed New York in honor of the Duke of York, the brother of England's king.

Answer:

Choice (A) is *not* the main idea. It describes only minor parts of the passage: Who Peter Stuyvesant was, and that New Netherland included what is now New York City. It fails to describe England's capture of New Amsterdam, which is a major part of the passage.

Choice (B) is also *not* the main idea. It describes just the one detail that England sent four ships to capture New Amsterdam. It doesn't describe anything about the conditions in New Amsterdam that made it so easy for the English to win, which is a major part of the passage.

Choice (C) *is* the MAIN IDEA. It says that England took New Amsterdam from the Dutch. It also describes when this happened (1664), how it happened (without a fight) and why it happened (people there were glad to be rid of Peter Stuyvesant, the Dutch governor). This statement describes exactly what the passage is about by including all the major points from the passage.

Choice (D) is *not* the main idea because it describes only the one detail about the naming of New York.

Use the type of thinking shown above to answer all "main idea" questions in this unit.

Try to achieve 100% accuracy on all questions in this unit. Reread each passage as many times as necessary until it is completely clear. For some questions you will be able to find specific lines in the passage that contain the answer. For other questions, you will need to combine details from different parts of the passage. In either case, you should feel you could, if asked, clearly explain to someone else *why* your answer is correct.

PASSAGE A

¹ In 1664 the king of England sent four ships to capture
² New Amsterdam (now New York City) from the Dutch.
³ Because of the explorations of John Cabot, England claimed
⁴ the whole area on which the colony of New Netherland was
⁵ built. Serving as the Dutch governor of New Netherland
⁶ was one-legged, vigorous Peter Stuyvesant. He was to be the
⁷ last Dutch governor of the colony. Stuyvesant tried to resist
⁸ the invading English and their demands to surrender. He
⁹ failed because the rich merchants of New Amsterdam were
¹⁰ tired of his rule. He could not enlist their help or their loy-
¹¹ alty. New Amsterdam and New Netherland thus fell to the
¹² English without a single shot being fired. New Amsterdam
¹³ was renamed New York, in honor of the Duke of York, the
¹⁴ brother of the king of England.

1. Below are three possible titles for this selection. In each blank, write the letter of the phrase (A, B or C) which best describes that title.

    _____ Peter Stuyvesant Resists English Invasion
    _____ Establishment of English Colonies Throughout the World
    _____ England Takes New York and Surrounding Area From the Dutch

    (A) too broad
    (B) too narrow
    (C) comprehensive title

2. One can conclude from the selection that John Cabot was

    ☐ (A) a Dutch governor of New Amsterdam
    ☐ (B) a Dutch explorer
    ☐ (C) an English governor of New Amsterdam
    ☐ (D) an English explorer

3. The English were able to take over New Amsterdam because

    ☐ (A) they fought bravely and conquered the people of New Amsterdam
    ☐ (B) the people of New Amsterdam did not oppose the English invasion
    ☐ (C) Peter Stuyvesant had only one leg
    ☐ (D) the Duke of York used better military planning (strategy)

4. The selection suggests that under the Dutch, the governor of New Amsterdam

    ☐ (A) could be easily removed from office by the rich merchants whenever they wanted a new governor
    ☐ (B) could not be easily removed from office by the rich merchants whenever they wanted a new governor

5. The main idea of this selection is:

    ☐ (A) Peter Stuyvesant was the one-legged, vigorous governor of New Netherland, the colony including what is now New York City.
    ☐ (B) England sent four ships to capture New Amsterdam (now New York City).
    ☐ (C) England took New Amsterdam from the Dutch in 1664 without a fight because the people there were glad to be rid of Peter Stuyvesant, the Dutch governor.
    ☐ (D) New Amsterdam was renamed New York in honor of the Duke of York, the brother of England's king.

PASSAGE B

¹ Recently scientists have begun to study in detail ² the ways that pets improve human health. ³ They've discovered that when we stroke friendly ⁴ animals or watch fish swimming in a tank, our ⁵ blood pressure goes down. (Lower blood pressure ⁶ means that the heart isn't working so hard to ⁷ pump blood through the body's arteries. It's a sign ⁸ of good health.)

⁹ Scientists have also found that pets make it ¹⁰ easier for us to meet people we don't know. If ¹¹ you've ever passed a new neighbor walking his or ¹² her dog, you know that this is true.

¹³ But what may be more important is the grow-¹⁴ ing evidence that pets help us get along with peo-¹⁵ ple we do know, especially our families. The pres-¹⁶ ence of a favorite cat or dog may help family ¹⁷ members talk and play more—and argue less.

1. Below are three possible titles for this passage. In each blank, write the letter of the phrase (A, B or C) which best describes that title.

_____ The Uses and Benefits of Animals
_____ Some Social and Health Benefits of Pets
_____ Stroking Animals Reduces Blood Pressure

    (A) too narrow
    (B) comprehensive title
    (C) too broad

2. According to the selection, pets

  ☐ (A) can stimulate conversation with both friends and strangers
  ☐ (B) can stimulate conversation with friends but not strangers
  ☐ (C) can stimulate conversation with strangers but not friends
  ☐ (D) cannot stimulate conversation with others

3. The main idea of this selection is:

  ☐ (A) Lower blood pressure means that the heart isn't working so hard to pump blood through the arteries.
  ☐ (B) Scientists have concluded that pets can make it easier for us to meet people we don't know.
  ☐ (C) Pets are good for both our physical and social well-being.
  ☐ (D) Pets can help family members talk and play together more.

4. Which statement is supported most strongly by the selection?

  ☐ (A) Talking to your pet will improve your conversation skills.
  ☐ (B) Everyone should pet animals for their health, even if they are afraid of them.
  ☐ (C) A pet can provide a way to begin a conversation with a stranger.
  ☐ (D) Staring at a fish tank can lull you to sleep or hypnotize you.

5. Is the following statement true or false? According to the selection, it is unhealthy for your blood pressure to go down.

  ☐ (A) True.
  ☐ (B) False.

6. As used in the context of line 3, "stroke" means

  ☐ (A) a physical armstroke in swimming
  ☐ (B) to quickly and suddenly appear
  ☐ (C) an illness caused by low blood pressure
  ☐ (D) to rub gently and lovingly

PASSAGE C

Vocabulary preview: **serpentine** (adjective)—winding and full of curves like a serpent (snake).

pursuer (noun)—one who pursues or chases something.

flaking (verb)—chipping, falling off in flakes.

mildewed (verb)—having been covered with mildew (fungus growth).

rubble (noun)—broken pieces resulting from the destruction of a building.

1   Conan set out at a run, keeping his balance as best he could,
2 half falling against the walls at every twisting of the alley, his
3 massive shoulders knocking more stucco from the flaking, mil-
4 dewed buildings. Another alley serpentined across the one he
5 followed; he dodged down it. Still another passage appeared,
6 winding cramped between dark walls, and he turned into that.
7 Behind the curses of his pursuers followed.
8   As he ran he realized that he was in a warren, a maze of
9 ancient passages in an area surrounded by more normal road-
10 ways. The buildings seemed ready to topple and fill those pas-
11 sages with rubble, for though they had begun long years past
12 with but single stories, as years and needs demanded more
13 room that could not be got by building outward, extra rooms
14 had been constructed atop the roofs, and more atop those, till
15 they resembled nothing so much as haphazard stacks of stuc-
16 coed and gray-tiled boxes.
17   In such a region, running like a fox before the hounds, it
18 would be a matter of luck if he found his way to the outside
19 before his pursuers seized him. And it seemed his luck was
20 sour that day. But there was another option, for one who had
21 been born among the icy crags and cliffs of Cimmeria.
22   With a mighty leap he caught the edge of a roof, and swung
23 himself up to lie flat on the slate tiles. The curses and shouts of
24 the Guardsmen came closer, were below him, were moving off.

1. Below are three possible titles for this passage. In each blank, write the letter of the phrase (A, B or C) which best describes that title.

_____ The Life of Conan the Defender
_____ Conan Runs and Then Hides From His Pursuers
_____ Conan Tries to Outrun His Pursuers

    (A) too narrow
    (B) too broad
    (C) comprehensive title

2. The main idea of the selection is:

☐ (A) Conan found he was in a warren, a maze of ancient passages in an area surrounded by more normal roadways.
☐ (B) Conan set out at a run, his massive shoulders knocking more stucco from the flaking buildings.
☐ (C) The buildings looked ready to topple and fill the streets with rubble.
☐ (D) Deciding that he could not outrun his pursuers in the warren, Conan hid on a roof.

3. Which statement about the roofs is best supported by the selection?

☐ (A) They were made of stucco.
☐ (B) They were made of slate.
☐ (C) They were covered by mildew.
☐ (D) They were covered with icy crags.

4. Use information from the third paragraph to complete this analogy. FOX is to HOUNDS as

☐ (A) GUARDSMEN is to CONAN
☐ (B) CONAN is to GUARDSMEN
☐ (C) GUARDSMEN is to PURSUERS
☐ (D) PURSUERS is to CONAN

5. The buildings appeared ready to topple because

☐ (A) Conan leaped onto the roof of one building which was so weak that it began to shake
☐ (B) they were originally only one-story buildings and the addition of upper floors was not carefully planned

6. Below are four correct definitions of "passage." Which one gives the meaning of "passage" as it is used in this selection?

☐ (A) a short section taken from a written work (book) or speech
☐ (B) a street or alley through which a person can pass
☐ (C) the right to be a passenger
☐ (D) the passing of a law

PASSAGE D

Vocabulary Preview: **incident** (noun)—an event, an occurrence.

¹ The *Short Story* is a short work of fiction that usually centers around
² a single incident. Because of its shorter length, the characters and situa-
³ tions are fewer and less complicated than those of a novel. A short story
⁴ may range in length from a *short short story* of 1,000 to 1,500 words to a
⁵ *novelette*, or short novel, of 12,000 to 30,000 words. The short story has
⁶ many qualities of the *ballad*, a story in verse form. It is also related to the
⁷ *folk tale*, a story handed down by word of mouth from generation to
⁸ generation. Many characteristics of the short story come from earlier
⁹ literary forms that tried to teach a lesson. These forms include the *fable*,
¹⁰ a story about animals, and the *parable*, a story with a religious lesson.

1. Below are three possible titles for this passage. In each blank, write the letter of the phrase (A, B or C) which best describes that title.

    _____ Historical Roots of the Short Story
    _____ Characteristics and Historical Roots of the Short Story
    _____ Characteristics and Roots of Literary Forms Including the Novel, Short Story, Play, Poem and Non-fiction Piece

    (A) too narrow
    (B) too broad
    (C) comprehensive title

2. The main idea of this selection is:

    ☐ (A) The short story is a work of fiction that usually centers around a single incident.
    ☐ (B) The short story is simpler and shorter than the novel.
    ☐ (C) The short story is related to several other literary forms, including the ballad, folk tale, fable and parable.
    ☐ (D) The short story is simpler and shorter than the novel (often focussing on one incident) and is related to the ballad, folk tale, fable and parable.

3. According to the context of this passage, the word "literary" means

    ☐ (A) of or about literature
    ☐ (B) able to speak
    ☐ (C) theater critic
    ☐ (D) a library

4. A story of twelve hundred words would be considered

    ☐ (A) a small short story
    ☐ (B) average in length for a short story
    ☐ (C) a long short story
    ☐ (D) none of the above

5. For each of the literary forms listed, write the letter (A, B, C or D) of its description.

    _____ folk tale
    _____ fable
    _____ novelette
    _____ parable

    (A) story with a religious lesson
    (B) story passed orally from one generation to the next
    (C) a short novel
    (D) story that teaches a lesson through the actions of animals

PASSAGE E

Vocabulary preview: **confined** (verb)—limited, restricted.

Renaissance (noun)—the period from the 14th to the 16th century during which art, literature and learning regained popularity, following a drop in their popularity during the Middle Ages (about the 6th to the 14th century).

¹ Music during the Middle Ages and the ² Renaissance, however, was not confined to ³ church music. Traveling singers called ⁴ *troubadours* (true'buh-doorz) in France, ⁵ *minnesingers* (min'uh-sing-erz) in Ger- ⁶ many, and *minstrels* in England wandered ⁷ about singing songs of adventure, love, and ⁸ war. They delighted their listeners in castle ⁹ halls, in public squares, and at fairs by ¹⁰ singing old ballads or composing new ¹¹ ones. In time, their melodies and the ¹² improved music of churchmen paved the ¹³ way for some of the greatest masters of mus- ¹⁴ ical composition of all time.

1. Below are three possible titles for this passage. In each blank, write the letter of the phrase (A, B or C) which best describes that title.

    _____ Complete History of Music
    _____ Traveling Singers Delighted Listeners in Castle Halls
    _____ Activities of Traveling Singers in the Middle Ages and the Renaissance

    (A) too narrow
    (B) comprehensive title
    (C) too broad

2. According to the passage, a troubadour would

    ☐ (A) sing only old ballads, since this is what French people liked best
    ☐ (B) compose and sing only new ballads because people always wanted something new
    ☐ (C) sing minstrels in England
    ☐ (D) compose new ballads and also sing old ones

3. Which pair of words best completes this analogy: TROUBADOUR is to FRANCE as

    ☐ (A) GERMANY is to MINNESINGER
    ☐ (B) ENGLAND is to MINSTREL
    ☐ (C) MINSTREL is to ENGLAND
    ☐ (D) MINNESINGER is to ENGLAND

4. Assuming this passage is taken from a longer article, the paragraph before this passage was probably about

    ☐ (A) traveling singers
    ☐ (B) ballads of the Middle Ages and the Renaissance
    ☐ (C) church music of the Middle Ages and the Renaissance
    ☐ (D) greatest masters of musical composition of all time

5. The main idea of this passage is:

    ☐ (A) Traveling singers were called troubadours in France, minnesingers in Germany and minstrels in England.
    ☐ (B) The music of churchmen was important during the Middle Ages and the Renaissance and paved the way for some of the greatest masters of musical composition of all time.
    ☐ (C) Traveling singers provided musical entertainment during the Middle Ages and the Renaissance which, combined with church music, formed the basis for some later musical masterpieces.
    ☐ (D) Castle halls, public squares and fairs were places of musical entertainment during the Middle Ages and the Renaissance.

PASSAGE F

¹   Argentina is so much like the United States in so many ways
² that it is often called the United States of South America. Both
³ countries are alike in that they have hot weather part of the time
⁴ and cold weather part of the time. But there is also a big differ-
⁵ ence between the two. Argentina has winter when the United
⁶ States has summer, and Argentina has summer when the United
⁷ States has winter. In Argentina, Christmas comes in the hot
⁸ weather. There are snow and ice in July and August, and flowers
⁹ and vegetables grow in January and February.
¹⁰   The seasons are caused by the amount of heat received from
¹¹ the sun. The earth spins on its axis as it moves around the sun.
¹² The earth does not stand straight up as it spins, but tilts on its
¹³ axis. Because the earth tilts, one hemisphere is closer to the sun
¹⁴ while the other is farther away. When the southern hemisphere is
¹⁵ closer to the sun, it has summer because the rays of the sun are
¹⁶ more direct. While the southern hemisphere is having summer,
¹⁷ the northern hemisphere is having winter because it is farther
¹⁸ away from the sun. In time the northern hemisphere comes
¹⁹ closer to the sun and has its summer. This is why it is summer
²⁰ in the United States at the same time it is winter in South
²¹ America.

1. Below are three possible titles for this passage. In each blank, write the letter of the phrase (A, B or C) which best describes that title.

    _____ Argentina's Weather at Christmas
    _____ Weather Patterns on Earth
    _____ Weather Differences Between Argentina and the United States: What Kind and Why

    (A) comprehensive title
    (B) too narrow
    (C) too broad

2. An "axis," as used in this article, is

    ☐ (A) a tool used for chopping wood
    ☐ (B) the spinning earth
    ☐ (C) a planet's orbit
    ☐ (D) an imaginary line through the earth's center around which the earth spins

3. According to the article,

    ☐ (A) because Argentina is in South America it is hot all the time
    ☐ (B) Argentina is cold all year round, so there is even snow and ice in July and August
    ☐ (C) in Argentina Christmas comes in July
    ☐ (D) Argentina has seasons that vary from cold to hot

4. The main idea of this article is:

    ☐ (A) In Argentina there is snow and ice in July, while flowers and plants grow in January.
    ☐ (B) In Argentina Christmas comes in the hot season.
    ☐ (C) Argentina has seasons like the United States, but the seasons are opposite because of the earth's tilt.
    ☐ (D) The United States has better weather than Argentina.

5. One can conclude from the article that

   ☐ (A) Argentina does not celebrate Christmas because there is no snow there in December
   ☐ (B) people will someday control the earth's tilts so Argentina can have snow for Christmas
   ☐ (C) people would not swim outdoors in Argentina during July and August
   ☐ (D) the United States has better weather than Argentina

6. Seasons in the southern hemisphere are caused by the fact that

   ☐ (A) the sun spins on its axis as the earth moves around it
   ☐ (B) the earth tilts, so the southern hemisphere gets more direct rays from the sun during part of the year and less direct rays at other times
   ☐ (C) Argentina has snow and ice in July and warm weather in January
   ☐ (D) All of the above.

7. Given that South America is in the southern hemisphere, one can conclude that during August

   ☐ (A) the southern hemisphere is further from the sun than the northern hemisphere
   ☐ (B) the southern hemisphere is closer to the sun than the northern hemisphere

PASSAGE G

Vocabulary Preview: **severe** (adjective)—causing great hardship and discomfort.

stress (noun)—force or pressure that can cause damage.

1 Sally Ride was the first American woman to
2 be shot into the heavens on a space flight. She
3 was not the first woman to ever go into space,
4 however. The Russians sent a woman named
5 Valentina Tereshkova into space several years
6 before Sally Ride's trip. However, Tereshkova
7 was not a trained pilot and she developed severe
8 space sickness. Ride is an experienced pilot who
9 even flew her own plane to her wedding. Her
10 husband, Steve Hawley, is also an astronaut and
11 is hoping to make his own space flight soon.
12 Going through the stress of being launched
13 into space requires top physical condition.
14 Ride's fitness comes from hard training and
15 competition in tennis. She was a teenage tennis
16 champion who ranked 18th in the nation in her
17 age group. In fact, for a time she considered
18 becoming a professional tennis player.
19 But it takes more than physical fitness and a
20 pilot's license to be chosen as an astronaut. Sally
21 Ride is a highly trained scientist as well. She
22 majored in physics at Stanford University and
23 earned a Ph.D. in astrophysics. In 1978 she and
24 five other women became the first females in the
25 astronaut training program. For Space Shuttles
26 2 and 3 she had an important job even though
27 she stayed on the ground. Her job was to pass
28 information back and forth between the scien-
29 tists up in space and the scientists that were
30 helping them back on earth. This meant she had
31 to understand all the scientific observations and
32 decisions made by both groups of experts.
33 Bob Crippen was the commander on Ride's
34 space flight. He said he chose her and another
35 engineer-astronaut, John Fabian, for the trip
36 because they helped design the mechanical arm
37 used to place scientific equipment in space, and
38 later to grab it and put it back into the ship's
39 storage area. Crippen decided Ride and Fabian
40 should be on board so they could operate the
41 arm and deal with any problems that might
42 develop.

1. Below are three possible titles for this passage. In each blank, write the letter of the phrase (A, B or C) which best describes that title.

   _____ Biographies of American Astronauts
   _____ Why Sally was Chosen to Ride
   _____ Russian Female Astronaut Becomes Space Sick

   (A) too narrow
   (B) too broad
   (C) comprehensive title

2. The main idea of this selection is:

   ☐ (A) Sally Ride was a teenage tennis champion, which made her physically fit to be an astronaut.
   ☐ (B) Sally Ride had the physical and educational requirements to be America's first woman in space.
   ☐ (C) Sally Ride's space flight was under the command of Bob Crippen.
   ☐ (D) The first woman in space from Russia was not as well prepared as Sally Ride.

3. As used in line 23, the letters "Ph.D." stand for

   ☐ (A) part of a secret code used by astronauts
   ☐ (B) a degree (diploma) given by a university

4. How many women entered the astronaut program in 1978?

   ☐ (A) 1
   ☐ (B) 4
   ☐ (C) 5
   ☐ (D) 6

5. How many American astronauts are mentioned by name in the selection?

   ☐ (A) 1
   ☐ (B) 3
   ☐ (C) 4
   ☐ (D) 5

6. The mechanical arm discussed in the selection was designed by

   ☐ (A) Sally Ride all by herself
   ☐ (B) John Fabian all by himself
   ☐ (C) Sally Ride and John Fabian
   ☐ (D) Sally Ride, John Fabian and others

7. The mechanical arm is used to

   ☐ (A) put equipment in space
   ☐ (B) retrieve (get back) equipment from space by loading it in the ship
   ☐ (C) do both (A) and (B)
   ☐ (D) do neither (A) nor (B)

8. The "scientists up in space" mentioned in lines 28 and 29 are also astronauts. True or false?

   ☐ (A) True.
   ☐ (B) False.

9. The commander on Ride's flight said he picked her because

   ☐ (A) she had been a tennis champion so he knew she was physically fit
   ☐ (B) she flew herself to her wedding, proving she was an excellent pilot
   ☐ (C) she was very familiar with an important piece of equipment that would be used on the flight
   ☐ (D) in 1978 only four other women joined the astronaut training program

ADDITIONAL ASSIGNMENTS

1. Pick a passage that is about 150 words long from one of your textbooks, an encyclopedia or a news article. On a separate piece of paper, write a "main idea" multiple-choice question. (Your question should look like any of the "main idea" questions in this unit, such as Passage A Question 5.) Be sure to make one of your choices clearly state the main idea. The other three choices should state *minor* details or facts from your passage.

    Ask a classmate or friend to read your passage and answer the question. Check that person's answer. If he or she has made an error, discuss it and explain your correct answer. If there is confusion about the correct answer, rewrite your choices until there is clearly a *best* answer stating the main idea.

2. *Write your own short passage* on a topic that interests you. Then write a "main idea" question like the one you wrote for Assignment 1. Ask someone to read your passage and answer your question. Check that person's answer to see if the main idea you think you wrote about is, in fact, the main idea a reader gets from the passage. Discuss any confusion that arises. Rewrite your passage or your question until it is perfectly clear what your main idea is.

3. Study the meaning of the word "flaking" on page 182. Write a sentence on the lines below in which the meaning of "flaking" is *stated without punctuation* (see Unit 2, CASE II).

    _____

    _____

    _____

4. Study the meaning of the word "serpentine" on page 182. Write a sentence on the lines below in which the meaning of "serpentine" is *given by contrast* (see Unit 2, CASE III).

    _____

    _____

    _____

5. Study the meaning of the word "severe" on page 188. Write a sentence on the lines below in which the meaning of "severe" can be *inferred from ideas in the sentence* (see Unit 2, CASE IV).

    _____

    _____

    _____

Comprehending Descriptions Of Order II

When you have completed this unit you will

- be able to comprehend the order (sequence) of things described in a written passage by using clues given by "comparatives", "transition" words and phrases, cause—effect relationships and contrast relationships;

- be able to make a diagram showing the order of several things described in a complex written passage;

- be able to identify sentences that state the correct order of things described in a complex written passage.

INTRODUCTION

This unit covers the same analytical reading process as Unit 5—that is, understanding passages describing the order in which things happen or are arranged. In Unit 5 you learned how to analyze orders of things by size, weight, birth date, date of discovery, and so on. This unit will strengthen your ability to understand these and other types of order.

In this unit the exercises are more challenging than in Unit 5. They will require you to read very carefully and think very precisely. In general, these exercises have a greater number of items that must be put in order. Also, they have more extra, superfluous (not needed) information. You will need to sort carefully through what you read to find the important facts and relationships. As with most textbooks, you must carry out many mental steps as you try to make sense of the information in these exercises.

EXERCISE INSTRUCTIONS

Follow the same procedure you used in Unit 5. (Look back at Unit 5 if you want to review.) The key is to work patiently and carefully. Read the difficult parts of an exercise several times, if necessary, until the facts are completely clear.

Remember that it can help to make separate working-diagrams for each main part of an exercise. Then combine your separate working-diagrams into one final answer diagram. Work with the same hard effort you used in Unit 5 and you will find it is easy to understand even the most complex descriptions of order.

EXERCISE 1

Clinita, a doctor, has the nickname Bones. Ada is a left-handed artist. Gayle is an English teacher in an all-girl high school. Joanne, the mother of two boys, plays French horn in the orchestra. The French horn player is older than the woman who teaches only girls but younger than the left-handed woman. Bones is older than the mother of two boys but younger than the artist.

Write the *first names* of the women in order on the diagram.

older

younger

EXERCISE 2

Among major religions, Hinduism has more followers than Buddhism but less than Islam. Confucianism has fewer followers than Buddhism, whereas Christianity has even more followers than Islam.

Write the five religions in order on the diagram.

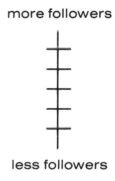

more followers

less followers

EXERCISE 3

Among the rulers of early England, King Richard I (known as "Richard the Lion-Hearted" because of his bravery during the Crusades) reigned in England after King William I (known as "William the Conqueror") but before King John, who granted the Magna Carta controlling the king's power. The Saxon King Alfred (known as "Alfred the Great") reigned before William I.

Write the names of the four kings in order on the diagram.

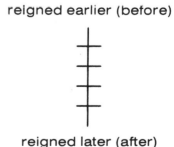

reigned earlier (before)

reigned later (after)

EXERCISE 4

Among the world's continents, Africa is larger than
South America. North America is between Africa and
South America in size. Antarctica and Europe are smaller
than South America, with Antarctica being larger than
Europe. Asia (including its surrounding islands) is the
largest of the continents, while Australia is the smallest.

A.   List the seven continents in order on the diagram.

larger

smaller

B.   Check (✓) the correct statement.

_____ (a) North America is smaller than Africa but larger than Asia.
_____ (b) North America is smaller than Africa but larger than Antarctica.
_____ (c) North America is smaller than Antarctica but larger than Africa.
_____ (d) North America is smaller than Asia but larger than Africa.

EXERCISE 5

Among noteworthy ancient Greeks, Sappho, the female
poet, lived before Pericles, the political leader in Athens.
Furthermore, Demosthenes, the great orator (public
speaker), lived after Pericles.

A.   Write the names of the three Greeks in order on the
diagram.

lived earlier

lived later

B.   Check (✓) the correct statement.

_____ (a) Pericles lived after Sappho and Demosthenes.
_____ (b) Pericles lived before Demosthenes and Sappho.
_____ (c) Pericles lived before Sappho but after Demosthenes.
_____ (d) Pericles lived before Demosthenes but after Sappho.

EXERCISE 6

Among famous ancient Greeks, Homer (the author of the books *Iliad* and *Odyssey*) lived before Aristophanes, who wrote comedies. However, the philosopher Aristotle lived after Aristophanes.

A. Write the names of the three Greeks in order on the diagram.

lived earlier

lived later

B. Check (✓) the correct statement.

_____ (a) Aristophanes lived before Aristotle and Homer.
_____ (b) Aristophanes lived before Aristotle but after Homer.
_____ (c) Aristophanes lived before Homer but after Aristotle.
_____ (d) Aristophanes lived after Homer and Aristotle.

EXERCISE 7

Many African countries have obtained their independence since 1955. Among them, Tanzania obtained its independence after Nigeria but before Algeria. Uganda and Algeria both became independent in 1962, which is before Kenya and Zambia obtained their independence. Zambia obtained its independence the year after Kenya did, and Botswana obtained its two years after Zambia. Ghana became independent before Nigeria.

A. List the seven countries in order on the diagram. Place the two countries which obtained their independence in the same year next to each other.

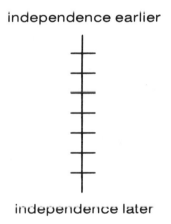

independence earlier

independence later

B. Check (✓) the correct fact.

_____ (a) Kenya obtained its independence before Zambia and Algeria.
_____ (b) Kenya obtained its independence before Algeria but after Zambia.
_____ (c) Kenya obtained its independence before Zambia but after Algeria.
_____ (d) Kenya obtained its independence after Zambia and Algeria.

EXERCISE 8

Among American poets, Ezra Pound died seven years after T.S. Eliot, but he was born before Eliot. Edgar Allan Poe, who wrote some of America's most stunning poetry as well as horror stories, lived a troubled life and died 33 years before another famous American poet, Henry Wadsworth Longfellow, although Poe was born two years after Longfellow. Walt Whitman was born after Poe but before Robert Frost, and Frost was born before Pound.

List the last names of the six poets in order on the diagram.

born earlier

born later

EXERCISE 9

West Germany has the largest population among western European nations, but it is not the largest in size. France, Spain and Italy are all larger. Italy has a larger population than France but is smaller in size. Spain's size falls between France's and Italy's. Greece and Portugal combined are smaller in size than West Germany, whereas Portugal and Switzerland combined are about the size of Greece. Switzerland is smaller in both size and population than Portugal.

A. Seven countries are mentioned in this passage. Write the seven countries in order *according to size* (not population) on the diagram.

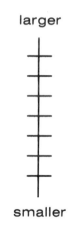

larger

smaller

B. Check (✓) the correct statement.

_____ (a) Italy is larger than Spain and West Germany.
_____ (b) Italy is larger than Spain but smaller than West Germany.
_____ (c) Italy is larger than West Germany but smaller than Spain.
_____ (d) Italy is smaller than Spain and West Germany.

EXERCISE 10

Francois Rabelais, a Frenchman who wrote *Gargantua*, was born before William Shakespeare, whose plays include *Hamlet* and *Macbeth*. Charles Dickens, who wrote *Oliver Twist*, was born after Victor Hugo, whose most popular work is *The Hunchback of Notre Dame*. Moreover, Jonathan Swift, whose satire *Gulliver's Travels* poked fun at many human activities, was born before Hugo. But Swift was born after Shakespeare. The Italian writer Dante, whose *Divine Comedy* summarized medieval thought, was born in 1265, about 200 years before Rabelais. Between Dante and Rabelais, Geoffrey Chaucer (*The Canterbury Tales*) was born in England.

List the last names of the seven writers in order on the diagram.

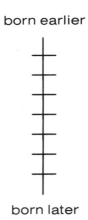

born earlier

born later

EXERCISE 11

Charlemagne (Charles the Magnificent) was the first powerful ruler in Europe after the long period of European ignorance and confusion known as the "Dark Ages" that followed the fall of Rome. Feudalism began with Charlemagne and reached its peak over the next several hundred years, but then it declined as the Crusades disrupted Europe and brought new ideas from the east. The Renaissance—the "rebirth" of European interest in science and man—only reached its full strength when Gutenberg invented the movable type printing press so books could be printed cheaply and read by everyone. However, the Renaissance had its beginning earlier than this when, as the Crusades continued for several hundred years, new ideas and commerce were brought to Europe.

Six historical events are listed below. Write them in order on the diagram.

Gutenberg invented movable type
Reign of Charlemagne
Dark Ages
Peak of feudalism
Fall of Rome
Beginning of Renaissance

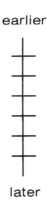

earlier

later

EXERCISE 12

[NOTE: In this selection the word "contemporary" is used. A contemporary is someone who lives at about the same time as someone else. For example, George Washington was a contemporary of Ben Franklin. **On your answer diagram, the names of people who are contemporaries should be written next to each other.**]

Copernicus (1473-1543) challenged the view of the ancient Greek astronomer Ptolemy (about 150 A.D.) that the earth was the center of our universe. Instead, Copernicus argued that the sun was the center. Born 98 years after Copernicus, Kepler discovered that the planets do not travel in perfect circles around the sun but in elliptical (oval) orbits. Kepler based his discovery on the many astronomical observations of Tycho Brahe, who was born between Copernicus and Kepler. After Kepler's work, about 80 more years had to pass before Newton discovered the law of gravity, explaining why the planets do not fly out of their orbits away from the sun. No discussion of the history of astronomy would be complete without mentioning Galileo, who got in trouble with the Church for arguing in his writings that the sun rather than the earth was the center of the universe. Galileo was a contemporary of Kepler, which means that he, too, lived about 90 years after Copernicus. But Galileo got into more trouble than Copernicus for having the same view of the universe because Galileo's writings were more widely read and therefore a greater threat to authority.

Write the names of the six astronomers in order on the diagram. Remember to put the names of the two astronomers who were contemporaries next to each other.

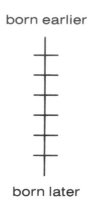

born earlier

born later

EXERCISE 13

Vocabulary preview: **vague** (adjective)—not certain, not definite.

Vague records suggest that a number of black American slaves made significant inventions for which they were never officially given credit. But after the Civil War outlawed slavery, black inventors were able to take out patents (official notices of invention) and get credit for their work. Among them, perhaps the most famous is George Washington Carver, who developed products from the soybean and peanut that revolutionized agriculture in the South by freeing it from its total dependence on cotton. Born several years before Carver, Granville Woods took out over 50 patents, including several that improved railroad transportation and safety. On the other hand, born almost 80 years after Carver, George Carruthers is a modern-day scientist who designed the ultraviolet camera/spectrograph placed on the moon in 1972. Two medical researchers who were born between Carver and Carruthers are Charles Drew and Percy Julian. Julian was a chemist who produced cortisone for arthritis sufferers and physostigmine, which is used in the treatment of the eye disease glaucoma. Charles Drew, born six years after Julian, was a medical doctor who developed ways of preserving blood for blood banks, which has saved countless lives.

born earlier

born later

A. Write the names of the five inventors in order on the diagram.

B. According to the selection,

- ☐ (a) there were no inventions by black American slaves
- ☐ (b) there is some reason to believe that American slaves made inventions for which they did not receive credit

C. Whose work is most directly used by the Red Cross in saving accident victims?

- ☐ (a) Carver
- ☐ (b) Drew
- ☐ (c) Woods
- ☐ (d) Percy

ADDITIONAL ASSIGNMENTS

1. Read the paragraph below and write the names of the five people in order on the diagram to the right.

   Lem was born before Jose and Jill, but after Vana. Jose was born after Jill, and Leslie was born before Vana.

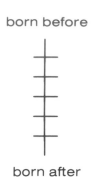

born before

born after

Now study this diagram on the right. On a separate piece of paper, write a paragraph like the one above that describes the order the diagram shows.

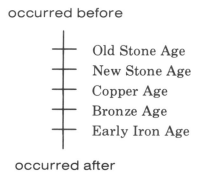

occurred before

Old Stone Age
New Stone Age
Copper Age
Bronze Age
Early Iron Age

occurred after

2. Reread Exercise 8 in this unit. Using information from that exercise, write a problem on a separate piece of paper about five American poets. *Write your problem by using the following pattern of sentences:*

   Poet A was born before poet D but after poet B. Poet A was born before poet B. Poet E was born after poet D.

   Have a classmate or friend solve your problem using the diagram to the right.

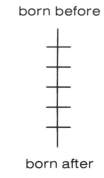

born before

born after

Supporting Evidence In Reading And Writing

OBJECTIVES

When you have completed this unit you will

- understand how "specific" statements are used to support or give evidence for a "general" statement;

- be able to select (from four choices) a specific statement that best supports or gives evidence for a given general statement.

INTRODUCTION

An excellent writing technique is to begin a paragraph with a *general statement* of a fact or idea. Then, the rest of the paragraph is made up of sentences that give *specific statements* that support or give evidence for the general statement. Study this short paragraph:

A home computer can often help students with their schoolwork. Students can use the computer to get extra practice on the reading, writing and math work they are learning in school.

The first sentence of this paragraph makes a general statement:

A home computer can often help students with their schoolwork.

This sentence makes a general statement because it does not give any reasons or evidence to explain why it is true.

The second sentence gives a specific statement that supports or gives some evidence for why the general statement is true:

Students can use the computer to get extra practice on the reading, writing and math work they are learning in school.

By telling the reader *how* the computer can help with schoolwork, this specific statement supports the general statement that a computer *can* help with a student's schoolwork. It gives some reasons or evidence for why the general statement is true.

Much of the material in textbooks is organized in this *general-specific* writing style. An author makes a major general point, and then provides specific information to support or give evidence of that major point. To fully understand the material, you must comprehend how the specific statements support or give evidence of the general statement.

The exercises in this unit will make it easier for you to comprehend this kind of writing. They will also help you to use this kind of writing in your own writing of essays, term papers and reports.

EXERCISE INSTRUCTIONS

Each exercise in this unit begins with a general statement. Then four other sentences are listed. *One* of these four sentences gives specific information that *supports or provides evidence for* the general statement.

Read the general statement and the four possible specific statements very carefully. Think about what they mean. Then check (✔) the choice that *best supports or gives evidence for* the general statement.

Try the example on the next page.

EXAMPLE: Check (✓) the choice that best supports or
provides evidence for the first sentence.

**When Egyptians died they were buried with many of their
possessions because Egyptians believed these would be used
in a life after death.**

_____ A. The Egyptian pyramids were the tombs (bur-
ial places) of ancient Egyptian nobles.

_____ B. The three largest pyramids, the Great
Pyramids, were the tombs of Egyptian kings.

_____ C. Each of the Great Pyramids required the
work of thousands of people working for
years with only primitive tools.

_____ D. Clothing, tools, weapons, jewelry and furniture were often found in Egyptian tombs.

ANSWER:

___✓___ D. Clothing, tools, weapons, jewelry and furniture were often found in Egyptian tombs.

Choice D best supports or provides evidence for the first
sentence. It lists the types of items found in Egyptian tombs,
and these items are examples of useful possessions. So, it
supports the first sentence by giving specific examples of useful possessions buried with Egyptians.

None of choices A, B or C provide specific evidence of the
things with which Egyptians were buried. So, they do not
support or give evidence for the first sentence.

Use this same kind of thinking to complete the exercises.
Remember to read all four of the choices carefully before making
your final selection.

General Directions: Check (✓) the choice that best supports or
provides evidence for the first sentence.

EXERCISE 1

Dogs can be trained to do important jobs for people.

_____ A. Dogs make better pets than cats, canaries, fish, tur-
tles or ponies.

_____ B. Dogs range in size from tiny Chihuahuas and mini-
ature poodles to giant Great Danes and Saint Ber-
nards.

_____ C. A seeing-eye dog helps a blind person cross streets
and avoid danger.

_____ D. The dog has been called "man's best friend."

EXERCISE 2

Camille was the best player on the women's basketball team.

_____ A. Cindy and Candy also played on the team.

_____ B. Camille won the Most Valuable Player award both
this year and last year.

_____ C. The team achieved a record of 14 wins and 5 losses.

_____ D. The team finished in third place at the state
tournament.

EXERCISE 3

Watching television can be educational.

_____ A. Children watch too much television.

_____ B. Some television shows explain topics in science and
art.

_____ C. TV keeps people from talking to each other or reading.

_____ D. The average person watches more than two hours of
television per day.

EXERCISE 4

You should buckle your seat belt even for short car trips.

_____ A. Shoulder seat belts are safer than lap seat belts.

_____ B. Accidents can be reduced by not speeding.

_____ C. The law requires that cars be equipped with seat belts.

_____ D. Most accidents occur within twenty miles of the driver's home.

EXERCISE 5

Football is the most popular sport in America.

_____ A. In a football game there are 11 players on each team.

_____ B. A football field is 100 yards long and 53-1/3 yards wide.

_____ C. More people watch football games than baseball games or other sporting events.

_____ D. American football is somewhat like the European games of soccer and rugby.

EXERCISE 6

Vitamins are necessary for your health.

_____ A. Vitamin C is contained in oranges and grapefruit.

_____ B. A person who does not get enough Vitamin C develops a disease called scurvy.

_____ C. Whole wheat bread is a good source of Vitamin B as well as minerals and protein.

_____ D. Most candy is mainly sugar and contains very little vitamins, minerals or protein.

EXERCISE 7

The climate of a place depends upon where it is located on earth.

_____ A. A place near either of the earth's poles is cold year-round, whereas a place near the equator is warm year-round.

_____ B. Halfway between the North and South Poles is called the equator.

_____ C. Milwaukee is located north of the equator.

_____ D. The place we call the North Pole is often thought of as being at the "top" of the earth.

EXERCISE 8

Tokyo, the capital of Japan, is the world's largest city.

_____ A. Residents of Tokyo may wear old Japanese-style clothing at home but modern, western clothing for business.

_____ B. A Japanese city named Osaka is a ship building center.

_____ C. Hundreds of theaters, nightclubs, tea houses and dance halls are found in Tokyo's huge entertainment area.

_____ D. Rice is an important part of the diet of most Tokyo residents.

EXERCISE 9

Land transportation between European countries has been greatly improved.

_____ A. Modern telephone and telegraph systems link the countries of Europe.

_____ B. Airlines provide quick transportation between European countries.

_____ C. European nations receive each other's radio and television broadcasts.

_____ D. The roadway between Italy and France was shortened when a tunnel was built through Mont Blanc in the Alps mountain range.

EXERCISE 10

The most important contribution made by ancient Rome was in the field of law.

_____ A. Although the Roman Senate made law, Rome's first dictator, Caesar, had great power that went beyond the Senate's laws.

_____ B. All European law until the 1800s was based upon Roman law.

_____ C. Wealthy Romans had brilliant Greeks tutor their children.

_____ D. During the Punic Wars, Rome developed a strong navy.

EXERCISE 11

A computer program is a list of the commands you want a computer to follow as it does a task for you.

_____ A. The price of home computers is dropping sharply.

_____ B. A computer program must contain at least one command, and can have a list of well over one hundred commands, that tells the computer what to do.

_____ C. A common home computer system is made up of a computer terminal (the computer itself), a monitor (like a TV screen) and a typewriter-like printing machine.

_____ D. Business computers are now a normal piece of office equipment.

EXERCISE 12

The Romans had a great respect for Greek culture.

_____ A. Styles that were developed in Greek architecture have been used in designing American buildings.

_____ B. The Greek general Alexander the Great took Greek culture to all of the lands he conquered.

_____ C. The works of Greek artists and scientists were carefully studied by the Romans.

_____ D. The greatest of the Greek sculptors (stone carvers) was Pheidias.

EXERCISE 13

In the middle 1900s people became aware that technology brought problems that were not easily solved.

_____ A. Thanks to technology, many jobs that had often caused injury to workers were made safer.

_____ B. Technology brought improved methods of transportation and communication.

_____ C. The standard of living for most people improved through the use of technology.

_____ D. Automobiles polluted the air, but there was no better way to transport goods to people or get workers to their jobs.

EXERCISE 14

Africa's greatest natural resource is its mineral deposits.

_____ A. Forest products are important in central Africa, where palm oil is produced along with hardwoods such as ebony that are used to make high-quality furniture.

_____ B. The world's richest diamond mines, as well as petroleum, gold, iron, copper and manganese are found in Africa.

_____ C. Most of the world's ivory comes from African elephant tusks, and the skins of African animals are in high demand all over the world.

_____ D. About two-fifths of Africa is made up of desert.

EXERCISE 15

Few people deserved to be president more than Thomas Jefferson.

_____ A. Jefferson was the first president to serve in the country's new capital of Washington, D.C.

_____ B. Jefferson had fought for democracy and human rights throughout his life and had written the Declaration of Independence.

_____ C. As president, Jefferson bought the Louisiana Territory from France, which greatly increased the land size of the United States.

_____ D. Jefferson was curious about the territory west of the Mississippi River and sent Pike out to explore this land.

EXERCISE 16

The astrolabe—the forerunner of the modern sextant used by ship captains to find their location at sea—was not too accurate.

_____ A. The astrolabe was used to observe the position of the stars.

_____ B. Tables had been made showing the position of the stars from different locations at sea, so a captain could find his location by observing the stars with an astrolabe.

_____ C. Sea captains often sailed far off their planned course before the astrolabe and compass came into use.

_____ D. It is believed that the captain of the Mayflower was using an astrolabe when the ship reached Massachusetts instead of his planned target of Virginia.

ADDITIONAL ASSIGNMENTS

1. Select a sentence from one of your textbooks in which the author makes a general statement or point about the topic. Then find a sentence that the author uses to support the general statement or point. (History books are good sources for these kinds of sentences.)

   On a separate piece of paper, write the general statement you chose. Below that sentence, *write three sentences of your own that* do not *support that general statement*, and also write the sentence that *does* support it that you took from the book. Write the four sentences in random order. You have now created an exercise like the ones in this unit.

   Ask a classmate or friend to read the general statement and the four other sentences. Tell that person to pick the sentence that supports the general statement. Check that person's work.

2. *Write your own general statement* about a topic that interests you. Then write four other sentences. One sentence should support your general statement and the other three should *not* support it.

   Ask a classmate or friend to read the general statement and the four other sentences. Tell that person to pick the sentence that supports the general statement. Check that person's work. Discuss any confusion he or she had, and rewrite your sentences if necessary.

Reading For
Full Comprehension III:
Recognizing Implied Ideas
And Analyzing Details

OBJECTIVES

When you have completed this unit you will

● understand what an "implied" idea is;

● be able to identify a statement that is implied but not directly stated in a reading passage;

● be able to answer questions about the main idea and specific details of a reading passage;

● be able to use context clues to figure out the meaning of a word as it is used in a certain reading passage.

INTRODUCTION

This final unit is similar to Units 6 and 11. It will add to your skill in reading material for full, total understanding of facts and relationships. As the final unit of this text, this unit will let you prove to yourself how much your reading has improved since Unit 2. (Remember Unit 2? You have probably become so good at that reading skill that you just do it naturally now whenever you read.)

Like Units 6 and 11, this unit contains reading passages with test-like questions. You will find the vocabulary and difficulty level of these passages to be a little harder than Units 6 and 11. Your reading is improving so you need tougher challenges to continue to grow. As before, use a dictionary whenever you need help with a word's meaning *and cannot figure it out from context clues*.

Among the questions that follow each passage, you will see a new type of question. This question asks you to identify an idea that is *not stated* in the passage but is only *implied*. Implied means "suggested but not directly stated." So, when an idea is *implied* in a passage, the writer is suggesting or hinting it without directly stating it in clear words. An idea that is implied is called an *implication*. Study this statement:

**Gilda and I have known each other for three years.
We have been close friends since last month.**

This statement directly states certain ideas. In addition, it implies—but does not directly state—another idea. The implied idea is that *Gilda and I were not friends during the time period from three years ago up to last month*. This is not directly stated in either sentence, but it is suggested by the meaning of the two sentences together.

This new type of question will help you "read between the lines" to discover the full meaning of a passage.

EXERCISE INSTRUCTIONS

Follow the same procedures you used in Units 6 and 11: Read the passage carefully; Read each question and its answer choices completely; Reread sections of the passage to uncover the *best* answer to each question. Aim for total accuracy—show your full comprehension of the material.

To practice answering the new "implied idea" questions, try the example given at the top of the next page.

EXAMPLE

Read this passage and answer the "implied idea" question beneath it. As you answer the question, keep these "rules" in mind:

(1) Some choices give correct ideas that *are directly stated* in the passage—these choices *do not answer* the question because an implied idea is an idea that is *not* directly stated.

(2) Some choices give ideas that are *wrong or false* according to the passage—these choices *do not answer* the question because an implied idea is a true idea.

(3) The *correct* choice gives a true idea that is not directly stated in the passage.

Passage:

1   Science in colonial America had a slow start.
2 It was held back by superstitions brought from
3 Europe and by concern with the more imme-
4 diate problems of surviving in the wilderness.
5 Yet some progress was made. The Franklin
6 stove which improved home heating, the
7 lightning rod which helped prevent fires, and
8 bifocal eyeglasses which made the wearer able
9 to see objects near and far—were all inventions
10 of Benjamin Franklin. Benjamin Banneker
11 was a free black who became an important
12 mathematician and astronomer. He published
13 an almanac which listed information about
14 the moon and tides. Later, he was to help plan
15 the city of Washington, D.C.

The passage *does not state but implies that*

☐ (A) Banneker's almanac listed information about the moon and tides
☐ (B) Benjamin Franklin was a lazy person
☐ (C) Benjamin Franklin was a man of
science in colonial America
☐ (D) scientific progress in colonial America was slow

Check your understanding with the answers on the next page.

Answer: C

Choice A is *not correct* because this fact *is directly stated* in the passage in lines 12-14.

Choice B is *not correct* because this is a *false* idea according to the passage. The list of inventions made by Franklin shows that he was not lazy.

Choice C *is correct*. The passage *does not directly state* that Franklin was a man of science, but it *does imply that this is true*. The passage is about science in colonial America and it lists a number of Franklin's inventions. In this way, it implies that Franklin was a colonial American scientist.

Choice D is *not correct* because this fact *is directly stated* in the first sentence of the passage.

Begin working now on the exercises that follow. Use careful reading and thinking and you can achieve 100% success.

PASSAGE A

1 Science in colonial America had a slow start.
2 It was held back by superstitions brought from
3 Europe and by concern with the more imme-
4 diate problems of surviving in the wilderness.
5 Yet some progress was made. The Franklin
6 stove which improved home heating, the
7 lightning rod which helped prevent fires, and
8 bifocal eyeglasses which made the wearer able
9 to see objects near and far—were all inventions
10 of Benjamin Franklin. Benjamin Banneker
11 was a free black who became an important
12 mathematician and astronomer. He published
13 an almanac which listed information about
14 the moon and tides. Later, he was to help plan
15 the city of Washington, D.C.

1. The main idea of this selection is that:

   ☐ (A) Benjamin Banneker, a free black man, helped plan Washington, D.C.
   ☐ (B) There was no scientific activity in early America.
   ☐ (C) Benjamin Franklin invented many things including a stove, the lightning rod and bifocal eyeglasses.
   ☐ (D) Although scientific activity in early America was limited, there was some.

2. Which pair of words best completes this analogy: FRANKLIN STOVE is to HOME HEATING as

   ☐ (A) BIFOCAL is to EYEGLASSES
   ☐ (B) BANNEKER is to WASHINGTON, D.C.
   ☐ (C) LIGHTNING ROD is to FIRE PREVENTION
   ☐ (D) BENJAMIN FRANKLIN is to INVENTIONS

3. According to the selection, one reason for the small amount of scientific activity in early America was

   ☐ (A) people's time and energy were taken up by other activities
   ☐ (B) superstition helped people make scientific discoveries
   ☐ (C) Franklin and Banneker were the two major scientists
   ☐ (D) living in the wilderness encourged scientific activity

4. The selection says the almanac on the moon and tides was written by

   ☐ (A) Benjamin Banneker
   ☐ (B) Benjamin Franklin
   ☐ (C) Banneker and Franklin together
   ☐ (D) none of the above

5. The selection *does not state* but *implies* that

   ☐ (A) superstitions were brought to colonial America from Europe
   ☐ (B) Washington, D.C., did not develop in a haphazard, unplanned manner
   ☐ (C) Banneker was a black mathematician and astronomer
   ☐ (D) there was a great deal of scientific activity in colonial America

PASSAGE B

1 The value of Garrett Morgan's "gas inhal-
2 ator" was first acknowledged during a suc-
3 cessful rescue operation of several men
4 trapped by a tunnel explosion in the Cleve-
5 land Waterworks some 200 feet below the
6 surface of Lake Erie. During the emergency,
7 Morgan, his brother and two other
8 volunteers—all wearing inhalators—were
9 the only men able to descend into the
10 smoky, gas-filled tunnel, and save several
11 workers from asphyxiation.
12 Orders for the Morgan inhalator soon
13 began to pour into Cleveland from fire
14 companies all over the nation but, as soon
15 as Morgan's racial identity became known,
16 many of them were cancelled. In the South,
17 it was necessary for Morgan to utilize the
18 services of a white man to demonstrate his
19 invention. During World War I, the Morgan
20 inhalator was transformed into a gas mask
21 used by combat troops.
22 Born in Paris, Kentucky, Morgan moved
23 to Cleveland at an early age. His first inven-
24 tion was an improvement on the sewing
25 machine which he sold for $150. In 1923,
26 having established his reputation with the
27 gas inhalator, he was able to command a
28 price of $40,000 from the General Electric
29 Company for his automatic traffic sign.
30 Morgan died in Cleveland, the city which
31 had awarded him a gold medal for his devo-
32 tion to public safety.

1. Below are three possible titles for this passage. In each blank, write the letter of the phrase (A, B or C) which best describes that title.

    _____ Tunnel Explosion in Cleveland Waterworks
    _____ The Gas Inhalator and Other Inventions of Garrett Morgan
    _____ Major Inventions by Black Americans

    (A) comprehensive title
    (B) too narrow
    (C) too broad

2. The main idea of this selection is:

    ☐ (A) There was a tunnel explosion in the Cleveland Waterworks.
    ☐ (B) Garrett Morgan invented the gas inhalator and other things, and although he met some difficulty from racism, these inventions brought him financial and personal rewards.
    ☐ (C) Several men were saved from death by use of the gas inhalator invented by Garrett Morgan.
    ☐ (D) Racial prejudice in the South and other places kept Garrett Morgan's gas inhalator from becoming popular.

3. The selection *implies* but does not state that

    ☐ (A) Morgan helped rescue several men in the Cleveland Waterworks explosion
    ☐ (B) Morgan was a black American

4. Where was Morgan born?

    ☐ (A) Cleveland, Kentucky
    ☐ (B) Cleveland, Ohio
    ☐ (C) Paris, France
    ☐ (D) Paris, Kentucky

5. The word *acknowledged* in the first sentence means

    ☐ (A) publicly noted or given credit
    ☐ (B) gained knowledge or learned
    ☐ (C) became unknown or lost
    ☐ (D) invented

6. The last word in the first paragraph, *asphyxiation*, means

    ☐ (A) death from drowning in water
    ☐ (B) death from lack of oxygen to breathe
    ☐ (C) safety device
    ☐ (D) gas inhalator

7. The article *implies* but does not state that

   ☐ (A) it was necessary for Morgan to have a white man demonstrate the gas inhalator in the South
   ☐ (B) racial prejudice was especially strong in the South
   ☐ (C) Morgan fought for France during World War I

8. The invention that Morgan sold for $40,000 was a

   ☐ (A) gas inhalator
   ☐ (B) sewing machine improvement
   ☐ (C) automatic traffic sign

9. Which conclusion can be drawn from the selection?

   ☐ (A) Racial prejudice prevented Morgan from selling any of his inventions.
   ☐ (B) Racial prejudice prevented the gas inhalator from being used during the first World War.
   ☐ (C) Morgan was a financially successful inventor in spite of the obstacle of racial prejudice.

10. According to the passage, the city of Cleveland felt Morgan had earned special praise for

    ☐ (A) inventing the Cleveland Waterworks
    ☐ (B) reducing injury and death
    ☐ (C) improving on the sewing machine
    ☐ (D) fighting racism

PASSAGE C

Vocabulary preview: **portrayed** (verb)—played (acted a role
on stage or movie screen.

¹ For all classes, whether highly educated or
² not, the theater of Elizabeth's time supplied out-
³ standing plays. Today, highschool students usu-
⁴ ally think of Shakespeare's plays as something
⁵ to be read in English classes. Had you lived in
⁶ the fast-growing city of London in Elizabeth's
⁷ day, however, you would have found people
⁸ flocking to the Globe Theater to see the much-
⁹ talked-of plays of William Shakespeare being
¹⁰ acted, with Shakespeare himself sometimes play-
¹¹ ing roles. Englishmen of all classes liked Shake-
¹² speare's plays, not only because the characters
¹³ were shrewdly portrayed but because some of
¹⁴ his historical plays stirred English pride by re-
¹⁵ calling half-forgotten events in their history.
¹⁶ Another famous playwright of those times was
¹⁷ Ben Jonson, who wrote comedies which pic-
¹⁸ tured English life as it was about 1600.

1. A playwright is a writer of plays. According to the selection, Shakespeare was

   ☐ (A) a playwright but not an actor
   ☐ (B) a playwright and occasional actor
   ☐ (C) an actor but not a playwright
   ☐ (D) neither an actor nor a playwright

2. England's ruler during Shakespeare's
   time was

   ☐ (A) Queen Elizabeth
   ☐ (B) Queen Mary
   ☐ (C) Henry VIII
   ☐ (D) Ben Jonson

3. Below are three possible titles for this
   passage. In each blank, write the letter of
   the phrase which best describes that title.

   _____ History of English Drama
   _____ Shakespeare and Jonson: Two Popular Elizabethan Playwrights
   _____ Ben Jonson: A Popular Elizabethan Playwright

   (A) too narrow
   (B) comprehensive title
   (C) too broad

4. In which city was the Globe Theater
   located?

   ☐ (A) England
   ☐ (B) New York City
   ☐ (C) Elizabeth City
   ☐ (D) London

5. The word *classes* appears in line 1 and
   also line 5. What are its two meanings?

   ☐ (A) Line 1—social groups
   Line 5—political groups
   ☐ (B) Line 1—school groups
   Line 5—political groups
   ☐ (C) Line 1—school groups
   Line 5—social groups
   ☐ (D) Line 1—social groups
   Line 5—school groups

6. The passage does not state but *implies*
   that today's highschool students usually

   ☐ (A) love to read Shakespeare's plays
   ☐ (B) do not read Shakespeare's plays
   outside of school
   ☐ (C) read Shakespeare's plays while
   travelling in England
   ☐ (D) read Shakespeare's plays during
   history lessons on England

7. During Shakespeare's lifetime, his plays
   were enjoyed

   ☐ (A) mainly by the educated, upper
   social class
   ☐ (B) by all social classes
   ☐ (C) mainly by the uneducated, lower
   social class
   ☐ (D) by students in English classes

PASSAGE D

Vocabulary preview: **comrade** (noun)—friend; fellow member
of the same organization or group.

1 "You have heard then, comrades," he said, "that we pigs
2 now sleep in the beds of the farmhouse? And why not? You
3 did not suppose, surely, that there was ever a ruling against
4 *beds*? A bed merely means a place to sleep in. A pile of straw
5 in a stall is a bed, properly regarded. The rule was against
6 *sheets*, which are a human invention. We have removed the
7 sheets from the farmhouse beds, and sleep between
8 blankets. And very comfortable beds they are too! But not
9 more comfortable than we need, I can tell you, comrades,
10 with all the brainwork we have to do nowadays. You would
11 not rob us of our repose, would you, comrades? You would
12 not have us too tired to carry out our duties? Surely none of
13 you wishes to see Jones back?"
14 The animals reassured him on this point immediately,
15 and no more was said about the pigs sleeping in the farm-
16 house beds. And when, some days afterwards, it was
17 announced that from now on the pigs would get up an hour
18 later in the mornings than the other animals, no complaint
19 was made about that either.

1. According to the passage, the speaker is

   ☐ (A) a cow
   ☐ (B) a pig
   ☐ (C) a human

2. The word *repose*, as used in line 11, means

   ☐ (A) brainwork
   ☐ (B) property
   ☐ (C) rest

3. According to the speaker, which one of these did mankind invent?

   ☐ (A) beds
   ☐ (B) blankets
   ☐ (C) sheets

4. The passage does not state but *implies* that

   ☐ (A) the pigs did the brainwork on the farm
   ☐ (B) the other animals (not pigs) did the brainwork on the farm
   ☐ (C) the other animals (not pigs) did not do much of the brainwork on the farm

5. This passage is probably from

   ☐ (A) a book about raising pigs on a farm
   ☐ (B) a story using animals to illustrate human characteristics such as greed
   ☐ (C) a book about how different animals are best suited for different work
   ☐ (D) a book explaining that pigs are the smartest kind of animal

6. Which situation below seems just like the situation in the passage?

   ☐ (A) A boss decides to give her workers a raise in salary.
   ☐ (B) A boss decides to give herself a raise in salary.

7. What seems to have occurred *before* the situation in the passage?

   ☐ (A) Animals have taken control of a farm and the pigs are trying to help the human farmers regain control.
   ☐ (B) Animals have taken control of a farm and the pigs are their leaders.

PASSAGE E

Vocabulary preview: **cycle** (noun)—a sequence of activities or events that happens over and over again. For example: getting out of bed, going through the day, going back to bed to sleep. This "cycle" repeats every day; it begins anew each morning.

erupt (verb)—break out; force out or release suddenly.

periodically (adverb)—happens again and again at approximately regular points in time (such as every five minutes or every hour).

1 One of the major attractions at Yellowstone
2 National Park in Wyoming is the geyser named
3 Old Faithful. A geyser is a deep hole in the
4 ground which periodically shoots hot water into
5 the air like a fountain.
6 The center of our earth, which is 4,000 miles
7 from the surface, is so hot that the stone from
8 which it is made has melted and is in liquid form.
9 As you move away from the center, the stone
10 becomes more and more solid but remains very
11 hot for some distance. A geyser is created when
12 there is a long, narrow hole reaching from the
13 earth's surface down into the hot rock. As this
14 hole fills with water from rain and underground
15 streams, the water at the bottom becomes so
16 hot that, were it on your kitchen stove, it would
17 boil off as steam. But in a very narrow hole, the
18 water at the bottom cannot easily bubble up and
19 boil off because cooler water entering the top of
20 the hole holds the hot water down. Slowly, how-
21 ever, more and more of the water becomes
22 boiling hot until there is not enough cooler water
23 on top to hold the hot water down. Then it boils
24 up violently, shooting hot water and steam up
25 the hole and high into the air above the ground.
26 After this eruption, cool water begins filling the
27 hole and the cycle begins again.
28 Old Faithful is not the only geyser in Yellow-
29 stone Park, but it has become very popular
30 because it erupts about every 66 minutes and
31 shoots water 150 feet into the air. Some geysers
32 do not erupt on such a regular schedule. For
33 example, one of the other geysers in Yellow-
34 stone erupts every 6 to 9½ hours. Also, the
35 water from other geysers may rise only a few
36 feet or even inches. But Old Faithful faithfully
37 gives a wonderful show for visitors approxi-
38 mately once an hour.

1. Below are three possible titles for this passage. In each blank, write the letter of the phrase (A, B or C) which best describes that title.

_____ Distance to the Earth's Center
_____ Old Faithful
_____ Geysers and Other Attractions at National Parks

(A) too broad
(B) too narrow
(C) comprehensive title

2. The main idea of the selection is:

☐ (A) The center of the earth is so hot that its stone has melted and is liquid not solid.

☐ (B) The surface of the earth is about 4,000 miles from the center.

☐ (C) Old Faithful shoots water (heated by hot rock within the earth) high into the air about once an hour in a great display.

3. The selection does not state but *implies* that

☐ (A) the earth's center is 4,000 miles from the surface

☐ (B) if a hole in the ground is narrow, cool water at its top may for a while keep hot water at its bottom from boiling off

☐ (C) if a hole in the ground is wide, it is not possible for an eruption like a geyser's to happen

4. As used in line 37, the word *wonderful* tells you that

   ☐ (A) Old Faithful's show is neither especially good nor bad
   ☐ (B) you will not enjoy Old Faithful's show
   ☐ (C) you will enjoy Old Faithful's show

5. Below are four steps in the eruption of a geyser. Which choice shows the correct order of these four steps?

   I. Cool water keeps the hot water from easily boiling off.
   II. Hot rock heats water in the bottom of a long, narrow hole in the ground.
   III. More and more water in the hole becomes boiling hot until it can no longer be kept from boiling off.
   IV. The hot water boils and forces its way up and out of the hole.

   ☐ (A) I, II, III, IV
   ☐ (B) II, I, III, IV
   ☐ (C) IV, II, I, III
   ☐ (D) II, I, IV, III

6. Pretend you are making a drawing of a geyser. Which statement best explains how to draw the hole in the ground?

   ☐ (A) Draw a rectangle one inch wide and six inches long, with one end of the six-inch sides at the earth's surface and the other end near the earth's center.
   ☐ (B) Draw a rectangle three inches wide and four inches long, with one end of the three-inch sides at the earth's surface and the other end near the earth's center.
   ☐ (C) Draw a rectangle one inch wide and six inches long, with one end of the one-inch sides at the earth's surface and the other end near the earth's center.

7. According to the context, the word *shoots* in line 4 means

   ☐ (A) takes a shot, as in basketball
   ☐ (B) fires a gun or cannon
   ☐ (C) slowly drips
   ☐ (D) forcefully sends off

8. Old Faithful was given its name because

   ☐ (A) it is in Yellowstone Park
   ☐ (B) it brings hot water from deep within the earth to the surface
   ☐ (C) it can be counted on to erupt about every 66 minutes
   ☐ (D) it helped mankind learn that nature could never be understood

PASSAGE F

Vocabulary preview: **limited** (adjective)—kept within certain kinds or amounts; not varied or open-ended.

captivity (noun)—the condition of being under control or restraint, not free.

1 If you saw the movie *Jaws*, you know how
2 frightening a great white shark can be. The
3 thrill they give visitors as they swim within a
4 few feet of the underwater glass tunnel at Sea
5 World has made them a popular attraction.
6 Yet the sharks are more delicate and difficult
7 to keep alive in captivity than many of the
8 gentler animals at Sea World.
9 The problem with sharks is not a limited or
10 unusual diet. In catching sharks, almost any
11 type of fish can be used as bait. Hunters use
12 tarpon, mullet, mackerel, sailfish, or whatever
13 else is available.
14 The real problem is that sharks are born
15 fighters. When caught, they struggle violently
16 in a blind rage, becoming completely
17 exhausted and often going into shock. This
18 weakened state frequently leads to death.
19 A second obstacle arises when a shark is
20 transported from where it is caught to where
21 it will be kept. Dolphins and whales, the other
22 big attractions at Sea World, travel better
23 because they are not really fish but mammals.
24 Like other mammals (such as dogs), dolphins
25 and whales have lungs. They have adapted to
26 living in water, but they come to the surface to
27 breathe. Sharks, however, have gills, which
28 are designed for breathing in water. Some
29 sharks must swim constantly so that new
30 water with fresh oxygen continually flows
31 across their gills. When a shark must be
32 transported, special equipment is required to
33 pump oxygen into the water and keep it circu-
34 lating past the gills. If this is not properly done,
35 the shark does not survive the trip.
36 Sharks illustrate the disadvantage that
37 comes with "specialization." The shark is a
38 specialist, very good at doing just one thing:
39 hunting and attacking prey. But the emotional
40 and physical characteristics that make it such
41 an effective hunter lead to its quick death when
42 adaptation to a new situation is required.

1. Below are three possible titles for this passage. In each blank, write the letter of the phrase (A, B or C) which best describes that title.

_____ Sharks: Fierce but Delicate
_____ Difficulties of Keeping Sea Animals in Captivity
_____ Sharks Use of Gills for Breathing

(A) too narrow
(B) too broad
(C) comprehensive title

2. The word *state*, as used in line 18, means

☐ (A) make a statement, speak
☐ (B) a political and geographical body such as Idaho or Arizona
☐ (C) condition, such as a person's mental condition

3. Based on how the words *adapted* and *adaptation* are used in the selection, the word "adapt" must mean

☐ (A) become the parent of someone else's child
☐ (B) adjust, make or become suited
☐ (C) fail to be successful

4. Which pair of words best completes this analogy: MAMMAL is to LUNGS as

☐ (A) ANIMAL is to GILLS
☐ (B) GILLS is to FISH
☐ (C) GILLS is to LUNGS
☐ (D) FISH is to GILLS

5. Select the correct statement.

☐ (A) The term mammals includes animals and fish.
☐ (B) The term animals includes fish and mammals.
☐ (C) The term whales includes fish and mammals.

6. The passage *implies* but does not state that

  ☐ (A) the normal diet of sharks consists of many different types of fish
  ☐ (B) sharks are easy to place in captivity
  ☐ (C) sharks are born fighters
  ☐ (D) whales have lungs and so do dogs and other mammals

7. All of the following are mentioned in this passage EXCEPT

  ☐ (A) dogs
  ☐ (B) mackerel
  ☐ (C) seals
  ☐ (D) tarpon

8. To avoid the danger of "specialization" described in the final paragraph, which plan of study should a student follow?

  ☐ (A) Study one subject until he/she is expert, and ignore all other subjects.
  ☐ (B) Study all subjects so that he/she knows something about all of them.

9. [HINT: Read all the choices carefully before selecting the *best* answer.]

  According to the selection, sharks are hard to keep alive in captivity because

  ☐ (A) there are very few things that sharks can eat
  ☐ (B) they fight so violently that they can become exhausted and die
  ☐ (C) water with fresh oxygen must be pumped across their gills while they are being transported so they can breathe
  ☐ (D) (A), (B) and (C) are all correct
  ☐ (E) (A) and (B) but not (C) are correct
  ☐ (F) (B) and (C) but not (A) are correct

10. [Read all the alternatives carefully before selecting the *best* answer.]

  The first paragraph has what purpose(s)?

  ☐ (A) To arouse your interest by reminding you of the frightening shark in *Jaws*.
  ☐ (B) To contrast the delicateness of sharks with how frightening they are.
  ☐ (C) To introduce the main topic—the delicateness of sharks in captivity.
  ☐ (D) (A) and (B) but not (C) are correct.
  ☐ (E) (B) and (C) but not (A) are correct.
  ☐ (F) (A), (B) and (C) are all correct.

ADDITIONAL ASSIGNMENTS

1. Pick a passage that is about 150 words long from one of your textbooks, an encyclopedia or a news article. On a separate piece of paper, write at least five multiple-choice questions that would test a reader's understanding of the passage.

   Try to make one of the questions a "best title" question. If you need help writing that question, refer to Assignment 1 on page 98. Also, try to write one "main idea" question (for help refer to Assignment 1 on page 190). The other questions can be about details mentioned in the passage. (If you think you can, write an "implied idea" question like those in this unit.)

   Ask a classmate or friend to read the passage and answer your questions. Check and discuss the answers. If necessary, rewrite your questions until there is clearly a *best* answer to each.

2. *Write your own short passage* on a topic that interests you. Then write at least five multiple-choice questions for that passage. Have a classmate or friend read your passage and answer the questions.

3. Study the meaning of the word "comrade" on page 219. Write a sentence on the lines below in which the meaning of "comrade" is *stated without punctuation* (see Unit 2, CASE II).

   _____

   _____

   _____

4. Study the meaning of the word "captivity" on page 222. Write a sentence on the lines below in which the meaning of "captivity" is *given by contrast* (see Unit 2, CASE III).

   _____

   _____

   _____

5. Study the meaning of the word "portrayed" on page 218. Write a sentence on the lines below in which the meaning of "portrayed" can be *inferred from ideas in the sentence* (see Unit 2, CASE IV).

   _____

   _____

   _____

Critical Reading: Biased Language, Fact Or Opinion, Propaganda

OBJECTIVES

When you have completed this unit you will

● understand how types of language called "biased language", "opinions" and "propaganda" can be used by people to influence your thinking;

● be able to distinguish between biased language and neutral language, and write an explanation of why a given sentence shows bias;

● be able to distinguish between statements of fact and opinion, and write an explanation of why a given statement is a fact or an opinion;

● be able to recognize and name four propaganda techniques.

INTRODUCTION

Should you believe everything you read? Of course, the answer is no. Companies want you to buy their products, travel agents want you to take vacations, politicians want you to believe they—not their opponents—know best. So, these people present information in ways that will influence (shape) your ideas and opinions. Sometimes, people even write in ways designed to trick you into believing what is not actually true or doing what may not be best for you. You can avoid being fooled this way through *critical reading*.

Critical reading is a special kind of analytical reading. When you read a math textbook analytically, your purpose is to fully understand the ideas and procedures used in solving math problems. But when you read an advertisement, your purpose should be different. In this case, you must decide if the ad is totally honest, or if it is written so as to deceive you or make you act in some way useful to the advertiser. Likewise, when friends try to convince you to believe or do something, you should think *critically* about what they are saying. Decide if you *really* agree with their statements completely.

One way to read critically is to separate statements of *fact* from *opinions*. Is a statement clearly true, or just a person's opinion or judgement about the truth? Another way is to recognize special words and methods people can use to fool you into believing what they are saying. When you recognize these words and methods, you can guard against being fooled. This unit will teach you these kinds of critical reading skills.

There are three parts to this unit. The first part will teach you to recognize *biased language*—words that can make you feel a certain way about something. The second part will give you practice in separating fact statements from opinions. The third part will teach you to recognize *propaganda*—statements designed to influence your opinion about something. These skills are all ingredients of good critical reading.

PART I: Biased Language

A writer's purpose in a math or science textbook is usually to present accurate information (facts). The writer does not give many personal opinions or try to get you to believe that certain things are good or bad, useful or useless, wanted or unwanted. On the other hand, the purpose of most advertisements *is* to shape your feelings and opinions—to get you to like something and want to buy it.

However, the purpose of much of the material you read falls between these two examples. For instance, in newspaper and magazine articles, the writer might be presenting information about a topic but might also have strong feelings about the information. By means of the language the writer uses to present the information, he or she may also be shaping *your* feelings about the information.

To see how this is so, read the three sentences below. They might be found in a history textbook or article.

The soldiers fought and defeated the *savage* Indians.
The soldiers fought and defeated the *innocent* Indians.
The soldiers fought and defeated the tribe of Indians.

The first sentence uses the word "savage" to describe the Indians. This word gives you a bad feeling about the Indians (maybe a feeling of anger or horror). Because of this feeling, you may believe that it was okay or good that the soldiers defeated the Indians.

The second sentence uses "innocent" to describe the Indians. This gives you a warm or good feeling about the Indians, perhaps making you feel sympathy for them. Because of this feeling, you may believe that the defeat of the Indians was bad or wrong.

The third sentence uses the words "tribe of" to describe the Indians. These are *neutral* words. Neutral words make you feel neither good nor bad about the information. They leave you to develop your own feelings about it.

These three sentences present the same basic information: The soldiers defeated the Indians. But your understanding of the information and your feeling about it are different for the three sentences. The first sentence *can make you feel* good about the defeat. The second sentence *can make you feel* bad about the defeat. But the third sentence *does not* make you feel either good or bad about the defeat; it is a neutral sentence.

Words that make you feel one way or another are called "emotionally-loaded" words. They are "loaded" because they arouse feelings rather than just give neutral information. A writer who uses loaded words is said to write with *biased language*. The word "biased" means the opposite of neutral. When a person has a strong feeling about something (good, bad, useful, useless, etc.), we say that he or she has a "bias" or a "biased view." Such a person may use biased language to try to shape *your* feelings to agree with theirs. A critical reader or listener will watch out for this.

The exercises in this part of the unit will make you more aware of when and how a person may be using biased language. This way, you will recognize a person's bias and not be fooled into accepting his or her feelings about something without first questioning them. Instead, you will separate the person's bias from the neutral information he or she is presenting. Then you can form your own feelings about the information.

EXERCISE INSTRUCTIONS: SET A

Each exercise has two sentences. One sentence contains biased language (loaded words). The other sentence has only neutral words. First, read the sentences carefully and decide which one has biased language. On the blank provided, write the LOADED WORD(S) that are used in the biased sentence. Then study the other sentence. On the blank provided, write the NEUTRAL WORD(S) that are used in that sentence to replace the "loaded word(s)" in the biased sentence.

Finally, fill in the blank labelled BIAS ANALYSIS. Stop and think. A person who used the loaded words wants to make you feel that something is good or bad. Write a sentence telling *what is said to be good or bad*.

Study Example #1. Then try Example #2 on your own.

Example 1: **You will eat three dinners during the trip.**

You will enjoy three dinners during the trip.

LOADED WORD(S): ___enjoy___

NEUTRAL WORD(S): ___eat___

BIAS ANALYSIS: ___The dinners will be good and___

___this will make the trip___

___pleasant.___

The second sentence contains biased language because it has the loaded word "enjoy." Enjoy suggests that the dinners will be good or pleasant. "Eat" is a neutral word—it does not suggest that the dinners will be either good or bad. Note that the BIAS ANALYSIS *explains what the writer feels* about the dinners.

Example 2: Complete this example on your own before checking the answers.

Judy left the meeting with her attitude unimproved.
Judy left the meeting with her attitude unchanged.

LOADED WORD(S): _____

NEUTRAL WORD(S): _____

BIAS ANALYSIS: _____

_____

_____

Answers: LOADED WORD(S): __unimproved__

NEUTRAL WORD(S): __unchanged__

BIAS ANALYSIS: __Judy has a bad attitude that__

__needs to be improved.__

_____

The first sentence contains biased language because of the loaded word "unimproved." This word gives the feeling that Judy's attitude is bad and should be improved. In the second sentence, the neutral word "unchanged" does not suggest that Judy's attitude is either good or bad.

Complete the exercises in this same way. *Use a dictionary whenever you need help with a word's meaning.*

SET A

EXERCISE 1

Fireworks are a bright display of color.
Fireworks are an awesome display of color.

LOADED WORD(S): _____

NEUTRAL WORD(S): _____

BIAS ANALYSIS: _____

_____

EXERCISE 2

Our dishonest mayor will run again in the next election.
Our present mayor will run again in the next election.

LOADED WORD(S): _____

NEUTRAL WORD(S): _____

BIAS ANALYSIS: _____

_____

EXERCISE 3

There was a large increase in the world population last year.
There was an alarming increase in the world population last year.

LOADED WORD(S): _____

NEUTRAL WORD(S): _____

BIAS ANALYSIS: _____

_____

EXERCISE 4

Congress passed a long-overdue anti-smoking law.
Congress passed a brand new anti-smoking law.

LOADED WORD(S): _____

NEUTRAL WORD(S): _____

BIAS ANALYSIS: _____

_____

EXERCISE 5

Joanne constantly refused her friend's offers of tutoring.
Joanne stubbornly refused her friend's offers of tutoring.

LOADED WORD(S): _____

NEUTRAL WORD(S): _____

BIAS ANALYSIS: _____

_____

EXERCISE 6

Juan is always volunteering different ideas.
Juan is always volunteering odd ideas.

LOADED WORD(S): _____

NEUTRAL WORD(S): _____

BIAS ANALYSIS: _____

_____

EXERCISE 7

The traps held several small beavers.
The traps held several helpless, frightened young beavers.

LOADED WORD(S): _____

NEUTRAL WORD(S): _____

BIAS ANALYSIS: _____

_____

EXERCISE 8

Benedict Arnold routinely located his troops around the city.
Benedict Arnold brilliantly located his troops around the city.

LOADED WORD(S): _____

NEUTRAL WORD(S): _____

BIAS ANALYSIS: _____

_____

SET B: EXERCISE INSTRUCTIONS

Nine words and their definitions are listed below. Read the words and study the definitions.

tramp: bum; dirty, homeless beggar or thief

mob: disorderly, unruly crowd that could easily become violent

matured: became older and wiser

democracy: form of government in which people vote for their leaders (often considered the best or highest form of government)

dishonesty: lack of honesty

plight: bad situation or condition

slaughtered: killed in a bloody or violent way

sentenced: given a punishment by some authority; made to suffer in some way

wreck: something broken or worn out

Each of the following exercises is a sentence with an underlined word. Read the sentence for its meaning. Then, cross out the underlined word and *above it write a word from the list that is more emotionally loaded.* The first one is done for you.

SET B

EXERCISE 1: The ~~man~~ *tramp* asked us for money.

EXERCISE 2: Does your mother really enjoy driving that <u>car</u>?

EXERCISE 3: His <u>personality</u> was shown by his actions in business dealings.

EXERCISE 4: I was <u>asked</u> to do the dishes every day next week.

EXERCISE 5: A large <u>group</u> of students entered the cafeteria.

EXERCISE 6: The hunters <u>caught</u> several dozen seals.

EXERCISE 7: The <u>situation</u> in which they found themselves was their own fault.

EXERCISE 8: Send money to support the <u>government</u> in this Central American country.

EXERCISE 9: Don's taste in music has not yet <u>changed</u> to the point of appreciating classical symphonies.

PART II: Fact or Opinion?

Sometimes when a person makes a statement we say, "That is not a *fact*, it is just your personal *opinion*." A fact is a clear, straightforward description of a situation. But an opinion is a statement someone believes is true, but which others may argue is not true. It is a judgement, not a straightforward description.

For example, a politician might say, "My last four years in office have been *very successful*, so vote for me in the next election." When he says "very successful" this is a judgement and his opinion. Some people might not agree with that statement. Before agreeing with him, you would want to know what he means by "very successful." Has the number of crimes gone down? Does the region have more money now? Do more people have jobs than before? Until questions like these are answered, his statement is his *opinion* and not a clear fact.

Compare these two statements. One is an opinion. The other is a fact.

> **OPINION:** **The building is tall.**
> **FACT:** **The building has 20 floors.**

The word "tall" is a judgement rather than a clear description. For a small farming town in Wyoming, a 20-floor building might be called tall. But in New York City or Los Angeles, a 20-floor building might be considered short. Therefore, saying the building is tall is an opinion—some people may agree and some may disagree. On the other hand, saying that the building has 20 floors is stating a fact. A 20-floor building has 20 floors whether it is located in Wyoming or New York City or anywhere else. The statement is a clear, straightforward description.

The exercises in this part of the unit will improve your ability to identify statements as facts or opinions. This is an important critical reading skill. It gives you the power to decide if what you read or hear is a straightforward description or simply someone's personal judgement which may not actually be true.

EXERCISE INSTRUCTIONS

Each exercise presents a statement that describes some situation. First, decide if the statement presents a *fact* about the situation or gives an *opinion* about the situation. Write your answer in the blank labelled FACT OR OPINION.

Then, in the space labelled EXPLANATION, write one or two sentences explaining your answer. If you said the statement is an *opinion*, explain which word or words give a judgement on which people might disagree. If you answered *fact*, explain which word or words present a clear description that is definitely true.

Try the following example. Write your answers before checking the ones given below.

EXAMPLE 1: I have the toughest math teacher in the school.

FACT OR OPINION: _____

EXPLANATION: _____

_____

_____

Answers: Here is how you could have answered this exercise. (The exact words you used to give your explanation may be different from those here, but should state the same ideas.)

FACT OR OPINION: _opinion_

EXPLANATION: "Toughest in the school"

is a judgement. Some students may disagree

with that and feel their own math teacher is

tougher.

Now try the next example.

EXAMPLE 2: My math teacher gives a quiz every Friday.

FACT OR OPINION: _____

EXPLANATION: _____

_____

_____

Check your answers against those on the next page. Again, the exact words you used to give your explanation may be different from those shown. Make sure, though, that they state the same ideas.

Answers: **FACT OR OPINION:** ___fact___

EXPLANATION: ___"A quiz every Friday" states a___

___definite fact.___

When you read this statement, you should have noted that it did not give a judgement. Rather, it gave a clear description of something definitely true. Now try the exercises.

EXERCISE 1

This cup of tea is too sweet.

FACT OR OPINION: _____

EXPLANATION: _____

_____

EXERCISE 2

This cup of tea has five teaspoons of sugar in it.

FACT OR OPINION: _____

EXPLANATION: _____

_____

EXERCISE 3

The temperature in St. Louis today is 85°.

FACT OR OPINION: _____

EXPLANATION: _____

_____

EXERCISE 4

It is uncomfortably hot in St. Louis today.

FACT OR OPINION: _____

EXPLANATION: _____

_____

EXERCISE 5

This is a 15-watt light bulb.

FACT OR OPINION: _____

EXPLANATION: _____

_____

EXERCISE 6

This is a very dim light bulb.

FACT OR OPINION: _____

EXPLANATION: _____

_____

EXERCISE 7

The military action has been successful.

FACT OR OPINION: _____

EXPLANATION: _____

_____

EXERCISE 8

The president of the enemy country surrendered.

FACT OR OPINION: _____

EXPLANATION: _____

_____

EXERCISE 9

I have the prettiest dress at the party.

FACT OR OPINION: _____

EXPLANATION: _____

_____

EXERCISE 10

That woman is a professional photographer.

FACT OR OPINION: _____

EXPLANATION: _____

_____

EXERCISE 11

That woman is a highly talented photographer.

FACT OR OPINION: _____

EXPLANATION: _____

_____

EXERCISE 12

Art owns a fast car.

FACT OR OPINION: _____

EXPLANATION: _____

_____

EXERCISE 13

The Grand Canyon is the most awesome sight on earth.

FACT OR OPINION: _____

EXPLANATION: _____

_____

EXERCISE 14

In land size, Europe is the smallest continent.

FACT OR OPINION: _____

EXPLANATION: _____

_____

PART III: Propaganda

The word *propaganda* refers to information presented by someone in order to influence (shape) other people's opinion about something. By influencing the other people's opinion, the person using propaganda hopes to get them to think or do something the people might not otherwise think or do.

Advertisers and others who try to influence your opinion use certain propaganda techniques (methods). With careful thinking, you can learn to recognize and guard against such propaganda. As an example, compare these two statements:

TV star Ed Mulligan feeds Chow Wow dog food to his dog.
A heavy-set, cheerful man feeds Chow Wow dog food to his dog.

The first sentence uses what is called the "Famous People" technique. Advertisers know that if you think a famous person uses their product, you will be more likely to buy it yourself. So, they try to influence your opinion about their product by telling you that a famous person uses it. The second sentence gives the same information, but without the "Famous People" technique. See the difference?

Below are some examples of other propaganda techniques commonly used to influence your opinion. Study each example and then the Critical Analysis. The Critical Analysis shows what a critical person should think about when he/she hears or reads that type of propaganda.

Expert From Another Field

Example: Dr. Arthur Whimbey, author of books to improve your mind, uses Hi-Vi vitamins.

Critical Analysis: The fact that Dr. Whimbey is an expert in improving the mind does not make him an expert on vitamins.

(NOTE: This is a little different from the "Famous People" technique. Scientific experts are generally not famous. But you may respect them and therefore their names might influence your opinion.)

Fancy Technical Language

Example: Our hair tonic contains two parts hydrogen combined with one part oxygen.

Critical Analysis: Two parts hydrogen combined with one part oxygen is water. The tonic contains water!

Many People Are Doing It (also called Smart People Know This)

Example: More than two million people have taken our speed reading
            course.

Critical Analysis: Maybe two million people wasted their time and
                money. It doesn't say that the course helped these two million
                people.

These are only some of the propaganda techniques used to influence your opinion. You can read about others in books about propaganda. But studying the main ones listed will give you an understanding of propaganda, and help you guard your mind against their influence. That is the purpose of this part of the unit.

EXERCISE INSTRUCTIONS

Here are the four propaganda techniques described in the Introduction:

Famous People
Expert From Another Field
Fancy Technical Language
Many People Are Doing It (Smart People Know This).

Each of the following exercises has two statements. The first statement uses one of the four propaganda techniques. The second statement does not. Decide which technique is being used in the first statement and write its title in the blank labelled PROPAGANDA TECHNIQUE. Try this example and then check your work below.

EXAMPLE:

All of my friends have 10-speed bicycles.
Some of my friends have 10-speed bicycles.

PROPAGANDA TECHNIQUE: _____

Answer:

PROPAGANDA TECHNIQUE: __Many People Are Doing It__

Now begin the exercises.

EXERCISE 1: Football star Mack Johnson shaves with Slick razors.
A tall, husky man shaves with Slick razors.

PROPAGANDA TECHNIQUE: _____

EXERCISE 2: All intelligent people agree that taxes must be reduced.
Some people hold the view that taxes must be reduced.
PROPAGANDA TECHNIQUE: _____

EXERCISE 3: This Blare stereo has a power-activation lever.
This Blare stereo has an on-off switch.

PROPAGANDA TECHNIQUE: _____

EXERCISE 4: Medical scientist Lloyd Jenkins wears Player Shirts.
A man named Lloyd Jenkins wears Player Shirts.

PROPAGANDA TECHNIQUE: _____

EXERCISE 5: More people use Stink Stick than any other deodorant.
Some people use Stink Stick deodorant.

PROPAGANDA TECHNIQUE: _____

EXERCISE 6: Don Wong, star of *Chinatown*, eats Moo Shu TV-dinners.
A middle-aged man eats Moo Shu TV-dinners.

PROPAGANDA TECHNIQUE: _____

EXERCISE 7: Work for Local Bell as a telecommunications coordinator.
Work for Local Bell as a telephone operator.

PROPAGANDA TECHNIQUE: _____

EXERCISE 8: Only a fool would not agree that a Corvette is the best car made.
Some people would not agree that a Corvette is the best car made.

PROPAGANDA TECHNIQUE: _____

EXERCISE 9: Our toothpaste is a decay-preventing dentifrice.
Our toothpaste cleans your teeth.

PROPAGANDA TECHNIQUE: _____

ADDITIONAL ASSIGNMENTS

1. On a separate piece of paper, write three exercises like the ones in Part I Set A of this unit. To create each exercise, first write a sentence that contains a "neutral" word or phrase. Then write that sentence again, but replace the neutral word or phrase with a "loaded" word or phrase.

   Ask a classmate or friend to read your sentences and to write the "loaded word(s)" and the "neutral word(s)." Then ask that person to explain aloud *why* the loaded word(s) makes the sentence biased (the "bias analysis").

2. Find an interesting *editorial* in your local newspaper or in a newsmagazine. Copy or cut out this editorial. Then follow these steps:

   a) Read carefully and find if the writer used any "loaded word(s)."

   b) Circle each instance of "loaded word(s)" and make a list of them on a separate piece of paper.

   c) Next to each "loaded word(s)" you listed, write a "neutral word(s)" that could replace the loaded one.

   d) On a new piece of paper, rewrite the editorial *using your "neutral word(s)" instead of the original "loaded word(s)."*

   e) Reread the original editorial and your new version. On the back of your new version, write a short essay *explaining the bias* that was used in the original editorial to shape your opinion about the subject.

3. Find another interesting editorial in a newspaper or newsmagazine. Copy or cut out this editorial. Read the editorial carefully. Draw a circle around every *opinion* that is given by the writer. Draw a line under every *fact* presented by the writer.

   Reread the editorial and study the opinions and facts. Does the writer use facts to support the opinions, or are the opinions given without supporting facts? On a separate piece of paper, write a short essay stating *your opinion about how well the writer supported opinions with facts*. In your essay, give examples from the editorial to support your opinion.

4. Pick one advertisement from a newspaper or magazine. Copy or cut out this ad. Then follow these steps:

   a) Put an "X" through every "loaded word(s)" used in the ad. List them on a separate piece of paper. Next to each one, write a "neutral word(s)" that could replace it.

   b) Draw a circle around every *opinion* given in the ad. Draw a line under every *fact* presented.

   c) Decide if the ad uses one of the four "propaganda techniques" you learned about on pages 238 and 239. Below your list of loaded words, write the name for the propaganda technique if one was used. If you think a propaganda technique was used but it wasn't one of the four you learned about, write a short description of this new type of propaganda. If you don't think a propaganda technique was used, write "NOT PROPAGANDA."

Reading For Full Comprehension IV: Putting It All Together

OBJECTIVES

When you have completed this unit you will

- be able to choose the best title that tells the overall topic of a reading passage;

- be able to identify titles that are too narrow and too broad for a given reading passage;

- be able to select a statement that best describes the main idea of a reading passage;

- be able to answer questions that ask you to interpret details presented in a reading passage;

- be able to identify a statement that is implied but not directly stated in a reading passage;

- be able to use context clues to figure out the meaning of a word as it is used in a certain reading passage.

INTRODUCTION

In the previous 15 units of this book you have made major gains in your reading ability. You have learned to:

- read carefully in order to fully comprehend a writer's meaning;
- use all of the information in a passage to understand the main idea;
- pay close attention to details to pinpoint facts;
- dissect a complex sentence to figure out its message;
- reason soundly to draw conclusions that are only implied by what is directly stated.

This unit will give you one more opportunity to sharpen your comprehension skills for mastering the type of reading material that you will encounter in advanced textbooks and also on standardized reading tests. The unit consists of reading passages followed by comprehension questions, similar to those you worked in Units 6, 11 and 14. Since this unit is the final one in your study of this book, the passages and questions will require you to use all of the skills you have been developing.

When you have completed this unit, you should feel confident that you have become better prepared to successfully tackle the reading material you will encounter throughout your schooling and later in the working world. You have become better equipped to succeed in school—and to advance upward to a good position in today's technological world.

EXERCISE INSTRUCTIONS

Since the format of this unit is similar to that of three units you have already completed, you will not need a practice exercise. Instead, the first reading selection is short and relatively easy, giving you a chance to warm-up your comprehension mental muscles. The remaining selections become increasingly complex. Read each selection thoughtfully, then reason accurately in answering the questions. Challenge yourself to achieve 100% accuracy!

PASSAGE A

1 Canine heartworm disease, once found
2 only in the southwestern United States, is
3 spreading north and west. Today it is a
4 problem for dog owners in 42 states and
5 Canada.
6 Heartworm disease is carried by mos-
7 quitoes. When a mosquito bites an infect-
8 ed dog, and then bites a healthy one, it
9 deposits infective larvae under the second
10 dog's skin. The larvae make their way
11 into the bloodstream, then to the heart. In
12 time they become adult heartworms, six
13 to 14 inches long.

1. Below are three possible titles for this passage. In each blank, write the letter of the phrase (A, B or C) which best describes that title.

    _____ Size of Adult Heartworms in Dogs
    Diseases of Dogs
    _____ Spread of Heartworm Disease in Dogs

    (A) comprehensive title
    (B) too narrow
    (C) too broad

2. Heartworm disease results when

    ☐ (A) an infected dog bites another dog
    ☐ (B) any mosquito bites a dog
    ☐ (C) a mosquito that has bitten an infected dog bites another dog
    ☐ (D) an infected heartworm bites a healthy dog

3. Previously, canine heartworm disease was found

    ☐ (A) in 42 states and Canada
    ☐ (B) in states like Georgia, South Carolina and Florida
    ☐ (C) in states like California, Nevada and Arizona
    ☐ (D) in states like New York, Maine and Connecticut

4. The word "canine" means

    ☐ (A) related to cans
    ☐ (B) related to dogs
    ☐ (C) related to the heart
    ☐ (D) related to worms

5. The passage does not state but *implies* that

    ☐ (A) heartworms grow inside a dog's heart
    ☐ (B) canine heartworm disease has spread to Europe
    ☐ (C) mosquitoes often die from canine heartworm disease
    ☐ (D) heartworms are a major part of a mosquito's diet

PASSAGE B

Vocabulary preview: **heir** (noun)—one who inherits the property or position of a person who has died.

triumvirate (noun)—a group or governing body made up of three persons.

¹ Caesar had made his grand-nephew and ² adopted son, Octavian, his heir. In 43 B.C., ³ Octavian, Mark Antony, and Lepidus ⁴ formed the Second Triumvirate. They ⁵ wanted to bring order to the Roman ⁶ Empire and to punish the murderers of ⁷ Caesar. They attacked Brutus and the oth- ⁸ ers, defeating them in the Battle of Philippi ⁹ in 42 B.C.
¹⁰ Now Octavian and Mark Antony, the two ¹¹ chief members of the Second Triumvirate, ¹² quarreled. Mark Antony wanted to rule the ¹³ East with Cleopatra, queen of Egypt. When ¹⁴ Mark Antony gave Cleopatra some Roman ¹⁵ lands, Octavian persuaded the Romans to ¹⁶ declare war on Egypt. He defeated Mark ¹⁷ Antony and the Egyptian navy at Actium, ¹⁸ off the coast of Greece, in 31 B.C. Mark ¹⁹ Antony and Cleopatra fled, and both killed ²⁰ themselves. Now Egypt, too, was complete- ²¹ ly subject to Rome.

1. Below are three possible titles for this passage. In each blank, write the letter of the phrase (A, B or C) which best describes that title.

    _____ Formation of the Second Trium-
    virate
    _____ The Second Triumvirate and
    Roman Expansion
    _____ History of Rome and Egypt

    (A) too broad
    (B) too narrow
    (C) comprehensive title

2. Caesar was Octavian's

    ☐ (A) grand-nephew
    ☐ (B) grand-father
    ☐ (C) grand-uncle
    ☐ (D) adopted son

3. The main idea of the selection is that

    ☐ (A) Caesar had made his grand-nephew and adopted son, Octavian, his heir
    ☐ (B) Octavian, Mark Antony, and Lepidus formed the Second Triumvirate
    ☐ (C) the Second Triumvirate was formed to bring order to Rome, but conflicts among its members destroyed it while enlarging the Roman Empire
    ☐ (D) Octavian defeated Mark Antony and the Egyptian navy at Actium

4. The selection *implies* that one of Caesar's murderers was

    ☐ (A) Brutus
    ☐ (B) Mark Antony
    ☐ (C) Cleopatra
    ☐ (D) Octavian

5. The selection does not state but *implies* that

    ☐ (A) there had been a triumvirate before the one formed by Octavian, Mark Antony, and Lepidus
    ☐ (B) Caesar had died of disease
    ☐ (C) Octavian, Mark Antony, and Lepidus formed the Second Triumvirate
    ☐ (D) Mark Antony wanted to rule the East with Cleopatra

6. Which statement is correct?

    ☐ (A) Mark Antony died fighting with the Egyptian navy at Actium
    ☐ (B) Mark Antony committed suicide
    ☐ (C) Mark Antony was the last surviving member of the Triumvirate

PASSAGE C

¹   The surface of the earth is divided into the eastern hemisphere
² and the western hemisphere. The continents of North America
³ and South America are the western hemisphere. But each of these
⁴ continents is also in another hemisphere, for the surface of the
⁵ earth is also divided into the northern hemisphere and the south-
⁶ ern hemisphere. The dividing line between these two hemi-
⁷ spheres is the equator. The equator is a line that goes all the way
⁸ around the globe and is always exactly halfway between the
⁹ North Pole and the South Pole. All the surface of the earth north
¹⁰ of the equator is in the northern hemisphere and all the surface
¹¹ of the earth south of the equator is in the southern hemisphere.
¹² North America is north of the equator from Panama and South
¹³ America is south of the equator from Panama.

1. Below are three possible titles for this passage. In each blank, write the letter of the phrase (A, B or C) which best describes that title.

_____ The Eastern and Western Hemispheres

_____ Hemispheres into Which the Earth is Divided

_____ Geographical Divisions of the Earth

   (A) too narrow
   (B) too broad
   (C) comprehensive title

2. The equator is a line which divides the earth into

   ☐ (A) eastern and western hemispheres
   ☐ (B) northern and southern hemispheres
   ☐ (C) northern and eastern hemispheres
   ☐ (D) southern and western hemispheres

3. The equator is a line that runs

   ☐ (A) east–north
   ☐ (B) west–north
   ☐ (C) east–west
   ☐ (D) north–south

4. The equator runs through which?

   ☐ (A) North America
   ☐ (B) North Pole
   ☐ (C) South America
   ☐ (D) Panama

5. India is north of the equator and on the opposite side of the earth from the Americas. Therefore, India is in the

   ☐ (A) northern and southern hemispheres
   ☐ (B) northern and western hemispheres
   ☐ (C) northern and eastern hemispheres
   ☐ (D) southern and eastern hemispheres

6. As it is used in this passage, the word *hemisphere* means

   ☐ (A) southern
   ☐ (B) a half of a round three-dimensional object, like half a ball
   ☐ (C) a round three-dimensional object, like a ball
   ☐ (D) western

7. Since "hemi" means "half," a sphere is

   ☐ (A) a half of a round three-dimensional object, like half a ball
   ☐ (B) a round three-dimensional object, like a ball
   ☐ (C) one-half of the land south of the equator
   ☐ (D) one-half of the land west of the equator

PASSAGE D

¹ In 1588 a combined Spanish and
² Portuguese fleet was sent to conquer
³ England. Proudly the Spanish monarch
⁴ called his ships the Invincible Armada. The
⁵ Spanish ships were huge and heavily armed,
⁶ but the smaller English vessels could sail
⁷ faster and shoot farther. Sir Francis Drake, by
⁸ then one of the English admirals, understood
⁹ clearly the changes in sea fighting made pos-
¹⁰ sible by gunpowder. When the lumbering
¹¹ Spanish and Portuguese vessels came up the
¹² English Channel, the English riddled the
¹³ enemy with shot before they could get near
¹⁴ enough to grapple the English ships and
¹⁵ board for hand-to-hand combat. The shat-
¹⁶ tered remnant of the Invincible Armada was
¹⁷ driven into the North Sea and scattered by
¹⁸ storms.

1. Below are three possible titles for this
   passage. In each blank, write the letter of
   the phrase (A, B or C) which best describes
   that title.

   _____ The Invincible Armada of Spain
           and Portugal
   _____ English Naval Victory Over
           Armada of Spain and Portugal
   _____ Major Naval Battles of the 1500s

   (A) too broad
   (B) too narrow
   (C) comprehensive title

2. The Armada was

   ☐ (A) the Spanish monarch
   ☐ (B) the ships of Sir Francis Drake
   ☐ (C) the Spanish and Portuguese fleet
   ☐ (D) the English and Spanish fleet

3. According to the selection, the Spanish
   fleet

   ☐ (A) had larger vessels but less effec-
         tive guns
   ☐ (B) had bigger guns that could shoot
         farther
   ☐ (C) had bigger, faster ships
   ☐ (D) had gunpowder for their guns

4. The selection suggests that boarding the
   enemy's ships was

   ☐ (A) the plan of Sir Francis Drake
   ☐ (B) successful and brought victory
   ☐ (C) the plan of the English
   ☐ (D) the plan of the Spanish and
         Portuguese

5. According to the context, in line 10 the
   word *lumbering* means

   ☐ (A) made of lumber
   ☐ (B) large and slow
   ☐ (C) very quick
   ☐ (D) ships used just for shipping lumber

6. According to the selection,

   ☐ (A) the Spanish defeated the English
         by fighting at a distance rather
         than close
   ☐ (B) the English defeated the Spanish
         by fighting at a distance rather
         than close
   ☐ (C) the Spanish defeated the English
         by fighting close rather than at a
         distance
   ☐ (D) the English defeated the Spanish
         by fighting close rather than at a
         distance

7. As used in this context, the word *grapple*
   in line 14 means

   ☐ (A) attach onto with hooks
   ☐ (B) sink with hooks
   ☐ (C) move away from during a struggle
   ☐ (D) blow up during a struggle

PASSAGE E

1 After the initial discoveries of Columbus, Spaniards were quick to explore the
2 New World. In 1513 Ponce de Leon discovered Florida. That same year Balboa
3 (ca. 1475-1519) and a small band of hardy adventurers hacked their way across
4 the fever-ridden Isthmus of Panama through jungles teeming with poisonous
5 snakes and hostile Indians until they reached the Pacific Ocean, which he named
6 the South Sea. In 1518-21, with only about 600 men, Cortes (1485-1546) con-
7 quered the splendid and rich state of Mexico. In 1531-33 Pizarro (ca. 1475-1541)
8 with even fewer men took Peru. Both conquests succeeded because of the personal
9 courage of the *Conquistadores* (Conquerors), in addition to their cruelty, duplici-
10 ty, and superior weapons. Besides, both the Aztecs of Mexico and the Incas of
11 Peru were politically divided at the time of the conquests. Cortes acquired Indian
12 allies in Mexico. Pizarro found the Incas in the middle of a civil war. In each case
13 the conquests cost the Spanish government nothing. These two expeditions had royal
14 authorization but were privately financed. Within a generation thereafter Spanish
15 explorers traveled widely through the western hemisphere. In 1541 Orellana made
16 a dramatic 3000-mile journey through the heart of South America, from the Andes
17 mountains eastward down the Amazon river to the Atlantic. In 1540-42 Coronado
18 explored North America as far north as the present state of Kansas. In 1542-43
19 Ferello explored the Pacific coast as far north as the present state of Oregon.

1. Below are three possible titles for this passage. In each blank, write the letter of the phrase (A, B or C) which best describes that title.

_____ Ponce de Leon's Discovery of Florida
_____ Early Spanish Explorers and Conquerors in the Americas
_____ History of South America

   (A) comprehensive title
   (B) too broad
   (C) too narrow

2. Florida, Kansas, and Oregon were explored, respectively, by

   ☐ (A) Coronado, Ferello, and Ponce de Leon
   ☐ (B) Ponce de Leon, Coronado, and Cortes
   ☐ (C) Ponce de Leon, Coronado, and Ferello
   ☐ (D) Ponce de Leon, Balboa, and Cortes

3. The selection indicates that Cortes

   ☐ (A) hacked through teeming jungles with poisonous snakes
   ☐ (B) conquered the Incas
   ☐ (C) conquered the Aztecs
   ☐ (D) sailed down the Amazon River

4. Which was not a factor in the conquest of the Incas and Aztecs?

   ☐ (A) The Spaniards had better tools of war.
   ☐ (B) The Spaniards had the financial support of their government.
   ☐ (C) The Spaniards were brave.
   ☐ (D) The Spaniards were cruel and deceptive.

5. According to the selection, the Indians

   ☐ (A) fought together bravely, but were beaten by the large Spanish army
   ☐ (B) did not present a joint defense, and this contributed to their defeat
   ☐ (C) trapped the Spaniards in the teeming jungles with poisonous snakes
   ☐ (D) were cruel, so were punished with defeat by the Spaniards

6. Which statement is true?

   ☐ (A) Pizzaro conquered the Incas before a Spaniard travelled down the Amazon river but after another Spaniard had reached what he called the South Sea.
   ☐ (B) The Incas were fighting a civil war after Cortes conquered Mexico but before the Spanish crossed Panama.
   ☐ (C) Both (A) and (B) are true.

PASSAGE F

1 What the study of anatomy needed was
2 careful observation and an open mind.
3 Renaissance artists and scholars brought
4 both to the field. Painters studied human
5 anatomy carefully so that they might
6 show the smallest details correctly. Some
7 of them, such as Leonardo da Vinci, even
8 dissected human bodies. They made care-
9 ful drawings of what they saw. Later they
10 published their findings so that scholars
11 could study them.
12 As they read more of the classical med-
13 ical texts discovered during the
14 Renaissance, European scholars found
15 that the ancients had disagreed with one
16 another. That gave sixteenth century
17 scholars the courage to challenge Galen,
18 as Copernicus had challenged Ptolemy on
19 astronomy. Andreas Vesalius, a professor
20 at the University of Padua, was the first
21 to contribute important new knowledge to
22 anatomy.
23 Even as a schoolboy, Vesalius showed
24 great curiosity about the structure of the
25 body. He dissected bodies of mice, rats,
26 dogs, and cats. At the university he stud-
27 ied with some of the best doctors of his
28 time. But Vesalius was disappointed to
29 learn that everything his teachers knew
30 came from Galen's ideas. They had done
31 little or no dissection to gain first-hand
32 knowledge.
33 Vesalius began looking in cemeteries
34 for skeletons to study. Once he took a
35 corpse down from the gallows in the mid-
36 dle of the night in order to examine it. He
37 did many dissections. In 1543 he pub-
38 lished a book with illustrations correctly
39 showing human veins and arteries.

1. Below are three possible titles for this passage. In each blank, write the letter of the phrase (A, B or C) which best describes that title.

   _____ History and Description of Human Anatomy
   _____ Contribution of Renaissance Artists and Scholars to Anatomy
   _____ Leonardo da Vinci's Contribution to Anatomy

   (A) comprehensive title
   (B) too narrow
   (C) too broad

2. Which date is included in the period called the Renaissance?

   ☐ (A) 500 B.C.
   ☐ (B) 500 A.D.
   ☐ (C) 1500 A.D.
   ☐ (D) 1900 A.D.

3. The best definition of "anatomy" is: The science of

   ☐ (A) the skeletons of corpses
   ☐ (B) the history of medical knowledge
   ☐ (C) illustrations showing human veins and arteries
   ☐ (D) the structures of animal and human bodies

4. Leonardo da Vinci was a

   ☐ (A) professor at the University of Padua
   ☐ (B) doctor
   ☐ (C) painter
   ☐ (D) astronomer

5. The selection does not state but *implies* that

   ☐ (A) Galen was an ancient authority on astronomy
   ☐ (B) Galen was an ancient authority on anatomy
   ☐ (C) Galen was a modern authority on astronomy
   ☐ (D) Galen was a modern authority on anatomy

6. Ptolemy and Copernicus studied

   ☐ (A) astronomy
   ☐ (B) anatomy
   ☐ (C) Renaissance art

7. Who among the following challenged Galen?

   ☐ (A) Vesalius
   ☐ (B) Ptolemy
   ☐ (C) Copernicus
   ☐ (D) All of the above

8. Which pair of words best completes this analogy: PTOLEMY is to COPERNICUS as

   ☐ (A) VESALIUS is to PADUA
   ☐ (B) VESALIUS is to GALEN
   ☐ (C) GALEN is to VESALIUS
   ☐ (D) DA VINCI is to VESALIUS

9. The main idea of the selection is:

   ☐ (A) During the Renaissance, Leonardo da Vinci dissected human bodies to learn anatomy
   ☐ (B) During the Renaissance, progress in anatomy was made by studying the writings of ancients such as Galen
   ☐ (C) During the Renaissance, progress in anatomy was made by studying human bodies rather than depending solely on the writings of the ancients
   ☐ (D) During the Ranaissance, Vesalius took a corpse down from the gallows to examine it

10. The selection *implies* that in the period immediately preceding Vesalius' work

    ☐ (A) corpses were not widely used in medical research
    ☐ (B) corpses were widely used in medical research
    ☐ (C) Renaissance artists never observed human anatomy
    ☐ (D) Vesalius' teachers had dissected bodies to study anatomy

11. Vesalius' teachers based their knowledge of anatomy on

    ☐ (A) a book by Vesalius published in 1563 with illustrations showing human veins and arteries
    ☐ (B) the writings of an ancient scholar rather than their own observations
    ☐ (C) the writings of a sixteenth century scholar rather than their own observations
    ☐ (D) their observations of animal and human bodies

12. Which statement is supported by the selection?

    ☐ (A) Outstanding researchers sometimes develop an interest in their area at a young age.
    ☐ (B) Before Vesalius, a number of doctors at the University of Padua dissected human bodies and made careful drawings of what they saw.
    ☐ (C) Painters could not contribute much to the study of anatomy.
    ☐ (D) Copernicus challenged old ideas on anatomy.

13. The selection *implies* but does not state that

    ☐ (A) Vesalius looked in cemeteries for skeletons to study
    ☐ (B) ancient medical authorities agreed with each other on anatomical facts
    ☐ (C) before the Renaissance, few ancient medical books were available and read
    ☐ (D) Vesalius was the first to contribute important new knowledge to anatomy

Note: The two final passages contain several challenging vocabulary words. When you encounter an unfamiliar word, use the skills you have learned in this book to try to figure out the word's meaning from the context. Hint — Read forward and backward a few sentences around each word to find context clues that tell what the word means.

PASSAGE G

1 Coal-mining was becoming a big business in
2 the eighteenth-century, partly because of the
3 increased demand for coal by iron-smelters. For
4 centuries, the smelters had used charcoal to
5 make iron from the raw ore, and they contin-
6 ued to do so in countries like Sweden that had
7 abundant wood for charcoal. But in England,
8 where almost all the great forests had been cut
9 down, the price of charcoal rose so high that it
10 constituted 80 per cent of the cost of producing
11 iron. By 1750, despite the abundant native sup-
12 ply of ore, the output of English smelters was
13 declining rapidly, and the country was relying
14 more and more on imported iron. Ordinary coal
15 could not replace charcoal as smelter fuel
16 because the chemicals in coal made the iron too
17 brittle. Here necessity mothered invention. The
18 Darby family of Coalbrookdale in Shropshire
19 discovered how to remove the chemical impuri-
20 ties from coal by converting it into coke
21 through an oven process. Since coke was almost
22 pure carbon, it produced iron of high quality.
23 In England, the Darbys and other private
24 firms were the pioneers in metallurgy. On the
25 Continent, governments took the lead—a signif-
26 icant exception to the rule about the inability of
27 states to solve economic problems. Warfare
28 required weapons and munitions in unprece-
29 dented quantities; France and Prussia met the
30 demand by setting up state-financed and state-
31 operated foundries and arms factories.

1. Below are three possible titles for this passage. In each blank, write the letter of the phrase (A, B or C) which best describes that title.

_____ Development of Coke in 18th-Century England
_____ The Iron Industry and Related Fuels in the 18th Century
_____ Development and Uses of Fuels Throughout History

(A) too narrow
(B) comprehensive title
(C) too broad

2. Iron production in England decreased because

☐ (A) the iron ore was being used up
☐ (B) there was a shortage of fuel needed in producing iron
☐ (C) the Darby family removed chemicals for coal
☐ (D) big business preferred to invest in coal-mining

3. According to the selection, the production of coal was stimulated by its use

☐ (A) in making charcoal
☐ (B) for heating homes
☐ (C) as a basic fuel that could be modified and substituted for wood
☐ (D) for adding chemicals to iron to make it brittle

4. By 1750, the price of charcoal in England had become extremely high because

☐ (A) there was very little wood left in England
☐ (B) there was very little wood left in countries like Sweden
☐ (C) there was very little coal left in countries like Sweden
☐ (D) there was very little coal left in England

5. Which statement is correct?

☐ (A) Charcoal is made from coke.
☐ (B) Coke is made from charcoal.
☐ (C) Charcoal and coke are made from wood and coal, respectively.
☐ (D) Coke and charcoal are made from wood and coal, respectively.

6. Which pair of words best completes this analogy: NECESSITY is to INVENTION as

☐ (A) BLACK is to GRAY
☐ (B) MOTHER is to CHILD
☐ (C) ILL is to SICK
☐ (D) FIRE is to LOG

7. As used in the selection in line 17, "necessity mothered invention" means:

☐ (A) because something was needed, someone produced a solution
☐ (B) because the problem was minor, there was no need to worry
☐ (C) because the Darby mother was an inventor, it was necessary for her to solve the problem

8. According to the selection, the production of iron was stimulated by its use in

☐ (A) making charcoal
☐ (B) making coke
☐ (C) providing a substitute for wood in England
☐ (D) making weapons

9. According to the selection, the iron industry was developed by

☐ (A) private enterprises in England, France, and Prussia
☐ (B) government in England, France, and Prussia
☐ (C) government in France and Prussia but private enterprise in England
☐ (D) government in England but private enterprise in France and Prussia

10. The author's opinion is that

☐ (A) in general, governments are ineffective in solving economic problems, although government made a positive contribution to the iron industry in England
☐ (B) in general, governments are ineffective in solving economic problems, although government made a positive contribution to the iron industry in France and Prussia
☐ (C) in general, governments are effective in solving economic problems, as illustrated by the iron industry in France and Prussia
☐ (D) in general, governments are effective in solving economic problems, but one exception is the government's failure to help the iron industry in England

PASSAGE H

1 Civilization is not improvised. It is complex, fragile, slow-growing; it
2 neither moves in a straight line, nor climbs indefinitely upward, nor
3 advances—or recedes—at the same pace on every segment of its jagged
4 front. The first signals indicating its birth are so early and so faint as
5 almost to escape detection. They can be accepted as incontrovertible evi-
6 dence only on assuming tangible form as artifacts, that is, tools and
7 weapons clearly conceived by human intelligence and shaped by human
8 hands. Driven always to seek a better life, man began in the Old Stone
9 (Paleolithic) Age to fashion various stone implements, numbers of which
10 are constantly being excavated throughout the world. Roughly chipped,
11 first by percussion, then by pressure, these tools evolved slowly toward
12 higher efficiency and specialized forms. When man fashioned his first
13 tool, technology was born, however humble in processes or crude in
14 results. In the Old Stone Age, too, esthetic appreciation began. The wild-
15 animal drawings with which Stone Age Man adorned his caves have real
16 artistic merit. The New Stone (Neolithic) Age saw a revolution in methods
17 of making a living; man turned from food gathering to stockbreeding and
18 agriculture; gained skill in creating and handling textiles and ways of con-
19 structing earthen vessels, first by hand, later with the earliest machine ever
20 made, the potter's wheel. More significantly still, he organized the first
21 political society of which we find definite records, his village, ruled by the
22 clan chief.

1. Below are three possible titles for this passage. In each blank, write the letter of the phrase (A, B or C) which best describes that title.

   _____ The Beginning of Civilization
   _____ The History of Civilization
   _____ The Paleolithic Age

   (A) comprehensive title
   (B) too broad
   (C) too narrow

2. According to the passage,

   ☐ (A) civilization is complex, but with the advent of technology it developed rapidly
   ☐ (B) civilization develops slowly, with continual forward progress
   ☐ (C) civilization develops gradually, with uneven progress and sometimes even backward movement
   ☐ (D) civilization developed at about the same rate in different parts of the world

3. The word *detection*, as used in line 5, means

   ☐ (A) prison
   ☐ (B) being noticed
   ☐ (C) borders
   ☐ (D) leaving the country

4. As used in line 6, the word *artifacts* means

   ☐ (A) artificial facts which scientists have questioned
   ☐ (B) objects made and used by people
   ☐ (C) art facts, such as the finding of wild-animal drawings in caves
   ☐ (D) a village ruler

5. The passage *implies* that during the Old Stone Age man satisfied his nutritional needs by

   ☐ (A) stockbreeding
   ☐ (B) using food found in nature
   ☐ (C) agriculture
   ☐ (D) both A and C, but not B

6. In Greek, "paleo" means "old" and "neo" means "new." From the way the words paleolithic and neolithic are used in the passage, what does "lithos" mean in Greek?

☐ (A) stone
☐ (B) civilization
☐ (C) primitive
☐ (D) early

7. According to the passage, technology began when

☐ (A) the potter's wheel was invented
☐ (B) man turned from food gathering to stockbreeding and agriculture
☐ (C) primitive tools were made from stone
☐ (D) man organized the first political society

8. Which pair of words best completes this analogy: WILD-ANIMAL DRAWING is to ART as

☐ (A) EATING is to FOOD
☐ (B) AGRICULTURE is to APPLE
☐ (C) POTTER is to WHEEL
☐ (D) TOOL is to TECHNOLOGY

9. As used in line 9, the word *implements* means

☐ (A) tools
☐ (B) tries
☐ (C) practices
☐ (D) buildings

10. Which of the following would the author say is evidence of the earliest beginnings of civilization?

☐ (A) a granite axe
☐ (B) a potter's wheel
☐ (C) a slate arrowhead
☐ (D) both A and C, but not B

11. It is the author's opinion that

☐ (A) man keeps making mistakes that cause a crude way of living
☐ (B) man will soon outlaw the use of weapons
☐ (C) man is not able to change his way of living, no matter how hard he tries
☐ (D) man is always trying to create an improved way of living

ADDITIONAL ASSIGNMENTS

1. Pick an interesting passage that is about 250 words long from one of your textbooks, an encyclopedia or a news article. On a separate piece of paper, write at least five multiple-choice questions that would test a reader's understanding of the passage.

   Ask a classmate or friend to read the passage and answer your questions. Check and discuss the answers. If necessary, rewrite your questions until there is clearly a best answer to each.

2. *Write your own short passage* on a topic that interests you. Then write at least five multiple-choice questions for that passage. Have a classmate or friend read your passage and answer the questions.

3. Turn back to Passage H on page 254. In this passage the author presents both his/her opinions about early civilization as well as facts. Reread the passage. Draw a circle around every opinion that is given by the author.

4. Study the meaning of the word "heir" on page 246. Write a sentence on the lines below in which the meaning of "heir" can be *inferred from ideas in the sentence* (see Unit 2, CASE IV).

   _____

   _____

   _____

WORD POWER

Power Words
For Powerful Vocabulary

Contents

Power Word Index

INTRODUCTION

This section contains 12 WORD POWER vocabulary sets like the sets you completed in Unit 2. In addition, there are two WRITING REVIEW sets. These vocabulary sets have two main purposes:

(1) To develop your ability to use context clues to *reason out* the meaning of any unfamiliar word you come across in your reading:

(2) To increase the power of your language skill by adding 96 Power Words to your vocabulary.

Therefore, as you study these sets, concentrate on *how* to reason out a word's meaning as well as on mastering each specific word. Use what you learned in Unit 2 about the four cases of context clues to figure out each word's meaning.

EXERCISE INSTRUCTIONS

Follow the directions provided with each WORD POWER set. Read slowly and carefully. Try to get every answer correct. Here are some study hints for completing the exercises.

Context Sentences: Each context sentence uses one of the four cases of context clues to show the meaning of the Power Word. Decide which type of context clue is used in a sentence. Then use that clue to reason out the Power Word's meaning.

Meaning Comprehension: For each Power Word, find the definition that matches the meaning you reasoned out from the context sentence. After you choose a definition, re-read that Power Word's context sentence. Try to replace the Power Word with your chosen definition. Does the sentence make sense? If not, choose another definition until you find one that does make sense in the sentence.

Context Completion: Each Context Completion sentence has *two* blanks. Decide which Power Word you think goes in each blank. Then read the completed sentence to make sure *both* words make sense. To double check your answers, replace each Power Word with its definition from "Meaning Comprehension." Does the sentence make sense?

Muscle Builder Analogies: First, study the pair of words in which both words are given and find how the two words are related. For example: Do they mean the same thing?; Do they mean opposite things?; Is one word a "cause" and the other an "effect"?; and so on. Then use that relationship to find the Power Word that goes in the blank. *The new pair of words must be related in exactly the same way as were the given pair of words.*

Word Power 1

Directions: Study the Power Words below. Note how each word is pronounced. Then read the sentences carefully and use context clues to figure out the meaning of each Power Word.

When you're sure you know the meaning of every Power Word, complete the exercises on the next page.

Power Words	standard	yielded	proposed	horizontal
	vertical	displayed	passions	campaign

---

1. **standard** | **stăn′** dərd |
   - The poster was not of *standard* size and the "Frame Shop" did not have a frame that fit it.

2. **vertical** | **vŭr′** tĭ kəl |
   - A line running from the top of a page straight down to the page bottom is a *vertical* line.

3. **yielded** | **yēl′** dĭd |
   - The farmland was rich and fertile and *yielded* a large harvest of wheat every year.

4. **displayed** | dĭ **splād′** |
   - Chico Carrasco is one artist who *displayed* paintings at the art show last week.

5. **proposed** | prə **pōzd′** |
   - One committee member *proposed* that the next meeting should be on Tuesday, but another member suggested Wednesday would be a better day to meet.

6. **passions** | **păsh′** ənz |
   - Love and hate are opposite *passions*.

7. **horizontal** | hôr′ ĭ **zŏn′** tl |
   - The lines above and below the set of Power Words on this page are *horizontal* not vertical lines.

8. **campaign** | kăm **pān′** |
   - Before the school election, each student running for office carried out a *campaign* that included putting up posters and making speeches to all the classes.

ă pat / ā pay / â care / ä father / ĕ pet / ē be / ĭ pit / ī pie / î fierce / ŏ pot / ō go / ô paw, for / oi oil / ŏŏ book /
ŏŏ boot / ou out / ŭ cut / ü fur / *th* the / th thin / hw which / zh vision / ə ago, item, pencil, atom, circus

Meaning Comprehension

Directions: In the blank next to each Power Word, write the letter of its correct definition.

Power Words

_____ standard

_____ vertical

_____ yielded

_____ displayed

_____ proposed

_____ passions

_____ horizontal

_____ campaign

Definitions

a. strong feelings or emotions
b. showed, put on view for others to see
c. from side to side; level or flat
d. up and down; upright, standing straight up
e. usual, typical, normal, average
f. produced, provided; gave up
g. a series of activities done in order to reach a goal
h. suggested, recommended

Context Completion

Directions: Each sentence below has two blanks. Choose and then write the Power Word that goes in each blank. Use each Power Word only once.

1. Some people are afraid to show their feelings, so they keep their _____ hidden rather than _____ .

2. Most telephone poles are _____ and the telephone wires strung between two poles are usually _____ .

3. When we cut the tray of fudge into _____ one-inch pieces, we found that two pounds of fudge _____ 32 pieces.

4. A group of policemen _____ that the chief of police start a _____ to get elected as mayor.

Muscle Builder Analogies

Directions: Each exercise below is an incomplete analogy. Choose the Power Word that best completes each analogy and write it in the blank. Write only Power Words in the blanks.

1. UPRIGHT is to VERTICAL _as_ LEVEL is to _____

2. HIDDEN is to DISPLAYED _as_ UNUSUAL is to _____

3. CARROT is to VEGETABLES _as_ LOVE is to _____

Word Power 2

Directions: Study the Power Words below. Note how each word is pronounced. Then read the sentences carefully and use context clues to figure out the meaning of each Power Word.

When you're sure you know the meaning of every Power Word, complete the exercises on the next page.

Power Words	legend	dispute	incident	municipal
	excess	heroic	sufficient	federal

1. **legend** | **lĕj′** ənd |
   - The *legend* of Robin Hood is a group of stories about an English outlaw famous for robbing from the rich and giving to the poor.

2. **excess** | **ĕk′** sĕs |
   - We had three cups of milk and needed only two for the recipe, so we had an *excess* of one cup of milk.

3. **dispute** | dĭ **spyōōt′** |
   - The loaf of bread had two price stickers on it, so we knew there would be a *dispute* about the correct price when we went to the cash register.

4. **heroic** | hĭ **rō′** ĭk |
   - The woman rushed onto the highway to grab the child before cars came and her *heroic* action surely saved the child's life.

5. **incident** | **ĭn′** sĭ dənt |
   - The incident I remember best from my childhood is receiving a silver star during the Scout awards.

6. **sufficient** | sə **fĭsh′** ənt |
   - Two cups of milk were *sufficient* for the recipe, so we drank the extra one cup left in the bottle.

7. **municipal** | myōō **nĭs′** ə pəl |
   - A *municipal* government can only make laws that affect people who live in that city.

8. **federal** | **fĕd′** ər əl |
   - A *federal* government can make laws that affect everybody who lives in that country, no matter which city or state they live in.

ă pat / ā pay / â care / ä father / ĕ pet / ē be / ĭ pit / ī pie / î fierce / ŏ pot / ō go / ô paw, for / oi oil / ŏŏ book /
ōō boot / ou out / ŭ cut / û fur / *th* the / th thin / hw which / zh vision / ə ago, item, pencil, atom, circus

Meaning Comprehension

Directions: In the blank next to each Power Word, write the letter of its correct definition.

Power Words

_____ legend

_____ excess

_____ dispute

_____ heroic

_____ incident

_____ sufficient

_____ municipal

_____ federal

Definitions

a. related to the government of a city

b. related to the government of a country made up of states

c. an argument, a disagreement

d. a story or group of stories handed down from earlier times

e. an event, something that happened

f. enough, as much of something as is needed

g. being like a hero, very brave

h. an extra amount

Context Completion

Directions: Each sentence below has two blanks. Choose and then write the Power Word that goes in each blank. Use each Power Word only once.

1. There was a nasty _____ at the party when there was a _____ about who owned a Rolling Stones album.

2. The _____ of The Alamo is about a _____ group of a few men who fought for hours against a much larger Mexican army.

3. A _____ is more powerful than a _____ government because it rules more people.

4. We had a four-foot board and a three-foot piece of wood was _____ for the shelf we were making, so we had an _____ of one foot of wood.

Muscle Builder Analogies

Directions: Each exercise below is an incomplete analogy. Choose the Power Word that best completes each analogy and write it in the blank. <u>Write only Power Words in the blanks.</u>

1. AGREE is to AGREEMENT *as* DISAGREE is to _____

2. COWARDLY is to FEAR *as* _____ is to COURAGE

3. EXTRA is to ENOUGH *as* EXCESS is to _____

Word Power 3

Directions: Study the Power Words below. Note how each word is pronounced. Then read the sentences carefully and use context clues to figure out the meaning of each Power Word.

When you're sure you know the meaning of every Power Word, complete the exercises on the next page.

Power Words	vital	sovereign	melee	monarch
	queue	gruff	prohibited	expelled

1. **vital** | vīt′ l |
   - Oxygen is *vital* to human beings since without it we cannot live.

2. **queue** | kyōo |
   - The *queue* to get tickets for the rock concert stretched from the box office to a bank four blocks away.

3. **sovereign** | sŏv′ ə rĭn |
   - As an adjective, *sovereign* means "independent," but as a noun, it means "king."

4. **gruff** | grŭf |
   - His *gruff* reply to her question hurt her feelings and brought tears to her eyes.

5. **melee** | mā′ lā′ |
   - The fight started between two players, but several players on each team joined in and the *melee* lasted almost 10 minutes.

6. **prohibited** | prō hĭb′ ĭ tĭd |
   - Selling liquor was *prohibited* in America during the Prohibition Era, but "bootleggers" broke the law and sold liquor anyway.

7. **monarch** | mŏn′ ərk |
   - The American Revolution was a revolt against England and the English *monarch*, King George III.

8. **expelled** | ĭk spĕld′ |
   - Three students were *expelled* from the military school for cheating on an exam.

ă pat / ā pay / â care / ä father / ĕ pet / ē be / ĭ pit / ī pie / î fierce / ŏ pot / ō go / ô paw, for / oi oil / ŏŏ book /
ŏŏ boot / ou out / ŭ cut / û fur / th the / th thin / hw which / zh vision / ə ago, item, pencil, atom, circus

Meaning Comprehension

Directions: In the blank next to each Power Word, write the letter of its correct definition.

Power Words

_____ vital

_____ queue

_____ sovereign

_____ gruff

_____ melee

_____ prohibited

_____ monarch

_____ expelled

Definitions

a. king, ruler (as an adjective, this word means independent)
b. king, ruler
c. forced out, driven out; dismissed
d. a free-for-all fight; a confused struggle
e. a line of people waiting for something
f. very important, essential; necessary for life
g. rough, stern, short-tempered
h. not allowed; forbidden by authority

Context Completion

Directions: Each sentence below has two blanks. Choose and then write the Power Word that goes in each blank. Use each Power Word only once.

1. It is _____ that a waiter or waitress always act politely and friendly, no matter how _____ a customer may be.

2. Smoking is _____ in the school and any student caught smoking will be _____ .

3. _____ and _____ are synonyms, but the first word is more common because a king is the head of a type of government called a "monarchy."

4. An argument among several people on the _____ for hockey tickets resulted in a _____ in which two people were injured.

Muscle Builder Analogies

Directions: Each exercise below is an incomplete analogy. Choose the Power Word that best completes each analogy and write it in the blank. Write only Power Words in the blanks.

1. MONARCH is to SOVEREIGN *as* _____ is to LINE

2. FRIENDLY is to GRUFF *as* UNIMPORTANT is to

_____

3. ALLOWED is to CAN *as* _____ is to CAN'T

Word Power 4

Directions: Study the Power Words below. Note how each word is pronounced. Then read the sentences carefully and use context clues to figure out the meaning of each Power Word.

When you're sure you know the meaning of every Power Word, complete the exercises on the next page.

Power Words	pangs	alias	truant	regal
	bleak	feeble	intercept	infuriated

---

1. **pangs** | păngz |
   - Jackie rushed by the blind beggar without giving him a penny, but later felt *pangs* of guilt about it.

2. **bleak** | blēk |
   - Trailing 9-0, we knew our chances of winning were *bleak*.

3. **alias** | ā′ lē əs |
   - To avoid being arrested, the escaped convict rented a car under an *alias* rather than his real name.

4. **feeble** | fē′ bəl |
   - That old man may look *feeble*, but he's actually stronger than many men half his age.

5. **truant** | trōō′ ənt |
   - Pierre never learned the basics of computer programming because he was *truant* when the class began the work.

6. **intercept** | ĭn′ tər sĕpt′ |
   - After mailing a nasty letter to her friend, Maria changed her mind and went to the post office to *intercept* it before it was delivered.

7. **regal** | rē′ gəl |
   - The young prince was trained in all the behaviors needed for the *regal* position he would take over when his father the king died.

8. **infuriated** | ĭn fyŏŏr′ ē ā′ tid |
   - A well-dressed customer became *infuriated* when a clumsy waiter dropped food in her lap, and she demanded that the waiter be fired.

ă pat / ā pay / â care / ä father / ĕ pet / ē be / ĭ pit / ī pie / î fierce / ŏ pot / ō go / ô paw, for / oi oil / ŏŏ book /
ŏŏ boot / ou out / ŭ cut / ü fur / *th* the / th thin / hw which / zh vision / ə ago, item, pencil, atom, circus

Meaning Comprehension

Directions: In the blank next to each Power Word, write the letter of its correct definition.

Power Words   ### Definitions

_____ pangs

_____ bleak

_____ alias

_____ feeble

_____ truant

_____ intercept

_____ regal

_____ infuriated

a. to stop something before it reaches its destination

b. a name one uses other than one's real name

c. not hopeful, gloomy, not optimistic

d. sharp feelings of physical or emotional pain

e. made angry or furious, enraged

f. lacking strength, weak, frail

g. royal, relating to a king

h. absent without permission (especially from school)

Context Completion

Directions: Each sentence below has two blanks. Choose and then write the Power Word that goes in each blank. Use each Power Word only once.

1. Mr. Hansen was _____ when the maid he hired complained that she was too _____ to wash dishes.

2. Because Princess Kalina did not want people to know she came from a _____ family, she traveled under an _____ rather than her real name.

3. Tom felt _____ of guilt after being _____ from school and lying about it to his parents.

4. During the Battle of Britain, British fighter pilots knew England's future would be _____ if they could not _____ the German bombers headed for London.

Muscle Builder Analogies

Directions: Each exercise below is an incomplete analogy. Choose the Power Word that best completes each analogy and write it in the blank. Write only Power Words in the blanks.

1. MIGHTY is to WEAK *as* POWERFUL is to _____

2. HAPPY is to JOYFUL *as* ANGRY is to _____

3. MASK is to FACE *as* _____ is to NAME

Word Power 5

Directions: Study the Power Words below. Note how each word is pronounced. Then read the sentences carefully and use context clues to figure out the meaning of each Power Word.

When you're sure you know the meaning of every Power Word, complete the exercises on the next page.

Power Words	despite	desperate	demolish	investigate
	abnormal	detected	traditional	minute

1. **despite** | dĭ **spīt′** |
   - Jack and Julius went to a movie *despite* the fact that they had not finished their homework.

2. **abnormal** | ăb **nôr′** məl |
   - A person whose behavior is often *abnormal* may be sent to a mental hospital to be tested for mental illness.

3. **desperate** | **dĕs′** pər ĭt |
   - Mrs. Low told the police she stole food from the grocery because she was *desperate*—she had no money and her children were starving.

4. **detected** | dĭ **tĕk′** tĭd |
   - The poisonous gases were *detected* by a special machine and the air in the coal mine was filtered clean.

5. **demolish** | dĭ **mŏl′** ĭsh |
   - The city wanted to *demolish* the small library and build a modern four-story library to replace it.

6. **traditional** | trə **dĭsh′** ə nəl |
   - As they have for hundreds of years, whole villages of people in southern France dress up in *traditional* costumes for holiday celebrations.

7. **investigate** | ĭn **vĕs′** tĭ gāt′ |
   - When Freida heard strange noises in her cellar, she bravely went down the cellar stairs to *investigate*.

8. **minute** | mī **noot′** |
   - Some of the worst diseases people catch are caused by *minute* germs that can only be seen through a microscope.

ă pat / ā pay / â care / ä father / ĕ pet / ē be / ĭ pit / ī pie / î fierce / ŏ pot / ō go / ô paw, for / oi oil / ŏŏ book /
ŏŏ boot / ou out / ŭ cut / ü fur / *th* the / th thin / hw which / zh vision / ə ago, item, pencil, atom, circus

Meaning Comprehension

Directions: In the blank next to each Power Word, write the letter of its correct definition.

Power Words

Definitions

_____ despite

_____ abnormal

_____ desperate

_____ detected

_____ demolish

_____ traditional

_____ investigate

_____ minute

a. done the same way for many years; handed down from one generation to the next
b. to look into or examine a situation in search of facts and explanations
c. tiny, very small
d. found, noticed, discovered
e. in spite of
f. not normal, strange, unusual
g. to have an urgent and serious need for something that makes you take risks to get it
h. tear down completely, destroy

Context Completion

Directions: Each sentence below has two blanks. Choose and then write the Power Word that goes in each blank. Use each Power Word only once.

1. A "haunted house" is a _____ display in an amusement park _____ the fact that few people believe in ghosts.

2. The farmer knew it was _____ for his pigs not to come when called, so he went to the barnyard to _____.

3. The people on the top floor of the hotel became _____ and began to jump when they realized that the earthquake would soon _____ the entire building.

4. Cracks in the metal that were too _____ to be seen by the eye were _____ by an X-ray machine.

Muscle Builder Analogies

Directions: Each exercise below is an incomplete analogy. Choose the Power Word that best completes each analogy and write it in the blank. Write only Power Words in the blanks.

1. EXAMINE is to INVESTIGATE *as* _____ is to DESTROY

2. MINOR is to MAJOR *as* _____ is to HUGE

3. NEW is to TRADITIONAL *as* USUAL is to _____

Word Power 6

Directions: Study the Power Words below. Note how each word is pronounced. Then read the sentences carefully and use context clues to figure out the meaning of each Power Word.

When you're sure you know the meaning of every Power Word, complete the exercises on the next page.

Power Words	mutiny	improbable	testimony	hamper
	forfeit	quest	journalist	obscure

1. **mutiny** | my$\overline{oo}$t′ n ē |
   - If a sea captain is cruel or unfair, his crew might *mutiny* and take over control of the ship.

2. **forfeit** | fôr′ fĭt |
   - If you break the rules while at the public swimming pool, you may *forfeit* your pool pass and your right to use the pool.

3. **improbable** | ĭm prŏb′ ə bəl |
   - It is *improbable* that you will win much money gambling because very few gamblers win more than they lose.

4. **quest** | kwĕst |
   - The modern explorers are on a *quest* for buried treasure they believe was left behind by Blue Beard the pirate.

5. **testimony** | tĕs′ tə mō′ nē |
   - If your *testimony* in a trial is proven false, you can go to jail for lying under oath (perjury).

6. **journalist** | jŭr′ nə lĭst |
   - A *journalist* may write news articles about local events, national events or world events.

7. **hamper** | hăm′ pər |
   - Refusing to answer a policeman's questions will *hamper* efforts to solve a crime.

8. **obscure** | əb skyŏŏr′ |
   - Mitchell Jackson thought he spotted an *obscure* figure dashing behind a tombstone, but he hoped the dim moonlight was tricking his eyes into seeing something that wasn't really there.

ă pat / ā pay / â care / ä father / ĕ pet / ē be / ĭ pit / ī pie / î fierce / ŏ pot / ō go / ô paw, for / oi oil / ŏŏ book /
ŏŏ boot / ou out / ŭ cut / ü fur / *th* the / th thin / hw which / zh vision / ə ago, item, pencil, atom, circus

Meaning Comprehension

Directions: In the blank next to each Power Word, write the letter of its correct definition.

Power Words

_____ mutiny

_____ forfeit

_____ improbable

_____ quest

_____ testimony

_____ journalist

_____ hamper

_____ obscure

Definitions

a. not likely to happen
b. newspaper or magazine writer
c. get in the way of, prevent the progress of
d. revolt against a leader
e. lose or give up a right (usually because of an error or poor behavior)
f. unclear, vague, difficult to see clearly
g. a search for something held valuable or precious
h. statement or answers given by a witness in a court trial

Context Completion

Directions: Each sentence below has two blanks. Choose and then write the Power Word that goes in each blank. Use each Power Word only once.

1. The angry sailors planned a _____ against their officers, but because they had no weapons it was _____ that they would succeed in taking over.

2. The jury's decision depended on the _____ of a single witness—a young girl who saw only an _____ face behind a rain-splattered window.

3. Juan Thomas was the _____ who wrote the story about Don Wang's around-the-world _____ to find the golden monkey.

4. "Anyone who tries to _____ the other players will _____ the game," the referee said.

Muscle Builder Analogies

Directions: Each exercise below is an incomplete analogy. Choose the Power Word that best completes each analogy and write it in the blank. Write only Power Words in the blanks.

1. BRIGHT is to DIM *as* CLEAR is to _____

2. LIKELY is to PROBABLE *as* UNLIKELY is to

   _____

3. JOURNALIST is to WRITER *as* _____ is to STATEMENT

WRITING REVIEW: Word Power 1-6

For the assignments below, you will be asked to write sentences
that show the meaning of certain Power Words from Word Power
1-6. Further, you will be asked to write each sentence by using
one of the four cases of context clues you learned in Unit 2. If
necessary, review Unit 2 before you begin.

1. Study the meaning and use of the word "standard" on pages 260-261. Write a sentence on the
   lines below in which the meaning of "standard" is *given by contrast* (CASE III).

   _____

   _____

   _____

2. Study the meaning and use of the word "horizontal" on pages 260-261. Write a sentence on the
   lines below in which the meaning of "horizontal" can be *inferred from ideas in the sentence*
   (CASE IV).

   _____

   _____

   _____

3. Study the meaning and use of the word "dispute" on pages 262-263. Write a sentence on the
   lines below in which the meaning of "dispute" is *stated without punctuation* (CASE II).

   _____

   _____

   _____

4. Study the meaning and use of the word "sufficient" on pages 262-263. Write a sentence on the
   lines below in which the meaning of "sufficient" is *stated with punctuation* (CASE I).

   _____

   _____

   _____

5. Study the meaning and use of the word "vital" on pages 264-265. Write a sentence on the lines below in which the meaning of "vital" is *stated with punctuation* (CASE I).

_____

_____

_____

6. Study the meaning and use of the word "bleak" on pages 266-267. Write a sentence on the lines below in which the meaning of "bleak" is *given by contrast* (CASE III).

_____

_____

_____

7. Study the meaning and use of the word "desperate" on pages 268-269. Write a sentence on the lines below in which the meaning of "desperate" can be *inferred from ideas in the sentence* (CASE IV).

_____

_____

_____

8. Study the meaning and use of the word "detected" on pages 268-269. Write a sentence on the lines below in which the meaning of "detected" is *stated without punctuation* (CASE II).

_____

_____

_____

9. Study the meaning and use of the word "improbable" on pages 270-271. Write a sentence on the lines below in which the meaning of "improbable" is *stated without punctuation* (CASE II).

_____

_____

_____

Word Power 7

Directions: Study the Power Words below. Note how each word is pronounced. Then read the sentences carefully and use context clues to figure out the meaning of each Power Word.

When you're sure you know the meaning of every Power Word, complete the exercises on the next page.

Power Words	apprentice	rancid	stipend	beseeched
	quiver	hazardous	clamor	humiliated

1. **apprentice** | ə **prĕn′** tĭs |
   - Like most untrained workers, the carpenter's *apprentice* made many mistakes before she gained the skill of an expert.

2. **quiver** | **kwĭv′** ər |
   - I knew Steve was nervous because I could see his hands *quiver*.

3. **rancid** | **răn′** sĭd |
   - When our refrigerator was broken for three days, some of the food became *rancid* and had to be thrown out.

4. **hazardous** | **hăz′** ər dəs |
   - Because accidents happen more easily on a slippery surface, even a few inches of snow can make roads *hazardous*.

5. **stipend** | **stī′** pĕnd′ |
   - The college awarded Carmine a four-year scholarship which included a *stipend* of $400 per month for living expenses.

6. **clamor** | **klăm′** ər |
   - A *clamor* interrupted the school play when several people spotted a snake slithering toward the stage.

7. **beseeched** | bĭ **sēch′** d |
   - Patty *beseeched* her father to cancel her "grounding" for one day so she could attend the skating party.

8. **humiliated** | hyo͞o **mĭl′** ē ā′ tĭd |
   - The chief of police was *humiliated* by his son who continued to get into trouble with the law.

ă pat / ā pay / â care / ä father / ĕ pet / ē be / ĭ pit / ī pie / î fierce / ŏ pot / ō go / ô paw, for / oi oil / o͝o book /
o͞o boot / ou out / ŭ cut / û fur / *th* the / th thin / hw which / zh vision / ə ago, item, pencil, atom, circus

Meaning Comprehension

Directions: In the blank next to each Power Word, write the letter of its correct definition.

Power Words

_____ apprentice

_____ quiver

_____ rancid

_____ hazardous

_____ stipend

_____ clamor

_____ beseeched

_____ humiliated

Definitions

a. slightly shake, tremble
b. loud noise, uproar, shouting
c. an allowance or salary, a regular payment of money
d. shamed, disgraced
e. begged, asked urgently and excitedly
f. having a bad smell or taste, spoiled
g. dangerous, risky
h. a person learning a job or business

Context Completion

Directions: Each sentence below has two blanks. Choose and then write the Power Word that goes in each blank. Use each Power Word only once.

1. Mrs. Spoletto was _____ by the _____ that her young grandchildren made while in the library.

2. The odor from Joe's Thermos told us that the milk was _____ and we _____ him to throw it away immediately.

3. Driving across the old wooden bridge is _____ : Whenever a car crosses, you can feed the bridge _____ .

4. "Since an _____ is one who is just learning a job, he or she usually is paid a smaller _____ than a skilled worker.

Muscle Builder Analogies

Directions: Each exercise below is an incomplete analogy. Choose the Power Word that best completes each analogy and write it in the blank. Write only Power Words in the blanks.

1. GOOD is to BAD *as* FRESH is to _____

2. EXCLAIMED is to SAID *as* _____ is to ASKED

3. QUIET is to LIBRARY *as* _____ is to CAFETERIA

Word Power 8

Directions: Study the Power Words below. Note how each word is pronounced. Then read the sentences carefully and use context clues to figure out the meaning of each Power Word.

When you're sure you know the meaning of every Power Word, complete the exercises on the next page.

Power Words	strategy	surplus	solar	revised
	radiates	reluctant	utilize	abundance

1. **strategy** | **străt′** ə jē |
   - The officer candidates learned military *strategy* by studying the war plans of past commanders.

2. **radiates** | **rā′** dē āts′ |
   - A "home heating radiator" has this name because it *radiates* (gives off) heat which is used to warm a home.

3. **surplus** | **sŭr′** plŭs′ |
   - We didn't need all the food we brought on the camping trip, so we gave the *surplus* to other campers.

4. **reluctant** | rĭ **lŭk′** tant |
   - Tina didn't really want to go to the movies, but she was *reluctant* to say no and hurt her brother's feelings.

5. **solar** | **sō′** lər |
   - The solar system consists of the sun and the nine planets and other bodies that orbit the sun.

6. **utilize** | **yōōt′** l īz′ |
   - A farmer is more likely to *utilize* a pickup truck while working than an office worker.

7. **revised** | rĭ **vīzd′** |
   - This dictionary is *revised* every 5 years to bring it up to date, since the definitions of many words change over time.

8. **abundance** | ə **bŭn′** dəns |
   - Alaska has an *abundance* of such natural resources as water, forests, oil and minerals.

ă pat / ā pay / â care / ä father / ĕ pet / ē be / ĭ pit / ī pie / î fierce / ŏ pot / ō go / ô paw, for / oi oil / ŏŏ book /
ōō boot / ou out / ŭ cut / û fur / *th* the / th thin / hw which / zh vision / ə ago, item, pencil, atom, circus

Meaning Comprehension

Directions: In the blank next to each Power Word, write the letter of its correct definition.

Power Words

_____ strategy

_____ radiates

_____ surplus

_____ reluctant

_____ solar

_____ utilize

_____ revised

_____ abundance

Definitions

a. use, put into service
b. unwilling to do something, tending not to do something
c. gives off, sends out (especially energy)
d. related to the sun
e. an extra amount, more than what is needed; opposite of shortage
f. a great amount, a large quantity
g. changed, improved; brought up to date
h. an overall or general plan of action

Context Completion

Directions: Each sentence below has two blanks. Choose and then write the Power Word that goes in each blank. Use each Power Word only once.

1. _____ power is power made from the energy which the sun _____ .

2. Saudi Arabia has an _____ of oil and it sells its great _____ to countries all over the world.

3. Mr. Pennypacker was _____ to buy any tools he would only _____ once, so he usually rented tools instead.

4. When General Halftrack found out that the enemy knew his battle plan, he _____ his _____ and surprised the enemy with a sneak attack.

Muscle Builder Analogies

Directions: Each exercise below is an incomplete analogy. Choose the Power Word that best completes each analogy and write it in the blank. Write only Power Words in the blanks.

1. LUNAR is to MOON as _____ is to SUN

2. GAME PLAN is to GAME as _____ is to WAR

3. TOO LITTLE is to SHORTAGE as TOO MUCH is to _____

Word Power 9

Directions: Study the Power Words below. Note how each word is pronounced. Then read the sentences carefully and use context clues to figure out the meaning of each Power Word.

When you're sure you know the meaning of every Power Word, complete the exercises on the next page.

Power Words	jeered	untidy	accumulate	proverb
	haggard	impudence	yearned	maxim

---

1. **jeered** | jĭrd |
   - The crowd *jeered* the overpaid baseball star when he struck out for the fourth straight time.

2. **haggard** | **hăg′** ərd |
   - The soldiers in the prison camp were *haggard* from lack of food and poor treatment.

3. **untidy** | ŭn **tī′** dē |
   - It is often said that a neat desk shows an organized mind and an *untidy* desk shows a disorganized or confused mind.

4. **impudence** | **ĭm′** pyə dəns |
   - Teenagers sometimes regard *impudence* as a sign of strength or independence; however, adults consider this rude behavior simply childish and improper.

5. **accumulate** | ə **kyōō′** myə lāt′ |
   - Mrs. Domingues had let so much furniture *accumulate* in her attic that she no longer remembered where each piece had come from.

6. **yearned** | yürnd |
   - After dieting for three days, Roland *yearned* for potato chips and ice cream.

7. **proverb** | **prŏv′** ərb |
   - The tale of the careful seamstress illustrates the *proverb*, "A stitch in time saves nine."

8. **maxim** | **măk′** sĭm |
   - "Early to bed, early to rise, makes a man healthy, wealthy and wise," is an example of a *maxim* that states that good sleeping habits can help a person be successful.

ă pat / ā pay / â care / ä father / ĕ pet / ē be / ĭ pit / ī pie / î fierce / ŏ pot / ō go / ô paw, for / oi oil / ŏŏ book /
ōō boot / ou out / ŭ cut / ü fur / *th* the / th thin / hw which / zh vision / ə ago, item, pencil, atom, circus

Meaning Comprehension

Directions: In the blank next to each Power Word, write the letter of its correct definition.

Power Words   ### Definitions

_____ jeered

_____ haggard

_____ untidy

_____ impudence

_____ accumulate

_____ yearned

_____ proverb

_____ maxim

a. a short saying which states a basic principle or rule of conduct

b. a brief saying which gives an example to illustrate a general truth (often connected to a story or fable)

c. looking worn and exhausted because of suffering or worry

d. rudeness, disrespectful behavior

e. pile up, gather together, collect (usually over a period of time)

f. shouted at in a mocking way, made fun of

g. greatly wanted or desired, longed for

h. not neat, messy

Context Completion

Directions: Each sentence below has two blanks. Choose and then write the Power Word that goes in each blank. Use each Power Word only once.

1. If you let dirty clothes and old papers _____ in your room, your room will soon look very _____.

2. After spending three days in a lifeboat without food, the shipwreck survivors were _____ and _____ for food and shelter.

3. Although both words mean a short saying, a _____ is often connected to a story, whereas a _____ is not.

4. When the disappointed player _____ at the referee, the official promptly penalized her team for her _____ .

Muscle Builder Analogies

Directions: Each exercise below is an incomplete analogy. Choose the Power Word that best completes each analogy and write it in the blank. <u>Write only Power Words in the blanks.</u>

1. SHIRT is to BLOUSE *as* PROVERB is to _____

2. POLITENESS is to PROPER *as* _____ is to IMPROPER

3. DEMANDED is to ASKED *as* _____ is to WANTED

Word Power 10

Directions: Study the Power Words below. Note how each word is pronounced. Then read the sentences carefully and use context clues to figure out the meaning of each Power Word.

When you're sure you know the meaning of every Power Word, complete the exercises on the next page.

Power Words	fraud	dauntless	elite	neophyte
	envoy	plural	ignite	singular

1. **fraud** | frôd |
   • When Maria scratched off the gold paint and saw the cheap metal, she knew the ring was a *fraud* and worthless.

2. **envoy** | ĕn′ voi′ |
   • The United States sent an *envoy* to Spain to discuss a new trade agreement.

3. **dauntless** | dônt′ lĭs |
   • Kareem was *dauntless*: He didn't even hesitate before leaping the 8-foot crevice that split the mountain path.

4. **plural** | plŏŏr′ əl |
   • The *plural* of goose is geese, not gooses.

5. **elite** | ĭ lēt′ |
   • Each season the *elite* of baseball players in the American and National Leagues are showcased in the All-Star Game.

6. **ignite** | ĭg nīt′ |
   • If you light a match in a room where there is a gas leak, the gas could *ignite* and blow up the room.

7. **neophyte** | nē′ ə fīt′ |
   • Because Fred was a *neophyte* in his job, he often asked for help from the workers who had been on that job longer.

8. **singular** | sĭng′ gyə lər |
   • If you are describing only one of something, then you name it with a *singular* noun.

ă pat / ā pay / â care / ä father / ĕ pet / ē be / ĭ pit / ī pie / î fierce / ŏ pot / ō go / ô paw, for / oi oil / ŏŏ book /
ŏŏ boot / ou out / ŭ cut / ü fur / *th* the / th thin / hw which / zh vision / ə ago, item, pencil, atom, circus

Meaning Comprehension

Directions: In the blank next to each Power Word, write the letter of its correct definition.

Power Words	Definitions

Power Words

_____ fraud

_____ envoy

_____ dauntless

_____ plural

_____ elite

_____ ignite

_____ neophyte

_____ singular

Definitions

a. a beginner, a person who is new to something, a novice

b. a group of people who are the best or the finest

c. a word form used to name one thing by itself

d. a word form used to name more than one of the same thing

e. not easily discouraged, brave, fearless

f. catch fire

g. a fake used to make money by tricking someone

h. a person sent by someone to carry a message or do a special job

Context Completion

Directions: Each sentence below has two blanks. Choose and then write the Power Word that goes in each blank. Use each Power Word only once.

1. The _____ that the French king sent with his secret message to the King of Denmark was a member of the _____ of French spies, known worldwide for their cunning and bravery.

2. For some words, the singular and plural forms are the same: The word "deer" may be _____ and mean just one animal, or it may be _____ and mean several.

3. The _____ police officer rescued the driver from the overturned gasoline truck despite the fact that he knew the gasoline could _____ at any moment.

4. A _____ in coin collecting should learn how to tell if a coin is a _____ so he or she can avoid being tricked into buying a worthless coin.

Muscle Builder Analogies

Directions: Each exercise below is an incomplete analogy. Choose the Power Word that best completes each analogy and write it in the blank. Write only Power Words in the blanks.

1. ONE is to SINGULAR *as* MANY is to _____

2. EXPERIENCED is to VETERAN *as* NEW is to

_____

3. FEARLESS is to COWARDLY *as* _____ is to AFRAID

Word Power 11

Directions: Study the Power Words below. Note how each word is pronounced. Then read the sentences carefully and use context clues to figure out the meaning of each Power Word.

When you're sure you know the meaning of every Power Word, complete the exercises on the next page.

Power Words	pact	refuge	irked	distinguished
	unceasing	residence	petty	antagonistic

1. **pact** | păkt |
   - The U.S., Britain and France signed a *pact* promising to come to each other's aid if any of them were attacked.

2. **unceasing** | ŭn sē′ sĭng |
   - The loud, *unceasing* noise from the street-paving machine made it impossible to have any group discussions in school today.

3. **refuge** | rĕf′ yo͞oj |
   - As the hurricane approached the coast, people fled to inland areas for *refuge*.

4. **residence** | rĕz′ ĭ dəns |
   - You must have a *residence* in a state in order to vote in that state.

5. **irked** | ürkd |
   - A mosquito buzzed around my room all night and *irked* me so much I couldn't sleep a wink.

6. **petty** | pĕt′ ē |
   - I thought his objections were *petty* and said only to give me a hard time, so I ignored them and went ahead with my plan.

7. **distinguished** | dĭ stĭng′ gwĭsht |
   - The *distinguished* professor was best known for his poetry, which had won many international awards.

8. **antagonistic** | ăn tăg′ ə nĭs′ tĭk |
   - Because their families had fought each other for years, Irma Hatfield and Emma McCoy were *antagonistic* toward each other.

ă pat / ā pay / â care / ä father / ĕ pet / ē be / ĭ pit / ī pie / î fierce / ŏ pot / ō go / ô paw, for / oi oil / o͞o book /
o͞o boot / ou out / ŭ cut / û fur / *th* the / th thin / hw which / zh vision / ə ago, item, pencil, atom, circus

Meaning Comprehension

Directions: In the blank next to each Power Word, write the letter of its correct definition.

Power Words

_____ pact

_____ unceasing

_____ refuge

_____ residence

_____ irked

_____ petty

_____ distinguished

_____ antagonistic

Definitions

a. famous, well known for high achievement or excellence
b. annoyed, bothered, irritated
c. safe shelter, protection
d. unfriendly, hostile
e. home, a place where someone lives
f. minor, small, unimportant, trivial
g. unending, never stopping, going on and on
h. a formal agreement; a treaty between two or more countries

Context Completion

Directions: Each sentence below has two blanks. Choose and then write the Power Word that goes in each blank. Use each Power Word only once.

1. I was really _____ by the child's rudeness, not just because it was obnoxious, but because it was _____ and went on all day long.

2. The hikers left the park and went to the nearest _____ to find _____ from the sudden thunderstorm.

3. After being _____ toward each other for two decades, Israel and Egypt signed a _____ promising to cooperate and live in peace.

4. The _____ scientist was irked when she read another scientist's criticisms of her work and she wrote a letter to that scientist in which she dismissed the criticisms as _____ .

Muscle Builder Analogies

Directions: Each exercise below is an incomplete analogy. Choose the Power Word that best completes each analogy and write it in the blank. Write only Power Words in the blanks.

1. MAJOR is to MINOR *as* IMPORTANT is to _____

2. SHIELD is to WEAPONS *as* _____ is to STORMS

3. ENDLESS is to UNENDING *as* CEASELESS is to _____

Word Power 12

Directions: Study the Power Words below. Note how each word is pronounced. Then read the sentences carefully and use context clues to figure out the meaning of each Power Word.

When you're sure you know the meaning of every Power Word, complete the exercises on the next page.

Power Words	enrich	elated	futile	dwindle
	replica	repeal	dismal	chided

1. **enrich** | ĕn **rĭch′** |
   - Mastering "Word Power" lists will *enrich* your vocabulary and improve your speaking, reading and writing.

2. **replica** | **rĕp′** lĭ kə |
   - The company produces *replicas* of old automobiles such as the Edsel for people who want an old-fashioned car.

3. **elated** | ĭ **lā′** tĭd |
   - Tanya was *elated* when she received a final grade of A in math.

4. **repeal** | rĭ **pēl′** |
   - If a law is no longer needed, the government can *repeal* it.

5. **futile** | **fyōō′** tĭl′ |
   - The firemen's efforts to put out the fire were *futile* because the warehouse contained hundreds of empty cardboard boxes which kept igniting.

6. **dismal** | **dĭz′** məl |
   - Four straight days of rain and wind put the campers in a *dismal* mood.

7. **dwindle** | **dwĭn′** dəl |
   - In America the need for unskilled labor will likely *dwindle* over the next 20 years, which will make it difficult for people without skills or education to find jobs.

8. **chided** | **chī′** dĭd |
   - When Coach Lombardo *chided* his halfback for smoking, the player promised to quit the habit.

ă pat / ā pay / â care / ä father / ĕ pet / ē be / ĭ pit / ī pie / î fierce / ŏ pot / ō go / ô paw, for / oi oil / ŏŏ book /
ōō boot / ou out / ŭ cut / ü fur / *th* the / th thin / hw which / zh vision / ə ago, item, pencil, atom, circus

Meaning Comprehension

Directions: In the blank next to each Power Word, write the letter of its correct definition.

Power Words

_____ enrich

_____ replica

_____ elated

_____ repeal

_____ futile

_____ dismal

_____ dwindle

_____ chided

Definitions

a. a copy made to look exactly like the original (especially in the arts)

b. scolded, criticized

c. sad, gloomy, depressing

d. to do away with a law by legal means; to withdraw any legal decision

e. very happy and lively, filled with joy

f. improve in quality by adding things, make fuller

g. useless, pointless, having no effect

h. become smaller and smaller, waste away, diminish

Context Completion

Directions: Each sentence below has two blanks. Choose and then write the Power Word that goes in each blank. Use each Power Word only once.

1. You can _____ your life by traveling overseas, but be careful not to spend too much money or your savings account may _____ down to nothing.

2. Several trucking companies asked the government to _____ the 55 m.p.h. speed limit law, but their request was _____ and the speed limit remained 55 m.p.h.

3. Coach Gibson was _____ with his team's winning record of 10-5, especially after their _____ start of 0 wins and 5 losses.

4. Monsieur Henri, the sculptor, _____ a young sculptor for making a _____ of a famous statue and displaying it as her own original work.

Muscle Builder Analogies

Directions: Each exercise below is an incomplete analogy. Choose the Power Word that best completes each analogy and write it in the blank. Write only Power Words in the blanks.

1. GENUINE is to ORIGINAL _as_ IMITATION is to

   _____

2. USEFUL is to USELESS _as_ WORTHWHILE is to

   _____

3. APPROVED is to PRAISED _as_ DISAPPROVED is to

   _____

WRITING REVIEW: Word Power 7-12

By now you have had a lot of practice in writing sentences in which a key word's meaning is given in the sentence by context clues. You have become especially skilled in using four main cases of context clues:

— CASE I: Meaning Stated With Punctuation
— CASE II: Meaning Stated Without Punctuation
— CASE III: Meaning Given By Contrast
— CASE IV: Meaning Inferred From Ideas In The Sentence.

For this assignment you are again asked to write context clue sentences. But this time, rather than tell you which case of context clue to use, you are free to use any one of the four cases in each sentence you write.

1. Choose two words from each of the Word Power sets 7-12. For each word, write a sentence on a separate piece of paper in which the meaning of that word is given in the sentence by context clues. Use any of the four cases of context clues.

2. Check how clearly your sentences were written. Ask a classmate or friend to read your sentences. Then point to the Word Power word in each sentence and ask that person to tell you its meaning. Ask him or her to identify the context clues in the sentence that helped to show the word's meaning.